GEORGE SAND
A Biography of the First Modern, Liberated Woman

Noel B. Gerson

SAPERE
BOOKS

GEORGE SAND

Published by Sapere Books.

20 Windermere Drive, Leeds, England, LS17 7UZ,
United Kingdom

saperebooks.com

ISBN: 978-1-80055-397-2.

For Cathy and Dick Libby

TABLE OF CONTENTS

That women differ from men, that heart and intellect are subject to the laws of sex, I do not doubt. But ought this difference, so essential to the general harmony of life, to constitute a moral inferiority? And does it necessarily follow that the souls and minds of women are inferior to those of men, whose vanity permits them to tolerate no other natural order?

GEORGE SAND

I

Although George Sand and her contemporaries didn't know it, and she herself would have been the first to deny it, she lived a century and a half before her time: the first member of her sex to become the trailblazer for the same sexual and economic freedom for women as for men. The facts of her life indicate the unique quality of her approach: she taught by example, seeking no followers.

Neither in Europe nor in the United States did any nineteenth-century woman achieve greater fame — or notoriety — yet she was supremely indifferent to the approval or disapproval of society. Wealthy all of her life, she was cursed by a streak of generosity that frequently made it necessary for her to earn large sums. Yet money meant so little to her that she habitually left her finances in the hands of others.

Her life was a succession of paradoxes, and so shaped her extraordinary character. On her father's side she was the direct descendant of royalty and of one of France's greatest generals; on the distaff side there had been camp followers and, perhaps, gypsies. The combination was explosive.

A meek, dutiful housewife and mother for the better part of a decade, a frustrated, hysterical woman who took refuge in hypochondria, she suddenly plunged into a Bohemian life in her late twenties, and although she had shown no particular talent for writing, she became an author because she needed money. Within two years she became one of the most renowned and popular novelists in Europe. She soon won her place as a leader in the new Romantic movement. Similarly, she turned to the theater in late middle age because she was in debt, and although she had no professional experience as a dramatist, she quickly became one of the most successful playwrights in Paris.

A self-proclaimed Socialist who spent many years fighting for liberty and equality on behalf of the poor workingmen of France, she nevertheless enjoyed a warm, genuine friendship with the petty tyrant of the century, Napoleon III. She believed it essential to educate men in the meaning of the democratic process of government, and herself held one of the most important posts in the Provisional Republican government during the Revolution of 1848. Although not given the title, she acted as Minister of Propaganda, and no other woman attained a post of equal rank in any democratic government until several decades passed in the next century.

At no time in her life was George Sand an attractive woman, either by the standards of her own time or of succeeding periods, although she took on a dignified appearance in her later years. Her hair was dark and nondescript, and her brown eyes were set in a long face, to which high cheekbones and forehead gave an even more lugubrious appearance. Her figure was ungainly; she loped rather than walked. She was deft when serving her guests or working in her garden, but admitted that bric-a-brac sometimes flew apart when she touched it.

Men who came to know her were fascinated by her and eventually came to believe she was beautiful. Many of the most prominent writers and artists were her friends — Honoré de Balzac, Eugène Sue, Théophile Gautier, both father and son Dumas, Delacroix, Lamartine, Heine, and Flaubert, among others, including such younger men as Zola. The list seems endless, and they not only thought of her as an equal, but swore she was a fascinating woman. The one exception was the dominating figure of the century, Victor Hugo, who tolerated her presence when necessary, but never sought her company. Yet it was he who wrote her funeral oration.

Accepted without question by authors, artists, and politicians, George Sand also won a place in the company of such aristocrats as the Empress Eugénie and Prince Jérôme Bonaparte. The common working people, both in Paris and the provinces, regarded her as their friend and champion. Knowing she would be recognized wherever she went, she could wander alone in the city or remote countryside without fear of being molested.

Only the middle class despised her, and with cause. She outraged bourgeois sensibilities and defied the conventions that merchants and shopkeepers considered absolute. She went everywhere dressed like a man, she smoked cigars in public, and she elected to use her masculine pen name as though it were her own. Despite these idiosyncrasies for her time, she was feminine in her interests and tastes; her books, most of which dealt with the theme of love, probably could have been written only by a woman, though Flaubert soon surpassed her in feminine realism.

George Sand's spectacular notoriety, caused by her appearance and by her highly publicized love affairs, led strangers to believe that she was brash, self-assertive, and boisterous. Those who came to know her were surprised to discover that she was painfully shy, rarely contributing much of substance to a social conversation. She was unable to make witty remarks, and remained so somber and silent at dinner parties and other affairs that fellow guests sometimes forgot her presence. Yet many commented on the sweet, utterly feminine quality of her soft voice.

George Sand's love affairs created her shocking reputation. She thought of herself as a woman of the highest moral standards, insisting that women had the right to enjoy the sexual freedom that society regarded as the exclusive prerogative of men. Never the philanderer, she became angry when accused of promiscuity. She went to bed with a man only when she loved him, and it was unfortunate for her public image that she so often imagined herself in love.

It is impossible to determine the number of her lovers, although biographers and historians have been playing guessing games for the better part of a century and a half. The gossip of her contemporaries contributed to the confusion, as did the rumors assiduously printed by the scandal-mongering Paris newspapers of her day, which took advantage of lax libel laws to print sensational stories about her to boost circulation. At one time or another, from the early 1830s to the mid-1870s, virtually every author, artist, and Republican politician in France was said to be one of her lovers.

Balzac, her close friend for many years, never slept with her, but did little to help her good name when he wrote that she had offered herself to him and that he had declined, not wanting to be number fourteen or fifteen. By the late 1840s he published the canard that twenty-five men had been her lovers up to that time. Everyone in Paris knew he habitually exaggerated, but people believed what they wanted to believe, and were duly shocked. Anyone who was well acquainted with George Sand knew that, aside from her few famous liaisons, which she made no attempt to hide, she took pains not to publicize her love life, so no friend was in a position to announce the score.

All the same, Balzac's reaction was significant. 'When I find myself in George's company,' this libertine wrote, 'I forget I am in the presence of a woman and think I am conversing with another man.'

The attitude of Victor Hugo, whose sexual exploits were unmatched in the century, and who may have bedded as many as two thousand women over a period of fifty years, was explicit and emphatic. He wrote: 'George Sand cannot determine whether she is a female or male. I entertain a high regard for all of my colleagues, but it is not my place to decide whether she is my sister or my brother.'

The perceptive Hugo may have penetrated to the core of George Sand's nature, by noting the kind of men who were her partners in her most celebrated affairs. Jules Sandeau, Alfred de Musset, and Frédéric Chopin were remarkably similar in many ways. All were some years younger than George Sand, all were of slender build and suffered from ill health. All were exceptionally handsome, reminding observers of delicate beauty, and each was narcissistically concerned with his wardrobe and appearance.

Even a cursory study of their relationships with George Sand reveals that she was the dominant partner, almost always assuming the aggressive role, while she pressed each in turn to become the passive partner. Her less important lovers fitted this same mold, and subjected themselves to her authority. Those who were masculine and aggressive — among them Prosper Mérimée — remained her lovers only a short time.

According to George Sand's own standards and those of the age in which she lived, she excelled in all of the 'feminine virtues'. She was a first-rate, efficient housekeeper, and demonstrated both taste and subtlety in the decoration of her various homes. She taught herself the art of cooking, and frequently prepared superb dishes for her guests. She believed herself a loving, devoted mother, not only to her own two children, but to the many whom she more or less adopted.

And she was duly enraged when her daughter, who achieved international notoriety of her own, accused her of neglect.

The extent of George Sand's sexual nature has been further revealed by correspondence and other documents which remained unpublished in private hands until after World War II and in America to this day. The letters clarify what only a few of her contemporaries suspected and just one dared to state. Alfred de Vigny, the handsome Romantic poet, had good cause for protesting the close friendship of George Sand and his bewitchingly beautiful mistress, Marie Dorval. Whether he knew the details of their relationship or merely guessed them, on at least two occasions he wrote firm letters to Mlle Dorval, demanding that she have no more to do with 'that damned Lesbian'.

The young actress ignored the directive, and her intimate friendship with George continued for many years. The older woman became the sole support of Marie's children after her tragic death.

Documentary evidence has also been unearthed in recent years to indicate affairs with other women, too — among them the notorious American actress, Adah Issacs Menken. And there may have been more than met the eye in her friendship with the ravishingly lovely aristocrat, Marie d'Agoult. For many years the mistress of Franz Liszt, Mme d'Agoult eventually emulated her one-time friend and wrote books under a man's name, that of Daniel Stern.

Although this phase of George Sand's life was hidden, her reputation was sufficiently bizarre to cause her to be shunned in the puritanical, Victorian world of the Anglo-Saxons. Elizabeth Barrett Browning, herself a rebel of sorts in her runaway marriage to Robert Browning and in the passionate release of her poetry, was sufficiently curious to pay a call on

George Sand in the 1850s. She subsequently wrote that although she admired her as an author, she could not respect her as a woman.

The literary influence of George Sand on the English women of the period who became major prose writers was relatively slight. But Jane Austen, the Brontë sisters, and George Eliot picked up her battle cry against the social conventions that fettered women, and they were loud in their demands for economic equality, but they sidestepped her bold insistence that women were entitled to sexual freedom. George Eliot suffered ostracism for her love affair, but herself considered it a marriage. Sedate English readers failed to appreciate feminine libertinism, and although a number of George Sand's books were published in London, they created no stir there. The most enthusiastic of her English supporters was Matthew Arnold, the distinguished critic, who dined at her country home as a young man, and thereafter unfailingly praised her work to an indifferent audience.

The reaction to George Sand on the far side of the Atlantic was tepid. The sales of her books there were unimpressive, in part because they were badly printed on shoddy paper. The letters of Ralph Waldo Emerson indicate that he was familiar with her work and admired her courage, although he found many of her romantic concepts and exaggerated plot devices difficult to swallow. Longfellow, Lowell, and Whittier read some of her books, making comments that were brief, cautious, and noncommittal. Adah Isaacs Menken, herself a minor poet, is the source of a statement that the romantic cape and soft hat worn by her friend, Walt Whitman, when he went to Pfaff's Restaurant in New York City, was inspired by the costume of the protagonist in George Sand's novel, *The Countess of Rudolstadt*, but there is no other clear evidence that he was in any way influenced by his French contemporary, though they held views in common.

Not until the end of the century did George Sand receive recognition from an American. In 1898, writing the first of a series of articles on her in the *North American Review*, Henry James called her a worthy successor to Goethe, even though she had written no *Faust*. A similar view had been expressed half a century earlier by the great German lyric poet, Heinrich Heine, who became one of George Sand's close friends and frequent dinner companions after he settled in Paris. Her work, he wrote, was similar in mood and inspiration to the best Romantic tradition of Goethe. Readers throughout Germany agreed, and her books enjoyed an enduring popularity there.

It was in Tsarist Russia that her books created an enthusiastic following as great during her lifetime as that in France. The Imperial censors banned the novels of many authors far more conservative than George Sand, but she was a subtle propagandist who never preached openly, and her pleas for freedom and justice were so well concealed in romantic trappings that, it appears, the Russian censors failed to notice and expunge these dangerous doctrines. Whatever the reason, most of George Sand's books were published in Russia, in their original editions, as French was the second language of all literate people there. The correspondence of Fyodor Dostoyevsky acknowledges that her work influenced his own writing, and Ivan Turgeniev was openly in her debt. He lived in Paris for a number of years, visiting her frequently during the period of her life when she and Flaubert were close. All three corresponded regularly, meeting when they could, and their discussions of literature were important in shaping Turgeniev's work.

George Sand's novels, however, suffered a rapid decline through the decades of the twentieth century, however. Today there are few, in France or elsewhere, who read her 'Romantic', her 'Pastoral', or her so-called political novels, most of which are closely related in theme, regardless of these pedantic labels.

Her life is significant, a century after her death, far more because of her accomplishments as a woman than for her books and plays. Certainly she was the prototype of modern woman. She was the first who published her challenge of institutions, mores, and customs that had enslaved members of her sex for thousands of years, the first who not only demanded sexual equality, but lived accordingly. Women had taken lovers and mistresses had always been common; George Sand was of a different mold.

Every modern woman who rejects the double standard, who combines a career with life as a mother, who demands personal fulfilment as a right, is indebted to her. Every woman who wears a pantsuit or slacks as a matter of course, who smokes in public, or chooses to cut her hair short is obligated to George Sand. It was she, wearing boots, trousers cut to fit her feminine figure, and a flowing cape, who first dared to join a party of men at a café and got away with it. All were her friends, accepting her as an equal, and it did not matter that one of the group happened to be her current lover. She earned her own way in the world in a profession of her own choice, and her fame was as great as that of any man at the table. She alone was responsible for people's willingness to accept her.

It was Balzac, half in jest, who mused, 'What will become of the world when all women are like George Sand?'

II

There were few in France, or anywhere else in nineteenth-century Europe, whose blue-blooded lineage was as distinguished as that of Aurore Dupin Dudevant, who called herself George Sand and was an ardent Republican devoted to the abolition of all monarchies. She was destined from her birth, as her good friend, Gustave Flaubert, observed, to lead a life of paradoxes.

Her great-grandfather on the paternal side was one of the most illustrious figures of the preceding century. Maurice de Saxe, illegitimate son of the King of Poland, was reared by his father to be a soldier, and became a Marshal of France. Universally recognized as the greatest general of his age, he amassed a vast fortune, none of which was inherited by his younger daughter, Aurore. He also tied himself to the royal family by arranging the marriage of his niece, Marie de Saxe, to the Dauphin, the eldest son of Louis XV. She was the mother of three kings, Louis XVI, Louis XVIII, and Charles X. Had she wished and had she been given the opportunity, George Sand could have called the reigning monarch, 'Cousin'. After the Revolution of 1830 she had every right to claim kinship with the new King of the French, Louis-Philippe, but by then she had formed her own political philosophy and heartily disapproved of the entire institution that the last of the Bourbons represented.

Aurore, the natural daughter of the Marshal, and grandmother of George Sand, was married as a child and became a widow at the unlikely age of fifteen. As Louis XV could not dispose of her hand in remarriage without providing the substantial dowry he was reluctant to pay, he granted a pension and sent her off to a convent, where she languished as a so-called guest for more than a decade. She was finally rescued from her life of indolent semi-isolation by her mother and through her old family friend, a M. du Pin de Francueil, who was more than twice her age. After 16 their marriage he took her off to his spacious estate, Nohant, in the Province of Berry, where he also owned a cotton mill. It was located on the Indre River, about halfway between the two principal towns, Châteauroux and La Châtre, in both of which he had extensive business interests.

Nohant was one hundred and fifty miles southwest of Paris, and Aurore's friends, who thought she would die of rustic boredom, were astonished by her devotion to her husband, whose intellectual interests she shared. Both were followers of Voltaire, which did not prevent them from forming a close friendship with his arch-enemy, Rousseau, who visited them frequently. To the further surprise of those who believed they had entered into a marriage of convenience, the elderly husband and young wife not only fell blissfully in love, but had a son, whom they named Maurice. He would achieve his greatest renown as the father of George Sand.

By the time the French Revolution exploded in 1789, old M. du Pin had died. His widow, who diplomatically changed the family name to the more democratic Dupin, was thrown into prison for a time during the Terror, but managed to survive. She retired to Nohant with her son, and with the aid of her faithful estate manager, a man named Deschartres, she lived through the worst days of the Revolution on shrinking proceeds.

As Napoleon Bonaparte came into prominence in the final years of the eighteenth century, Widow Dupin's various economic interests revived. She began to think of a suitable match for her son, who had been reared as a gentleman. But Maurice had ideas of his own regarding his future. The grandson of the Marshal de Saxe, he said, refused to be branded as a coward, so he ignored his mother's strenuous opposition and enlisted as a private in the Army.

His education and talents as a warrior won him a battlefield promotion to the rank of ensign, the lowest commissioned grade, and he continued to distinguish himself sufficiently to win two more promotions, and not only became a captain, but was assigned as aide-de-camp to a general serving in Italy. In this capacity he met the general's mistress, a young woman four years his senior, who bore the impressive name of Antoinette-Sophie-Victoire Delaborde, who was lively if not beautiful, shrewdly intelligent if not intellectual.

According to George Sand's romantic account of her parents, Maurice and the girl he called Sophie fell in love, and he won her from her lover. Perhaps it was an author's literary prerogative to indulge in flights of fancy, but the tale bore no relation to the truth. An aide-de-camp did not steal his general's mistress and keep his post as an aide. According to the more prosaic — albeit prejudiced — story told by Maurice's mother, the general grew tired of her, and in order to be rid of her persuaded his young aide to become her protector.

In any event, Maurice was willing, and Sophie was relieved to have found a new haven. She had known poverty, privation, and suffering most of her life, and was delighted to form a liaison with someone who demonstrated remarkable loyalty to her... Her father had been a peddler of birds on the bridges of the Seine, but the poor man had dreamed beyond his station, and his daughter had learned to read and write, accomplishments which few members of her class could boast.

There was only one way an attractive, ambitious girl who had no particular talents could escape from the slums of Paris, and Sophie took it, discarding whatever moral scruples she might have possessed. George Sand, in her *History* of *My Life*, described her with a candor burnished by no more than a slight romantic gloss:

> My mother was one of the world's gypsies, spiritual heir of a degraded and vagabond race. At one time she was a dancer, or, rather, something lower than a dancer, in one of the most disreputable of the Paris theaters, but a wealthy man rescued her from this abject condition, only to impose upon her one that was still more abject. She was thirty when my father first fell in love with her, and living in a whirl of wild indiscipline. But he had a big heart, and quickly realized that the beautiful creature still had a capacity for love.

George Sand neglected to mention that her mother was also burdened by an illegitimate daughter, whom she called Caroline, and for whose support she was responsible. The little-girl did not accompany her mother when she travelled with the general in the Army of Italy.

Mme Dupin made strenuous attempts to terminate her son's liaison, but neither she nor Deschartres could persuade or force Maurice to abandon her. When he came home on a leave, he performed the difficult feat of becoming reconciled with his mother while refusing to give up his mistress. Thereafter he married Sophie in a civil ceremony, and when he finally found the courage to tell his mother, an act requiring all the daring of Maurice de Saxe, she insisted that they come to Nohant and marry again in the local church.

Maurice was promoted to the rank of major in the Elite Guards of Napoleon, who had made himself Emperor, and was assigned to a regiment based in Paris, where his duties were ceremonial. It was there, in a small flat, that Sophie gave birth to a daughter on July 1, 1804. The baby was named Amantine Lucile Aurore, and immediately was known by the third of her Christian names, which pleased her grandmother, who had little else to celebrate.

When she was only a few months old, her father was transferred to the Army of Italy, and her mother accompanied him, leaving the baby with a cousin, Clotilde Marechal, with whom little Aurore spent the first three years of her life. Occasionally she visited her grandmother at Nohant and played with her half-brother; Hippolyte, the product of a previous liaison between Maurice and a peasant girl. These interludes were pleasant, although Hippolyte was something of a bully, but the small child spent most of her waking hours pining for her mother, about whom Clotilde had told her countless romantic tales, all of them untrue.

Early in 1808, Maurice, now a colonel, was sent to Madrid to join the staff of the dashing Marshal Joachim Murat, and Sophie returned to Paris to collect her two daughters. Pregnant with her third child, a boy who died in infancy, she followed her husband to Spain, accompanied by Caroline and Aurore, who became acquainted with her parents for the first time.

They reached Madrid in time for Sophie to participate in the planning for a week of gala festivities in honor of Joseph Bonaparte, the elder brother of Napoleon, whom the Emperor had placed on the throne of Spain. Sophie was a clever seamstress, and when she learned that her younger child had been taught to ride horseback by Deschartres, she made the little girl an exact replica of the Hussar uniform worn by

Murat's cavalry honor guard. The climax of the ceremonies in Joseph Bonaparte's honor was a mammoth military review, and when the day arrived, Aurore rode onto the parade ground alone, with her hair cut short, wearing her uniform and carrying a tiny sword made for the occasion by a Spanish armorer.

The little girl created a sensation. The entire crowd applauded, Marshal Murat insisted that she ride at the head of his Hussars, and King Joseph called a temporary halt to the proceedings while he went onto the field himself and escorted her to a place at his side in the reviewing stand. The influence of the occasion on the future of Aurore Dupin cannot be exaggerated. The lonely little girl was not only the center of admiring attention, but won the approval of the parents for whose company and love she had longed. The significance of this single traumatic experience in shaping the life of the future George Sand was overwhelming.

But Aurore's happiness was short-lived. She and Caroline were stricken with 'camp fever', a form of typhoid, and as medical facilities in Madrid were cramped, due to the refusal of the Spaniards to cooperate with their conquerors, Colonel Dupin decided to send his family off to Nohant, where his mother and Deschartres could care for them. Sophie and her infant son were taken ill on the journey, and soon after they reached their destination the baby died. Maurice followed his family to Nohant, riding a stallion named Leopardo he had acquired in Spain.

He obtained a leave of absence and stayed there with Sophie, Aurore, and Caroline while they recuperated. But he found sickroom attendance tedious, and one day relieved his boredom by going hunting. He foolishly rode his new stallion, an animal difficult to control under the best circumstances, and the horse threw him, then trampled him, killing him before his companions could intervene. Aurore was sufficiently recovered from her fever to attend her father's funeral in the village church, and in later years she repeatedly referred to the occasion as the dreariest, most sorrowful day of her life.

At best Sophie and her aristocratic mother-in-law had maintained a polite truce, but now the strains became so great that the younger Mme Dupin felt she could not remain at Nohant, and returned to Paris with her daughters. There Sophie was forced to recall the harsh realities she had forgotten during the years of her marriage. Maurice, at the time of his death, had not yet inherited his fortune, so he had left her nothing. No longer attractive, she knew it was virtually impossible to find another protector, so she was forced to do needlework to support herself and her children.

Aurore, who was too young to understand her mother's financial struggle, was ecstatically happy in her company. Sophie was witty and charming, cooked delicious meals by throwing scraps into a pot, and sang all day, no matter how great her worries. She also taught the little girl to sew, and Aurore would be comforted by that skill for over six decades.

The strain of trying to provide for three proved too great for Sophie, so she gave in to the requests of her mother-in-law, who wanted to bring up Aurore. Deschartres came to Paris to fetch the child, who promptly became hysterical, and who found no joy in the promise that she would spend a part of each winter with her mother in Paris.

Tears did not prevent the inevitable. Screaming and fainting, Aurore was taken off to live with the old lady who never for a moment forgot she was the granddaughter of a Polish king, the daughter of a great marshal of France, the cousin of a queen of France, or, for that matter, that her first husband had been an illegitimate son of Louis XV. The little girl's carefree life came to an abrupt end.

Tutors were hired for her, and her formal education was supervised by Deschartres, who had been an Abbé for a number of years before returning to the secular fold. Aurore spent long hours each day at her studies, and although she found it difficult to master mathematics, she learned to relish literature. She also became proficient in foreign languages, and soon could read, write, and speak English, Spanish, Italian, German, and Latin. Only because Deschartres was weak in Greek was she spared the need to learn that tongue. Her religious education was not neglected, either, and the elderly parish priest came to Nohant for an hour each day to instruct her.

Mme Dupin also made certain that the social conventions were not ignored. Aurore learned the proper use of forks and glasses and chinaware, she was taught what clothes were to be worn at different hours of the day, and her grandmother personally supervised the task of transforming her into a lady. Mme Dupin instructed her at length in the glorious history of her illustrious ancestors.

There were compensations, to be sure, not the least of them the comfortable manor house, which Mme Dupin called a 'simple' dwelling. Aurore occupied a sumptuous suite of her own, and a large staff of servants took care of her. Reared as a member of the highest nobility, in accordance with the standards of a bygone era, it is understandable that, in later years — even at the height of her rebellion — George Sand always remembered she was a lady, and insisted that others remain aware of it, too.

The lonely child found her greatest pleasures in the woods and fields, where she could daydream. She watched her grandmother's gardeners at work and studied the wildflowers she found, but took care never to pick them, a practice she followed all of her life. She taught herself to swim in the river, and formed the habit of taking a daily dip, no matter what the weather. She roamed the countryside incessantly, sometimes on foot, sometimes on horseback, and she came to know the peasants of the neighborhood so well that her later portrayals of them were marvellously detailed.

George Sand's so-called Pastoral novels, more than anything else she wrote, have won her an enduring place in the world's literature. Her self-acquired appreciation of nature grew directly from the childhood years she spent at Nohant. She observed everything, including the subtleties that others never noticed, and her love of the open countryside continued as long as she lived.

Her only companion of her own generation was Hippolyte who, after the manner of an older boy, tolerated her company only when he was in a generous mood. He was a stronger swimmer, a better rider, a tireless hiker. He did not feel squeamish when he baited a fishing hook with a worm, and he could handle a catch with assurance. Sometimes he took her hunting, a sport she failed to enjoy because she hated killing, but she envied his freedom when he climbed to the top of the highest trees at the far end of the formal garden. Sometimes, when her grandmother was taking an afternoon nap, Aurore shed her voluminous skirts and petticoats, and donning the peasant trousers she kept hidden at the back of a wardrobe, she practiced her own tree-climbing in a futile attempt to climb higher than Hippolyte.

Grand'maman did not care if Hippolyte paid a visit to a peasant's cottage, but Aurore was questioned interminably when she paid a neighborly visit. *Grand'maman* only smiled indulgently if Hippolyte's face was streaked with dirt, or his hands smelled of fish, but Aurore was reprimanded severely if her clothes were not immaculate, her hair not curled or her face lacking a coat of powder. When Hippolyte did particularly well in his day's lessons, Deschartres rewarded him by permitting him to swim for an extra hour, or sometimes allowed him to ride one of the more spirited horses in the Nohant stable. But perfection was expected of Aurore, and no matter how thoroughly she mastered her day's lessons, she was required to join *Grand'maman* in the salon for the daily lesson on deportment.

Aurore observed that females were forced to accept their supposedly natural inferiority. She complained to Deschartres and her tutors, who told her she would cause herself untold trouble if she forgot her place. She complained to the priest, who scolded her and read to her from Scriptures to prove that men were dominant. She complained to *Grand'maman*, who was shocked, and delivered even longer lectures on the art of becoming a lady.

As Aurore grew older, she began to seek her own answers to the questions that crowded her mind. She found little satisfaction in any of the books that filled the shelves of *Grand'maman*'s library. Aristotle and Plato took the superiority of men for granted. St Paul and St Augustine appeared to entertain a positive dislike for members of the female sex. And in the plays of Racine and Moliere, it seemed, men were always the aggressors and instigators, while women were the objects of their passion.

On her infrequent visits to her adored mother, the solemn child tried to probe the subject. But the harassed Sophie, who had little in common with her intellectual daughter, lacked the mind, the patience, and the wit to deal with the subject. She could speak only in terms of her own bitter experiences, and expressed her opinions of men in terms as blunt as they were emphatic. Aurore was horrified to learn that, in her mother's eyes, her education was a waste, and some day she would be forced to make her way in the world subject to the lusts of men.

The troubled girl found her first hope in the acidulous pages of Voltaire's work. In his correspondence she discovered his remarkable mistress, Émilie due Châtelet, who had been a distinguished philosopher, scientist, and author in her own right. What Mme du Châtelet had achieved, perhaps a woman who lived in the next century could also accomplish.

Her arms filled with books by Voltaire and Mme du Châtelet, Aurore confronted her grandmother, and received the setback of her young life. Voltaire, Mme Dupin said, was right to decry the inferior place women were forced to assume, and she herself had long admired the independence of Mme du Châtelet. But the session ended on a familiar note. One accepted the world realistically, because one had no choice, and the wise girl prepared for womanhood in accordance with society's inflexible rules.

At this time Aurore was fourteen years of age, and Mme Dupin, who was old and ailing, felt that the girl needed firmer guidance than she herself could provide. She sent her granddaughter off to complete her education at the most aristocratic school for young ladies in Paris, the Convent of the Dames Augustines Anglaises, where all of the nuns were English. Only English was spoken there, and English customs were observed so rigorously that, after spending more than three years there, Aurore habitually spoke English as often as she conversed in her native tongue. For the rest of her life she also preferred tea to coffee.

The girl left Nohant without a qualm, rejoicing in the thought that she would be near her mother and would see her often. But Sophie had lost all interest in the daughter she had seen so infrequently and with whom she had so little in common. The expensively gowned adolescent was completely out of place in the cramped, shabby flat where Sophie struggled to make ends meet; the latter made it plain that their first meeting would be their last. The fact that Aurore would be attending a convent school only a quarter of an hour's walk from her flat was a matter of supreme indifference to her. Some day they might meet again, but for the present her sewing kept her too busy to entertain wealthy young visitors.

The convent doors closed behind the heartbroken Aurore, who made a deeply significant entry in the *Diary* that would be replaced, a decade and a half later, by her *Intimate Journal*. She wrote the plaintive cry, '*Oh, darling mama, why is it you do not love me, while I love you so truly?*'

Throughout her adult life, George Sand would assert and reassert a maternal role, in her heterosexual and homosexual love affairs, in her fiercely protective relationships with her own children, and in her dealing with the many young people to whom she offered unlimited guidance, moral support, and financial help. Even her enemies grudgingly admitted that her sympathetic interest in the young was so intense, so obviously sincere, that she achieved an almost magical rapport with them.

Certainly she understood, better than most, the feelings of insecurity and loneliness endemic in the adolescent. Rejected by her mother and believing herself rejected by her grandmother, she barricaded herself, emotionally and to some extent physically, inside the walls of the convent. She lost none of her natural ebullience, her tomboy characteristics, or her love of simple practical jokes. Living in a dormitory with several younger girls, she soon became a leader of the group, and the chaplains who came to the convent daily to conduct services and hear confessions sometimes shook their heads when they heard of her pranks. But they were men, and therefore failed to understand that her high spirits were free of malice. The sisters, who knew her far better, accepted her mischief as an outlet for her ever-present frustrations.

The religious life of the convent was of very little interest to Aurore. Her previous education had been supervised by her grandmother, a nominal Catholic who admired Voltaire, and by Deschartres, who had found the demands of the clergy too exacting. Writing in her *History of My Life*, George Sand said she never felt a need to confess her sins because she had committed none. At the same time, she was being exposed to firm, conservative views on ethics and morality, and in her later life, no matter how unorthodox her ways, she remained convinced she was following the precepts she had learned at the convent.

In her second year under the roof of the English nuns, a marked change took place in her manner and conduct. Aurore was beginning to mature, and the sisters, when they became aware of the process, moved her to a tiny room of her own. It was the custom of the nuns to pay special attention to a girl who, in their opinion, showed greater promise than the rest, and Aurore decided she wanted to be 'adopted' by them. She particularly sought the favor of one nun, Sister Mary Alicia, for whom she had formed a schoolgirl infatuation, and seeking a substitute for the mother love that had been denied her, she often begged the nun to go beyond the customs of the convent school and formally adopt her as a daughter.

To the astonishment of the other girls, Aurore's high spirits vanished. Emulating Sister Mary Alicia, she became grave, scholarly, and introspective; she studied books on the lives of the saints, she pored over the Gospels, and she almost ruined her eyesight reading theology. One evening she went alone to the chapel to pray, and her experience is best described in her *History of My Life*:

> One star lost in the immensity of the night was, as it were, framed in the glazed tracery, and seemed to be watching me fixedly. The whole place breathed a calm, a loveliness, a composure and a mystery such as I had never dreamed. The birds were singing outside the windows of stained glass, and suddenly I was shaken in some strange way to the very core of my being. I felt dizzy, and then I seemed to hear the murmur of a voice saying, *Tolle, lege*. The tears gushed from my eyes. At that moment I felt that I loved God truly. It was as though some obstacle, until then impenetrable, which had stood between the ardor of my spirit and this burning center of ineffable adoration, suddenly had melted away.

Some might call the incident a manifestation of adolescent hysteria, but others would insist that it was a genuine mystical experience. Aurore herself firmly believed it to be the latter, and it profoundly influenced her for the rest of her life. As an adult she informally abandoned Catholicism, yet refused to leave the Church. At one point she came close to espousing Protestantism, but drew back at the last moment. And always she considered herself a religious woman, one who was close to God and communicated directly with Him, needing no cleric to interpret His Will to her.

In the days immediately following the experience, the young girl was ecstatic, and predictably decided she wanted to enter the Order as a novice. Her confessor, the Abbé de Prémord, was a worldly, experienced man whose judgement told him she was not suited to the disciplines required of a nun. He tried to dissuade her, but Aurore refused to listen to him, and he finally turned the problem over to Sister Mary Alicia.

The nun may have been the only person in the world to whom Aurore would have listened, but, in any event, Sister Mary Alicia performed the near-impossible. First she persuaded the girl not to do anything rash, and then, over a period of weeks, she gently helped her to change her mind. The process was not accomplished overnight, however, and Aurore wrestled with her dilemma for six months. During this period she did not neglect her studies, but took virtually no part in the social life of the school. Each day, after she finished her classes, she retired alone to the room she called her 'cell', and there brooded in self-imposed silence. Even at meals she rarely spoke, and her self-scrutiny was so intense that the worried nuns finally wrote to her grandmother.

Mme Dupin was alarmed by the possibility that the girl might take the veil and retire permanently from the world. So she handled the matter in her own forthright way, and sent a letter to Aurore ordering her to give up any thoughts of becoming a nun and to remain where she was.

The blunt communication, so similar in tone to the approach that George Sand herself employed later in life when dealing with the young, soon cleared away the mists of religious fervor. Aurore realized that Sister Mary Alicia was right, and promptly abandoning all thought of taking Orders, she became the director and principal actress in the next school play. Although she did not realize it until late in life, she owed her grandmother a great debt. In, spite of surface differences, her adult character was becoming remarkably similar to that of the worldly, pragmatic old lady.

At the end of her third year at the convent, Aurore received another urgent letter from her grandmother. Mme Dupin's health was failing, and although she refused to summon her physicians, she became convinced she was slowly dying. One major task remained before she was ready to confront her Maker, she declared: it was her duty and desire to see her granddaughter happily and properly married. She directed the girl to return to Nohant.

Locked away in a community of women, Aurore had given no thought to men, and the mere idea of marriage terrified her. In fact, she had never known any men other than the chaplains at the convent and Deschartres, the former abbe, so she knew nothing whatever about the lordly male creatures who ruled the world. She begged the nuns not to send her away, but they pointed out to her that it was her duty to obey her grandmother.

Frightened, bewildered, and cut off from the only affection she had known in her seventeen years, Aurore Dupin left the English nuns. Deschartres was sent to meet her, as it was considered unseemly for a young lady to travel unchaperoned, and returned with her on the stagecoach to Châteauroux, where the private carriage of Mme Dupin awaited them.

One astonishing aspect of George Sand's life up to this time requires comment. Virtually every major author in the history of literature began writing at a very early age, driven to a greater or lesser extent by the compulsions that characterize creative work. Aurore Dupin was an exception. She had received an education superior to that of most women of her time, and she had read extensively. But her only writing had been the lines she had penned to herself in her schoolgirl Diary. Nothing in her background indicated that she was destined to become one of the foremost authors of her time, and the first of her sex in France to achieve professional success in a demanding profession.

III

Nohant was unchanged. The old manor house, built to survive the centuries, was comfortable, austere, and tranquil. Flowers were in bloom everywhere, the paths through the woods were dark and cool, and the waters of the river were inviting. Aurore's home was Nohant, and for the first time in her life she appreciated its solidity.

Yet everything was different. The peasants who had always called her by her Christian name now tipped their worn hats and addressed her as 'Mademoiselle'. The villagers were uneasy in her presence, and treated her with unaccustomed respect. Even the servants at the manor house, many of whom had known her from early childhood, were deferential now. And her half-brother, Hippolyte, who was a lieutenant in the cavalry, displayed an embarrassed reserve when he came home on a leave of absence.

The heiress to a great fortune, Aurore discovered, was forced to live in luxurious isolation. She was also besieged by suitors, all of them total strangers, and many of whom wrote her letters in which they swore they loved her. Uninvited swains often appeared at the gates of Nohant, but Aurore was grateful that she was spared their company. Deschartres sent most of them on their way, but *Grand'maman* personally attended to those whose social position warranted her personal intervention. It was a relief that none was considered worthy of her hand.

There was one compensation for the lonely life Aurore was leading: for the first time, as a young adult, she really came to know her grandmother. She spent at least two hours each day with Mme Dupin, who spoke to her with candor about life and love, the problems of the wealthy, and the motives of men. The girl listened, asked countless questions, and began to appreciate the character of the old lady she had always considered so remote and forbidding. Mme Dupin was failing, a prospect that filled Aurore with dread, but her grandmother made strenuous efforts to prepare her for the day when she would be forced to face the world alone.

Late in the summer of 1821, Mme Dupin suffered a stroke that confined her permanently to her bed, and Deschartres overnight began to report on the management of the estate to the young, future mistress. Aurore knew nothing of farm products, real estate in La Châtre, and mills where cloth was made, but she learned quickly and was endowed with common sense. Within a surprisingly short time, she began to play an active, intelligent role in the management of the estate.

During this period Aurore unexpectedly received a letter from her mother, who had made no attempt to get in touch with her for years. Showing a solicitude unique since the girl's early childhood, Sophie inquired tenderly and at length about her interests and habits and showed an almost overwhelming curiosity about the steps that were being taken to protect her from fortune hunters.

Aurore saw through the flimsy façade, but remembered her training as a lady, and her reply was couched in terms of appropriate filial respect. Showing both patience and politeness, she replied to her mother's questions, and only when discussing the protection of her inheritance from the greedy did she show a sign of the future George Sand. The illness of her grandmother forced her to depend upon her own resources, she said, but she could look after herself and could always see through the front of mock concern. The final sentence was both a challenge and a dismissal: 'Leading-strings were necessary to me when I was a child, but I am now seventeen, and have learned to walk by myself.'

On Christmas Day, 1821, old Mme Dupin died. She was lucid to the end, and her final words, addressed to her granddaughter, haunted Aurore to the end of her own days: 'You are losing your best friend.'

In an attempt to provide for the girl's future the old lady had named two people as her guardians until she came of age, but they had no opportunity to act on her behalf. Less than a week after the daughter of Maurice de Saxe died, Sophie Dupin, seamstress and one-time army mistress, appeared at Nohant to claim custody of her daughter and as much of the inheritance as she could garner. Family friends in La Châtre and Châteauroux were horrified, but could do nothing, and even the Archbishop of Arles, a relative of sorts, was helpless. Several of the best lawyers in Châteauroux and Paris were consulted, and all gave the same answer: no law prevented Sophie from taking custody of her minor daughter.

Aurore was hauled off to her mother's cramped, ill-furnished Paris flat, and in the months that followed she was forced to endure the worst nightmare of her life. Sophie was a tyrant determined to even the score, at the expense of her daughter, for the abuses she imagined she had suffered. Intent upon sadistically humiliating the daughter who had enjoyed all of the luxuries she herself had been denied, she drove the girl mercilessly. Aurore, who had never endured physical labor, was compelled to wash floors, scrub dirty sheets, cook meals, and act as a personal maidservant. Her own clothes were taken from her, Sophie made her a serving maid's uniform, and she was compelled to wear it when neighborhood women dropped in for a chat and a cheap glass of brandy.

The girl made no complaint as the indignities mounted. Recognizing the helplessness of her position, she met the abuse and mockery in silence, meekly obeyed orders, and showed every sign of filial deference while Sophie, sometimes half drunk, abused her in language that not even Nohant stable hands had used in her presence.

In only one respect did Aurore stand up for herself. Sophie concocted a scheme whereby she would go to court and request that she be appointed guardian of the estate her daughter had inherited; but inevitably the justices would ask if the seventeen-year-old girl agreed to this transfer. As one who was approaching her majority, her opinion would carry weight.

Aurore quietly made it clear that she would speak her own mind in court, that she considered her mother an unfit guardian who would squander her wealth as quickly as it came into her hands. The girl promised that, on gaining control of her inheritance, she would be willing to give her mother a reasonable sum each year, a pension large enough to make it unnecessary for her to work again. Under no circumstances, however, would she permit her mother to disburse revenues or buy and sell property as she saw fit.

This display of independence infuriated Sophie, who created daily scenes and sometimes punished her daughter physically. But Aurore held firmly to her position; neither threats nor force could alter it. When Sophie, in what she regarded as the supreme insult, told her she was as stubborn as her grandmother, the girl accepted the accusation as a compliment.

Always restless, Sophie found an opportunity to travel in April, 1822. Taking money that had been sent by Deschartres for Aurore's living expenses, she decided to pay a visit to an army comrade of her husband, Colonel James Roettiers du Plessis, who lived on an estate near Melun with his handsome young wife and their five daughters. As an afterthought, in order to avoid possible trouble with the managers of Mme Dupin's estate, she decided to take Aurore with her.

James and Angèle Roettiers du Plessis were delighted by the girl, although they received Sophie coolly, and Aurore was happy because she could wander again in gardens and forests. After a few days Sophie became bored and accepted the offer of her husband's old friend to keep the girl with his family for a time. This arrangement satisfied everyone, and Aurore felt infinite relief when her mother departed.

The visit, originally scheduled for a week or two, stretched out for months. The Colonel and Mme du Plessis bought a new wardrobe for Aurore, as she had no acceptable clothes of her own. She became an older sister to the du Plessis girls. The kindness of the family was so great that both the parents and children became George Sand's lifelong friends.

Sophie, as happy to be rid of her daughter as she was to pocket the year's allowance Deschartres had sent, vanished again from Aurore's life, and the girl knew she would not reappear until her need for money once more became pressing.

One day in the early summer of 1822 she accompanied the Colonel and his wife on a shopping expedition to Paris, and in mid-afternoon they stopped at a café for a cooling drink. No sooner had they made themselves comfortable when an imposing young man rose from his own table to greet them.

His name was Casimir Dudevant; he held the rank of colonel in the cavalry reserves, and was the natural son of a baron, whose title and estate he would some day inherit, as there were no other heirs. His father, as it happened, had served along with Colonel Maurice Dupin, so he was already familiar with some parts of Aurore's story. Casimir was slender and handsome, he wore his expensive clothes with an air of elegance, and his terse speech made him appear strong and wise, at least in the eyes of the unhappy young girl.

He accepted the invitation of the du Plessis family to visit them, and at Melun he delighted Aurore by participating without reserve in the games of the children. Then, in the evenings, after the youngsters had gone to bed, he accompanied the lonely girl on long walks down country lanes. Inevitably she told him her problems, inevitably he offered her solemn advice, and it was not surprising that in a very short time the inexperienced Aurore fell madly in love.

Certainly she would not have listened had anyone told her that she and Casimir had far different interests. He rarely bothered to read a book, and his favorite pastimes were hunting during the day and drinking at night. The girl knew too little of men to realize he took women for granted, and although he was polite to Mme du Plessis, he found little to say to her. The terseness Aurore admired was one phase of a deep-rooted morose nature, and only violent physical exercise or the bottle gave him relief.

It was true that he was an eligible bachelor, an aristocrat whose estate some day would be worth more than Aurore would inherit. She had every reason to believe, as his interest in her grew, that her money was not the magnet that attracted him to her. In all probability she was right. Casimir was perhaps drawn to this intense, shy girl with dark hair and a breath-taking figure because it was so obvious that she was in love with him. But it would be difficult to determine his motives. He was as complicated as he was dour, and no one, including George Sand and her biographers, has ever truly understood the man.

There was one person who doubted him from the outset. No sooner had he proposed marriage and been accepted than

Sophie Dupin reappeared on the scene, swearing he wanted to marry her daughter so he could gain control of her inheritance. Aurore protested in vain that his own father was giving him a marriage settlement of sixty thousand gold francs, a considerable sum. Sophie replied that; no matter how solid and respectable the gift might be, it was worth only a small fraction of the Dupin estate, and her logic was unassailable.

For months Sophie refused to consent to the marriage, which could not take place without her approval, As week after dreary week passed, she created scenes, tried to demand that Casimir be given no part in either the principal or the interest his wife would inherit, and when everything else failed, she invented outrageous lies in a desperate attempt to break up the romance. Casimir, she said, was a professional fortune hunter who had already spent the inheritance of two previous wives, whom he had divorced in pagan, Protestant Geneva. He was not the son of a baron, as he claimed, but was a former café waiter who had lived off the earnings of prostitutes for years.

Sophie's charges became increasingly wild, and eventually the young couple gave up their efforts to deny them. Early in September their patience was exhausted. Aurore presented Sophie with an ultimatum: either she would sign the necessary papers, or the girl was prepared to elope with Casimir. They had found a priest who was sympathetic to thwarted young lovers, and he had agreed to marry them, even though the bride was still a minor.

Unable to hold out any longer and afraid she would permanently alienate the couple whose generosity could make her own life easier, Sophie finally capitulated. So, on September 10, 1822, the eighteen-year-old Aurore Dupin, the descendant of a Marshal of France and a bird peddler, was given in marriage by Colonel du Plessis to Casimir Dudevant, Gascon gentleman, former soldier and future baron.

The bride and groom immediately set out for Nohant, where they planned to make their home, and Aurore, the girl from the convent, tried to acclimate herself to marriage. 'I was still completely innocent at that time,' she later wrote in her *Intimate Journal*, and added, 'I knew nothing of the demands a man could make on his wife.'

The convent-bred virgin was surprised by the persistence of her husband's ardor, but submitted to him with the good grace expected of a bride. Neither her *Diary* nor the extensive correspondence she was maintaining with former schoolmates indicated a lively sexual curiosity, but too much could be made of her silence. Ladies simply didn't write about such matters, and Aurore was something of a prude.

In letters to her friends during the months that followed the wedding she made all the appropriate comments expected of a bride. Casimir was the most wonderful of men, their relationship was tender, and their rapport was close. Marriage was the best of all the institutions ever developed by society.

The truth first appeared many years later in *Lélia*, perhaps the most famous of George Sand's novels and the most frankly autobiographical. Once the dam of reticence had been broken there, she repeated her admissions many times in other books, her *Intimate Journal*, and her extensive correspondence. She revealed that the physical aspects of marriage left her unmoved. For a long time it did not occur to her that the woman, like the man, might become aroused; she merely considered it her duty to submit to her husband and give him pleasure.

Eventually, when it dawned on her that she, too, might find erotic enjoyment, she blamed Casimir for selfishly seeking only his own release. Not until she had experienced several affairs did she become aware that the flaw lay within herself, and in *Lélia* she emphasized the fear that she was frigid. Her homosexual relationships proved she was mistaken, but she did not gauge them as she did her affairs with men, and to the end of her life clung to the belief that she was something of an emotional cripple who could find only mild enjoyment and no release in sexual relations.

Aurore also found it difficult to adjust to marriage in other ways, and it was at this time that she developed her lifelong indignation against the French legal and social traditions that robbed women of their rights. Nohant was her property, as were the mills and other real estate she had inherited from her grandmother, yet she had no voice in their management or in the disposition of the income that the various investments earned. During the months prior to her grandmothers death she had taken an active role in making business decisions, encouraged by Deschartres. Now, she found herself excluded.

Deschartres, who planned to retire in a few months, was required to report only to Casimir, who gave all of the orders and did not bother to consult with Aurore before making a decision. According to law and custom, he was under no obligation to seek her advice or abide by her wishes, though the properties still belonged exclusively to her.

In later years, particularly at the time of her legal separation from Casimir, when she submitted a long petition to the courts, George Sand bitterly attacked the system so manifestly unfair to her sex. 'A woman,' she declared, 'is an adult, and has a mind of her own. We dwell under a system both archaic and pathetic in which woman must remain mute and bow to the supposedly superior wisdom of man, who may excel only in his physical strength. With all members of my sex, I eagerly await the day when the women of France will receive their equitable due under the law.'

With Deschartres' amiable supervision, Nohant was an estate of great charm and little efficiency. There had always been an income sufficient for old Mme Dupin's needs, so he had changed little during the decades he had been in charge. But Casimir was shocked by the wasted land, and ordered woods cut, pastures burned, and productive farms expanded. Aurore had always loved the rustic, half-wild estate, yet did not dare to protest her husband's decision. Retiring to her bedchamber, she wept for the solitude of the woods that would vanish forever.

But she refused to prostrate herself completely before her husband, and in the realm of finances apparently made enough scenes to convince him she would create far more trouble for him if he failed to heed her wishes. Her estate brought in an income of seventeen to eighteen thousand gold francs a year, a considerable sum. Aurore felt that a portion was needed to fulfil moral obligations. When Deschartres retired after a lifetime of faithful, dependable service, she wanted to pay him a yearly pension of three thousand francs. She also wanted to give her mother three thousand, and earmarked an additional two thousand as pensions for various elderly servants.

Casimir was happy enough to make the payments to his mother-in-law. He had already seen more than enough of Sophie during the trying period when she had attempted to prevent the marriage. He hoped the pension would keep her permanently at a distance. But he thought the pension for Deschartres was too much, and wanted to cut the allowances of the retired servants in half.

Aurore told him they required no more than nine thousand francs to live in style, and threatened household economies

43

that would interfere with his comfort if he did not alter his stand. Casimir capitulated, but for an altogether different reason, as his correspondence with Hippolyte, his brother-in-law, clearly reveals. He was a newcomer to Berry, and being a French country boy himself, he knew that the peasants and villagers of such small towns as La Châtre regarded all outsiders with resentful suspicion. If he displayed too great a reluctance to reward long service, he would lose more in the long run. Vegetable produce, cattle, sheep, and poultry would disappear mysteriously from Nohant, and the constabulary of La Châtre and Châteauroux would be unable to find the culprits. Grape vines would be cut just as they were on the verge of producing fruit, and firewood would vanish from the sheds behind the manor house. So his parsimony would cost him dearly, and he would be wise to pay Deschartres and the retired servants the pensions that the extravagantly good-hearted Aurore wanted them to receive.

Hippolyte sympathized with his brother-in-law; he not only agreed with him but suggested in a letter that Casimir should find some way to silence Aurore. There had been no need for the household staff to know the pension figures in her mind, but as usual, he said, she talked too much. Casimir may have tried to persuade his wife to exercise greater discretion; if he made the attempt, it failed. Even now, years before Aurore Dupin Dudevant transformed herself into George Sand, it was impossible for anyone to silence her when she wanted to make her voice heard.

Casimir and Hippolyte soon proved to be cut from the same bolt of cloth. They enjoyed hunting together every day, and at the end of their day's activities they went to the house of one or the other, Hippolyte having settled on a small estate of his own in the neighborhood. And there they spent several convivial hours drinking together.

Aurore discovered that, in many ways, her life as a married woman was similar to what it had been before she had left Nohant. She spent most of each day alone, read in the library, wrote letters to fellow alumnae of the convent school, went for walks in what was left of the woods, and sometimes went out for a canter. Her riding was curtailed, as she was a married woman now, and it did not become the matron who was the mistress of Nohant to behave like a tomboy.

Aurore and Casimir spent their evenings together, and the bride had imagined they would sit together by the fire, reading and chatting. The snowfall was heavy at Nohant that winter, which made the prospect all the more appealing to her. She quickly learned that Casimir was bored by books, and disliked reading for more than short periods. When he became restless, he usually resumed drinking after his day of hunting with Hippolyte. Aurore tried to interest him in chess, but he refused to concentrate. He finally learned to tolerate backgammon, an ancient game long popular in the countries of the eastern Mediterranean that had made its way to France from England after the fall of Napoleon. So they played several games before bedtime, which cut down his drinking.

Early in the winter of 1822-23, Aurore found she was pregnant, and her correspondence indicates she was neither elated nor displeased. Babies were to be expected. Casimir showed her greater attention and concern during the months of her pregnancy than he ever again displayed, and although he curtailed neither his hunting trips with Hippolyte nor his drinking, he spent far more time with his wife. He also took it upon himself to send off to Paris for a variety of luxuries he thought she would enjoy.

Deschartres postponed his retirement until the birth of the baby in the summer of 1823, and made it his business to prevent his beloved young mistress from engaging in too much physical activity. In accordance with the custom of the period he insisted that she spend the sixth month of her pregnancy in bed, and she followed his instructions. For five weeks she remained beneath the coverlet of heavy silk, and never had the active girl felt so useless or miserable. But she recovered her good humor when she was permitted to move around once again, and early in June Casimir took her off to Paris, where they moved into a furnished hotel suite. Only those who could not afford the luxury of bringing their children into the civilized world in its capital, Paris, had their babies in rural retreats, and the young M. and Mme Dudevant were very much aware of what the social leaders of the era considered chic. Aurore, with little else to occupy her time, had been reading the gossip of the city in its many newspapers.

In midsummer she gave birth, after an easy delivery, to a healthy son, and ever-conscious of her antecedents, named him Maurice, after both her father and the Marshal de Saxe. Most young mothers of quality hired wet-nurses, a custom French aristocrats had followed for over three hundred years. But Aurore insisted on nursing her infant herself. She would be the perfect mother, giving her children what she herself had been denied, and it amused her when she received a long letter from Sophie, praising her because she was nursing the baby.

The retirement of Deschartres forced Casimir to cut short his family's stay in Paris. He was needed at Nohant to supervise the operations of the estate, so he indulged in the extravagance of hiring a carriage with a padded interior, and only three weeks after his son's birth they returned to Aurore's ancestral home. There husband and wife took up their familiar routines, but there were differences. Casimir, who still rode and hunted and drank with Hippolyte, now spent his mornings attending to the management of his wife's properties. The baby occupied several hours of Aurore's time each day, but she still had ample opportunity to read, correspond with her friends, wander through the woods, and daydream.

Those dreams sustained her, nourishing her spirit when she felt crushed by the stultifying routine of her existence. She conducted an almost frenzied search for a 'perfect' philosophy that would reconcile the worlds of God and man, and when she could not find it, she began to realize she was almost hopelessly idealistic. It also occurred to her that she was a romantic who still had not received the love she had so long believed her due, and for the first time she wondered whether she had made the right marriage.

Casimir seldom spent more than short periods in her company. They rarely saw each other during the day, and although he always dined with her in the evening, his pleasures took him elsewhere after they left the table. Aurore read herself to sleep every night, and sometimes Casimir, returning home after drinking too much, awakened her by forcing his attentions on her. She submitted, in spite of her growing disgust with him, largely because it did not cross her mind that she had any alternative.

In the spring of 1824 the strains of marriage and loneliness became overwhelming, and at the climax of an insignificant quarrel Aurore succumbed to protracted hysterics. She referred to the incident in her *History of My Life*, wryly observing that, at the time, she was convinced she was a worthless creature who had become mentally unbalanced.

Her tears frightened Casimir, so later in the spring he took her and little Maurice, for a visit to their good friends, James and Angèle du Plessis. A number of other guests were entertained there at the same time, and the pendulum of Aurore's mood soared to the other extreme. She was gay and witty, and surprised to discover that she had natural, highly developed talents as a flirt. It did not occur to her that she was seeking compensations for Casimir's growing indifference to her.

For a short time the unexpected blossoming of his shy wallflower amused him, but soon he became jealous and ordered her to desist. Aurore had won a victory, but failed to recognize it, and like the George Sand she would become, refused to obey. She continued to flirt with other men at the house party until Casimir lost his self-control and slapped her across the face, embarrassing both of them.

A day or two later it became necessary for him to return to the management of the Nohant estates, while Aurore, the baby, and a nursemaid remained behind at the du Plessis home. Casimir's reluctance to leave should have told Aurore that she had achieved a significant triumph, but she spoiled it by writing him a series of long, apologetic letters in which she promised never to indulge in such shameful conduct again.

There was no improvement in the marital malaise after she and Maurice returned to Nohant. The bored dissatisfaction of husband and wife had become mutual, and they quarrelled incessantly, usually over trifles. The guilt-ridden young wife considered the blame all her own and conceived the idea of going to the only real home she had ever known, the convent of the English Ladies, for a protracted retreat. There, she hoped, she would find God again, and with His help achieve inner peace. Casimir agreed with such alacrity that it is difficult to refrain from assuming he was eager to be rid of her for a time.

The convent was still a cool, tranquil oasis, far removed from the world's problems, but the people who had guided and helped a lonely young schoolgirl were older now, and appeared to have become more rigid in their thinking. The chaplains and the Mother Superior, Mme Eugénie, gave what sounded like stock answers to her questions, and although she spent long hours praying in the chapel where she had enjoyed her ecstatic religious experience, she found no peace there. Perhaps the most catastrophic blow was the inability of the all-wise Sister Mary Alicia to assist or comfort her. In fact, the nun made no attempt to pour balm on her wounds, but lectured her severely, telling her she had become a pampered, lazy matron who should be offering thanks to God for her husband, child, and comfortable, secure life.

Aurore struggled, making a supreme effort to count her blessings, but her efforts were in vain. Then, suddenly, she had to cut short her retreat when she received word from Nohant that her son Maurice was ill. She returned home and quickly nursed him back to health, but could not arrange another visit to the convent, and the loveless marriage was resumed.

Several young ladies who had attended school with Aurore visited Nohant, these intervals affording her only temporary relief. Then she received word that Deschartres had died, and her melancholy grew worse. She had to give up riding entirely because of dizzy spells, she suffered heart palpitations that sent her to her bed, and she became the victim of headaches so severe she wept. Casimir summoned several physicians to the manor house, and after making thorough examinations they expressed the unanimous belief that nothing whatever was wrong with her health. Casimir was right when he told her that her ailments existed only in her bored, dissatisfied head.

By the summer of 1825, it was Casimir who longed for a change, but he was curiously dependent on his wife and insisted that she and Maurice accompany him to Gascony for a visit to his father and stepmother. Aurore agreed to go, but had hysterics when their carriage pulled out of the long Nohant driveway. According to her own account, told with complete candor in her autobiography, she had convinced herself she would die on the journey and would never see her beloved home again.

The senior Dudevants lived in a miniature Gascon castle, perched on a cliff, that was more impressive than comfortable. The Baron approved of the demure young lady his son had married and immediately carted off his grandson to the homes of his friends. The satisfactions of showing off the baby in person were great, and the Baron and Maurice daily disappeared soon after breakfast, rarely returning until sundown.

The Baroness was far more reserved. Casimir, Aurore, and Maurice represented a grave threat to her own financial future, at least in her own opinion. Aside from the sixty thousand gold francs that had been placed in reserve for Casimir at the time of his marriage, the Baron was leaving his entire estate to his widow, and Casimir would not inherit the castle until her death. But an attractive young woman who flirted expertly with her father-in-law and a laughing little boy who held tightly to his grandfather's hand could change all that. The moment the Baron left each morning, his wife's attitude became distinctly chilly.

Casimir spent his days indulging in his favorite pastime, hunting, leaving Aurore alone with her husband's hostile stepmother and her loyal servants. The young wife's tensions became worse, and Casimir, not only aware of her condition but sympathizing with her, insisted that she take a long walk each day and join him in the hills for a picnic lunch. The suggestion was the lesser evil, and Aurore agreed.

Her strolls through the rugged Gascon countryside proved far from dull, thanks to an unexpected escort. Aurélien de Sèze was a promising young attorney from Bordeaux, a slender, exceptionally handsome man who was fond of poetry and was romantic in his approach to life. He, too, was a visitor to Gascony, spending several weeks with his betrothed, Zoé Leroy, and her family. The girl's parents were friends of Casimir's father and his wife, so the young people met on a minor social occasion. Aurélien loved to walk, although Zoé did not, and Aurore accepted his invitation to accompany her on her daily jaunt to meet Casimir.

Within a few days Aurélien fell madly in love with Aurore, and the romance-starved young wife and mother responded, in spite of her attempt not to permit herself to become involved. Within a week Aurélien was writing her passionate letters, and soon thereafter she began to correspond with him, too. She admitted she had developed deep feelings for him, but insisted their relationship be maintained on a purely spiritual level. Remembering her convent training, she had no intention of engaging in an affair, and from the remnants of the correspondence that have survived, Aurélien wanted to maintain an honorable relationship, too. All the same, he was so smitten that he felt compelled to terminate his betrothal, which created an embarrassing scandal. No one suspected the cause.

Before Aurélien returned to Bordeaux he sent yet another letter to Aurore, informing her of his love for her and begging her to admit that she loved him, too. She refrained, continuing to display a sense of propriety far removed from the dissolute public image the future George Sand would create. It was enough, at least, for the moment, that she felt loved, and she had no need to consummate that love.

She persuaded Casimir to pay a brief visit to Bordeaux on their homeward journey, although it would take them out of their way. Aurélien immediately called on them at their hotel, and during the course of his visit he and Aurore were left alone in the sitting room for a few moments. He could not resist the opportunity to embrace her, and she, in a moment of weakness, returned his kiss.

In a situation worthy of the ancient traditions of French farce, Casimir chose that moment to re-enter the room. The startled husband had no chance to remonstrate: Aurore became hysterical, and dropping to her knees before him, begged him to forgive her. And Aurélien, who was shocked by his own temerity, swore he held the young woman in the highest regard and had no intention of trying to seduce her.

The outcome of the incident reveals Casimir Dudevant's fundamental weakness. Had he ordered Aurélien to get out, after recovering from his initial shock, that might have been the end of the matter. But it occurred to him, for the first time, that he might be losing his wife, and the fear numbed him. If he could not love her, at least as she wanted to be loved, he was attached to her in his own way, and did not want their lives disrupted. It appears that the conventions were important to him, too, and he questioned them at length before accepting their word that no one else ever dreamed of the 'spiritual' relationship they had established.

In any event, Aurore had found an outlet for her extravagant emotions, and after she, Casimir, and their small son returned to Nohant she corresponded regularly and at considerable length with Aurélien. They discussed the details of their day-today activities, they devoted long, sentimental passages to their thoughts of each other, and they unceasingly congratulated themselves for maintaining their relationship on a noble, elevated level.

Just when Casimir became aware of the correspondence is unknown, but he did learn of it, as seemingly casual references in Aurore's letters reveal. Apparently she did not want to stress the matter too hard for fear that Aurélien would stop writing. Ultimately, however, she told him the full story. She offered to let Casimir read every letter she sent and every letter Aurélien sent to her, but he told her the truth when he revealed that he had no interest in the correspondence. He had no appreciation of the poetry they quoted at length, and was bored by their ecstatic descriptions of the sound of a brook running or the song of a bird at daybreak. It was enough that they lived far apart, which rendered their relationship harmless, and it is possible that he was wise enough to believe Aurore needed a safe outlet for her over-abundant feelings. With evidence to the contrary lacking, it is fair to give Casimir the benefit of at least this one doubt.

Life at Nohant became more peaceful, which made it easier for both husband and wife to tolerate their marriage, although they were drifting apart rapidly. Casimir spent even more of his time hunting and drinking with Hippolyte, and Aurore, when not writing her effusive letters to Aurélien or smothering her small son with affection, retired to the library of the manor house and buried herself in reading.

Casimir's father fell ill, so it was necessary, in the early months of 1826, to pay another visit to Gascony. Aurore managed, in some way known only to herself, to persuade Casimir to travel there via Bordeaux, which gave her an opportunity to see Aurélien again. But the visit there was cut short when word was received that Casimir's father had died.

Upon their arrival at the estate, the younger Dudevants discovered that, for the present, Casimir had inherited nothing but his father's title, as the old Baroness had made certain that every sou of the considerable sum earned by her husband's investments would go to her as long as she lived. She retained life possession of the castle and other properties he had left.

This state of financial affairs had unhappy repercussions for Aurore. Casimir would be forced to depend on her estate for his living until the day in the dim future when his stepmother, who enjoyed remarkably good health, finally died. Aurore, looking forward to the day when she could manage Nohant herself, was as frustrated as Casimir.

Nevertheless, her relations with Casimir improved somewhat in 1826. The autocratic attitudes displayed by the restored Bourbon monarchy and its ministers were a constant source of irritation to landowners who found their operations hampered by petty new laws that made no sense to them. All of France was stirring under the authoritarian yoke of Charles X, and the dissatisfactions that would lead to the Revolution of 1830 were spreading very rapidly. It is something of a surprise to find that Aurore and Casimir, who seldom thought alike, shared increasing Republican sentiments. They began to play an active role in the politics of Berry, and when they found that a number of other young landowners felt as they did, their social circle expanded. Aurore renewed childhood friendships in La Châtre and Châteauroux, and Casimir became acquainted with men who not only felt as he did, but who proved to be splendid hunting companions too.

Meanwhile rifts were beginning to appear in the ideal romance of Aurore and Aurélien de Sèze. The young lawyer, a confirmed monarchist, not only despised Republicanism, but felt real contempt for the Bonapartist cause. This attitude outraged Aurore, who would never forget her childhood triumph at the Spanish court of Napoleon's brother.

They argued politics by mail. Aurore made no attempt to conceal her annoyance with v/hat she felt was her spiritual partner's stupidity, and by 1827 the exchange of letters dwindled. In fact, Casimir considered the correspondence so harmless that, on his trios to Bordeaux, where he had brought suit against his stepmother in an attempt to gain access to at least a portion of his father's estate, he acted as a mailman and delivered the idealists' letters to each other.

By 1827, however, the fundamental rifts in the Dudevant marriage grew more pronounced. Aurore had abandoned her attempts to interest her husband in philosophy, theology, or the classics, flirted with gentlemen at every social gathering at Nohant and other estates, and began to acquire a faintly dubious reputation. She could not tolerate it, some of the indignant ladies told each other, that a man failed to take due notice of her presence when he entered a room in which she was sitting.

Reacting strongly to the frustrations of marriage and the lack of excitement her own nature craved, the twenty-three-year-old matron became something of a madcap. During a dinner party she would organize a mushroom hunt in the woods, or would persuade several of the men to ride several miles to the farm of a peasant whose hens laid eggs that she considered perfect for the making of a souffle. She was the life of every party, and if her gaiety was forced, no one else seemed to realize it. Her activities did no more to cement her friendships with the conservative provincial ladies than the intellectual prowess she displayed. She was criticized severely because she could speak to the men on subjects ranging from politics to the management and operations of a working estate.

By now Casimir knew he had married a woman whose keen mind and unflagging energy were beyond him, and he developed a sense of inferiority toward her that remained unalleviated for the rest of his life. On the infrequent occasions when he made love to her she made no attempt to hide her indifference, which compounded his problem, and he became angry when her flirtatiousness indicated that, on the surface, she could become interested in any other man. He began to drink far more heavily, remaining sober only until he finished supervising Nohant's affairs at noon each day. He took his first wine before going out hunting at noon, the pace increased through the rest of the day, and, more often than not, he tumbled into bed as soon as he and Aurore finished dinner at night.

At this critical period, early in 1827, another man entered the life of Aurore, posing a far greater threat to her equilibrium than Aurélien de Sèze. Stéphane Ajasson de Grandsagne was a fellow aristocrat from Berry whom she had known as a child and young girl, and had become the type of man she would find irresistible as long as she lived. He was remarkably handsome, some of his La Châtre neighbors calling him 'as pretty as a girl', and he suffered from chronic ill health, which was a magnet whose pull Aurore could not escape. In later years she sometimes wondered, whether she had missed her calling and should have spent her life nursing the sick.

Stéphane was a student of natural history, and spent much of his time in Paris, where he was working on a monumental translation of ancient Greek and Latin scientists. Atheism had just become popular in intellectual radical circles, and he called himself one. He was also the first self-acknowledged Socialist of the Berry upper crust. He was headstrong and didactic, opinionated in all things, and would tolerate no disagreement with his views. Most of his old friends were amused, and refused to argue with him when he made one of his frequent trips to La Châtre.

Aurore was fascinated by this frail, slender male creature whom she could have subdued physically but who appeared so far beyond her intellectual reach. His answers to her questions, no matter what the subject, were positive, firm, and permitted no discussion. Stéphane's world was that of the supposedly objective nineteenth-century scientist who saw the world in terms of blacks and whites. He would not tolerate indecision or dissent, taking it for granted that any who wanted his friendship also accepted his opinions.

The combination of his wan beauty, physical weakness, and intellectual strength overpowered Aurore. On his visits to Berry, Stéphane was the guest of honor at Nohant dinner parties large and small, and often stopped in for an afternoon's chat with the young woman who sat unmoving, listening raptly while he expounded on his cures for all the ailments of humanity. At this time, Hippolyte had rented a small Paris apartment at the request of his wife, Émilie, and Aurore sometimes accompanied them when they went into the city for visits of two or three days. It was common knowledge in La Châtre and Châteauroux that she dined with Stéphane on these occasions, going with him to the obscure, inexpensive restaurants which were frequented by intellectual radicals and were avoided by provincials of substance and respectability. The correspondence of various Berry neighbors indicates that most of Aurore's contemporaries assumed she was having an affair with Stéphane, a view shared by a sympathetic but cautious Émilie and a thoroughly disapproving Hippolyte.

In the autumn of 1827 Casimir encountered difficulty collecting the rents on some of his wife's Paris properties, and his presence was also required in Bordeaux, where a hearing was scheduled in his suit against his stepmother. So he took care of both matters during the course of a long, single journey, first traveling north to Paris and then south to Bordeaux, absenting himself from Nohant for a period of about five or six weeks in October and November, 1827.

Perhaps it was accidental that Stéphane de Grandsagne chose this particular time to pay a visit of five or six weeks to his brother, whose estate near La Châtre was no more than a thirty-minute ride from Nohant. It could not have been accidental, however, that he paid frequent visits to his childhood friend and neighbor. When he called on her in the afternoon, he showed a due regard for the proprieties, and was escorted by his brother or some other suitable chaperon. It was rumored, however, that he often returned there after dark, and on these occasions he came alone.

Aurore's correspondence with her husband during these weeks reveals a genuine talent for ambiguity and clever double-dealing, and her letters were so polished they make her appear both candid and innocent. She unfailingly mentioned Stéphane's afternoon visits, including his name among the many who dropped in to see her, but her references to him were so casual they contained no hint that he was anything but an old, rather odd friend whose occasional company she found amusing.

The true situation was not revealed for another century and a quarter. A number of years after World War II several boxes of old correspondence were unearthed in the Berry attic of a house belonging to a descendant of Stéphane de Grandsagne, and exhaustive studies by a panel of experts indicated they had been written by Aurore Dudevant. More than forty of these communications, all of them passionate love letters, were from Aurore to Stéphane, and many of them obviously were sent in reply to similar letters he had written to her.

This correspondence authenticates the rumors and stories that kept the gentry of Berry preoccupied in 1827 and 1828. Stéphane was seen leaving Nohant soon after sunrise one morning. Aurore and Stéphane, holding hands, were seen dining together in a Paris café located in a district that no respectable person would visit. There are other clues, too.

In September, 1828, Aurore gave birth to a daughter, whom she named Solange, and when Aurélien de Sèze heard the news in Bordeaux, his friends were afraid he would lose his mind. His correspondence with Aurore had diminished, yet he still maintained his idealistic love for her, and had been content to accept her assurances that she had been chaste, avoiding relations with all men, including her husband.

News of the birth of Solange may have been the best thing that had ever happened to Aurélien de Sèze. Thereafter he concentrated on his career, and not only became wealthy and powerful, but won the universal respect of his fellow citizens. In time he married and became the father of a large brood of healthy, active children; many years later two of his sons joined his law office and achieved distinction of their own.

The salvation of Aurélien, to be sure, was only a side effect. The importance of Aurore's relationship with Stéphane is that he gave her the courage to escape from the bondage imposed on her by an unhappy marriage. It was Stéphane, too, who introduced her to the working class district of Paris, later to become known as the Latin Quarter on the Left Bank, which she would be one of the first to make famous as a Bohemian neighborhood. It was in the cafés on the Place Saint-Michel where she first sat with Stéphane and some of his radical friends from the Sorbonne that she enjoyed her first taste of the rebellious freedom that thumbs its nose at all respectable institutions. University students and embryo philosophers, would-be novelists, critics and playwrights, struggling lawyers and young men who dreamed of making their mark in politics drank cheap wine or coffee and damned the Bourbon Establishment that tried to turn back the clock to the era before the French Revolution and made unending efforts to nullify the personal freedoms achieved under Napoleon.

The convent-bred Aurore sipped her weak tea, listened to the strong talk, and became increasingly convinced she had found her own milieu. She had read Plato and Thomas More and all the others who had written so magnificently of the Utopias they envisioned. Here were men actively working to create one version or another of a brave new world, and is scarcely mattered that no two of them could agree on anything. What mattered was that they were not content to accept a stultifying status quo, and the idealistic, sheltered young woman felt as they did. Change was in the air, and she was sensitive enough, intelligent enough, to feel the breezes.

As she subsequently wrote with such intensity in her *History of My Life* and *Intimate Journal*, Aurore felt she had come home when she sat listening to Stéphane and his friends in a Paris café or an underfurnished flat. Their courage appealed to her, as did their fresh ideas, for which they argued with such passionate conviction. And these men treated her as an equal. She was not one whose presence they tolerated because she was attractive or an accomplished flirt, but was a fellow intellectual, a companion to whom they could expound their views. When she was able to overcome her shyness, they listened to her with the respect they accorded each other. She treasured — and remembered — the experience.

Solange was a beautiful baby and she may have resembled Stéphane, but Casimir accepted her without question as his own child. In the unlikely event that he had sired her, the night she had been conceived probably had been the last time Aurore had allowed him to make love to her. His drinking had become uncontrolled, and it was a scandal of the neighborhood that he was having affairs with several of his wife's serving maids, taking them to bed at Nohant while Aurore was on the premises. For centuries ladies and gentlemen had observed unwritten but rigidly fixed rules in the conduct of romantic affairs, but Casimir was breaking all of them. No one sympathized with him except his drinking companion, Hippolyte.

The circumstances surrounding the birth of Solange was so traumatic that George Sand was never able to forget them, and in later years wrote disguised versions of the incidents in several of her books. She was reading in the library at Nohant when her labor began, so she hastily dispatched a groom for the physician at La Châtre whose house was a thirty-or forty-minute ride closer to town. Then, attended only by a frightened and inexperienced young serving maid, she retired to her bed.

Before the physician arrived, however, Casimir came home, accompanied by Hippolyte, both intoxicated. Aurore's labor pains were intense now, and she tried to send them from the bedroom, but Hippolyte was so drunk he fell to the floor and there lost consciousness. No one moved him, and he remained in the same spot, groaning occasionally, until after the birth of the baby.

Meanwhile Casimir retired to the adjoining sitting room of his wife's suite, and there he trapped a willing serving maid with whom he amused himself. Every sound could be heard through the open bedroom door, which he neglected to close, and at the precise moment Aurore was giving birth to Solange, her drunken husband was engaging in noisy fornication with the serving girl.

The incident was beyond Aurore's capacity to forgive or forget, and was directly responsible for the decision that had been growing within her for a long time — to lead her own life.

IV

An outsider might have thought that all was as it had been at Nohant, but everything was changed. Casimir Dudevant continued to manage his wife's estate, but he had grown careless, and made many errors, none of which escaped her attention. It was surprising he did not make even more mistakes: he drank steadily, daily, and now openly engaged in affairs with two of the house servants, making no attempt to conceal anything from Aurore.

She tolerated the indignity because of the probability that, being otherwise occupied, he would not molest her. She took no chances, however, and rearranged the sleeping quarters so that her new bedroom stood beyond those of Maurice and Solange and could be reached only by way of the children's rooms. If necessary she could barricade the entire suite, which was well within earshot of the chambers occupied by the baby's nursemaid and the young tutor she had just hired for Maurice. Even when Casimir was drunk, she reasoned, he had too much pride to break down her door within the hearing of servants.

Perhaps, as she later wrote in her autobiography, she was being unnecessarily cautious, because Casimir had no desire to become intimate with her. On the other hand, he sometimes became abusive and she wanted to place herself and the children beyond his reach.

Aurore's explanations may well have been self-serving. The children were never in any physical danger from Casimir; he did all he could within the limits of his ability, to be a good father to them. Each morning, when he was sober enough to mount a horse, he took Maurice for a canter, and he paid a regular morning visit to the nursery, to play with Solange. Such an attitude, in the light of his later relationship with her, made it unlikely that he thought someone else might have sired her.

Regardless of Casimir, Stéphane was a frequent visitor to Nohant in 1829. By evening the master of the house was always in his cups, too far gone to appear at the table, so Stéphane dined alone with the mistress of the house, an arrangement which both found more pleasant.

Aurore gave no more dinner parties and accepted no social invitations. As her friends subsequently testified when she and Casimir aired their trouble in court, creating Berry's greatest sensation in generations, everyone assumed she was reluctant to leave her children at the mercy of a man who might harm the youngsters without realizing what he was doing. If Aurore made mistakes as a mother, none was due to inattention to her children. Under no circumstances would she subject them to the neglect she had suffered at Sophie's hands.

Although her new existence was restricted, Aurore was busier than ever before in her life. The collapse of her marriage revived her interest in projects that had occupied her during her childhood, and she took them up again with renewed energy. She collected fossils on the banks of the river and in fields newly turned by the peasants. She collected living plant specimens, and so many varieties soon filled her bedchamber that she had to convert the adjoining dressing room into a makeshift greenhouse.

But these hobbies did no more than occupy her spare time. She was absorbed in a daring plan that would have seemed insane to anyone else. Knowing that there was no way to regain control of her properties and attain financial independence until Casimir's stepmother died, she could escape only by supporting herself and her children. With more logic than common sense, she decided to write novels.

Aurore had never written or attempted to write a single word for publication, either as a schoolgirl or as a young matron. She knew no authors, and had made no formal study of a writer's profession. The usual lady's letters and some scraps of a diary were all she had ever written.

Ignoring insurmountable obstacles, displaying supreme confidence, she took the most significant step George Sand would ever take in her most memorable life. Yet this was accepted casually by most of her literary contemporaries as well as by her subsequent biographers. All assumed she was a professional writer, and none questioned her plunging into an uncharted sea, sustained only by her unquenchable faith in her own ability.

According to her own reasoning, at least, she was literate, endowed with a spirited imagination that made it seem easy for her to envision characters and the complicated, dramatic lives they would lead on paper. In her letter writing, she had discovered, she possessed a talent for expressing subtle shades of feeling and meaning.

The single most important cause of her choice was that she could turn in no other direction. For the first time in her life she demonstrated the shrewdness that was her maternal heritage, for there were virtually no other fields of endeavor open to her as a gentlewoman.

The most obvious employment would have been the stage, but Aurore had neither the talent nor the desire to become an actress. Already in her late twenties, she knew she was too old for such a career, since the passports to a theatrical career were beauty and youth. She faced still another obstacle, one which made life as an actress repugnant to her. It was common knowledge that any woman who went onto the stage was available to men for a price, and some of the better known actresses of Paris were among the city's higher priced courtesans. Under no circumstances was she willing to sell herself, or contemplate giving herself to a man, as she had done with Stéphane, except that she loved him.

The doors of other professions were closed to her. Even if she had been interested in attending medical school, she would not have been admitted. Men became lawyers or university professors; women were not allowed to vote. In spite of her growing interest in politics, to attempt candidacy for public office would have been ludicrous.

A dreary future of genteel poverty and insecurity awaited her if she chose to move into the fields usually selected by impoverished ladies. She was a clever needlewoman, it was true, but her mother's life as a seamstress discouraged her from even thinking of emulating Sophie. Only one, equally unhappy alternative remained: she might be accepted as a governess in a wealthy family, where her own children, if she were fortunate, would be treated as poor relations. The very idea appalled her.

Certainly no clear road spread out before Aurore in the literary world. Published authors of books were men, and no woman wrote for newspapers or magazines, either. Partly through instinct, partly through conversations with the would-be young authors in Paris who were Stéphane's friends, she felt that it might be easier to break down the walls of prejudice in the literary world than it would be elsewhere. If necessary, she could adopt a man's pen name, at least until she became known.

Needing only a desk, pen, and paper, she went to work in a corner of her bedroom. Trial and error soon convinced her that she worked best at night, after the children were asleep and no other distractions interrupted her. The cool self-confidence she displayed from the start was remarkable. Not even at the beginning did she grope, stumble over words, or search in vain for ideas. The words flowed onto paper in a smooth, unending stream, and she filled page after page of foolscap. She soon learned that she was too impatient to revise and polish her work, though she knew that most successful authors of the day including those she most admired, Victor Hugo and Honoré de Balzac, spent long hours revising their work, rewriting. She confessed in her autobiography that she put a sentence or paragraph on paper, never to alter it.

During this trial period, Aurore wrote two complete novels, *La Marraine* and *Aimée*, both romantic stories about frustrated young women. Into them she poured her own emotions, and the results, predictably, were an undisciplined jumble. But she learned from the exercise, losing nothing, and eventually, when she understood her craft, she broke her own rule, made major changes in both novels, and published them. So her attitude, from the outset, was thoroughly professional: words were her tools, and she hated to waste them.

On her brief trips to Paris she haunted the bookshops, buying every contemporary work she could afford, then devouring, studying, and analyzing it when she returned to Nohant. She daydreamed incessantly, and in her *Intimate Journal* she wrote, 'I would gladly ride ten leagues just to see M. de Balzac pass by.' Balzac, who became one of her close friends for almost two decades, never knew of this hero worship.

Victor Hugo filled her with even greater awe. Although he was just in the process of establishing his reputation as the greatest poet-novelist-dramatist-literary critic of the century, he was already becoming a figure of such Olympian majesty that Aurore was overwhelmed. She could never rid herself of this sense of inferiority toward Hugo, even after she herself achieved international renown. She attained a friendly relationship with everyone else in the publishing world, but invariably remained shy, almost inarticulate in Hugo's presence. More than forty years later, after the Franco-Prussian War of 1870, when Hugo and George Sand were both elderly grandparents and both had made enduring places for themselves in the annals of literature, she finally summoned the courage to tell him of the feelings he inspired in her. 'When I am in your presence,' she said, 'I am stricken dumb.'

Hugo's reply was typical. 'I have spent my entire life searching for a silent woman,' he said, 'and I regret that George Sand, the only woman of our time whose thoughts are worth hearing, should be that one.'

Hugo's comment was made when a distinguished career and a trail-blazing life were drawing to a close. Certainly the young Mme Dudevant, writing by the light of an oil lamp in her country house, alert to the chance that her drunken husband might molest her or disturb the children, could not imagine what lay in store for her. She had no plan, and apparently was not concerned about publishing her books. She was ambitious, but took no first step toward the creation of a career, and gave no thought to the mechanics of making her dreams come true.

In the summer of 1830, fate intervened in the unlikely person of a nineteen-year-old youth. On one of her infrequent excursions Aurore went to a small gathering of friends at a neighboring château, and among the guests was an extraordinarily handsome young man, the son of the tax collector of La Châtre, whom she had never before met.

Jules Sandeau had golden blond curls, classical features, and a build as slender and supple as a girl's. A brilliant student, he had spent the past two years in Paris, presumably studying law, but developing far greater interests in literature and the theater. Incurably romantic, he knew almost nothing about the revolution that had broken out in Paris prior to his return to La Châtre on a holiday, and politics held no interest for him. He did not care who would become the head of state, replacing the Bourbon Charles X sent into exile that same week, and he was indifferent to the possibility that a republic might replace the monarchy.

Guests tried to draw him out. Everyone was vitally concerned with the news of what was taking place in Paris, but Sandeau was so shy that he withdrew to the far side of his host's garden. According to separate accounts he and George Sand wrote in later years, she followed him and finally persuaded him to talk. The incident was one of the few about which they ever told the same story.

Sandeau was fascinated by this intense young matron, seven years his senior, who knew even more than he did about the current state of French literature, and expressed her convictions in such a forceful manner. He eagerly accepted her invitation to visit Nohant the following day.

Casimir held the rank of colonel in the National Guard, thanks to his previous military experience, and the next day his regiment was mobilized, as no one knew how serious the mounting revolution in Paris might become. So he was away from home when Jules Sandeau called. When the dust settled a week later, Sandeau had been a daily visitor to the house, and the revolution had come to an abrupt end when the elderly Marquis de Lafayette had thrown his support to the so-called bourgeois Bourbon, Louis-Philippe, the former university lecturer, who not only preserved a monarchy of sorts, but mounted the throne under a new, amorphous title, King of the French.

By this time Jules Sandeau was in love with 'the only woman who has ever spoken with a tongue I can understand'.

At the very least, Aurore imagined herself in love with him, too. Over a chasm of almost a century and a half it is difficult to judge the sincerity and depth of any individual's feelings. Although there can be little doubt that the frustrated young wife and mother believed her love to be real, she and Sandeau had little in common beyond their incurable romanticism. Beyond this, they were probably drawn together by forces far more potent: Aurore was endowed with great strength; Sandeau, lacking in self-recognition, was weak-willed. The opposing qualities proved to be irresistible magnets.

Aurore best expressed her own sentiments in a frank letter she wrote to a friend:

> If only you knew how I love that poor young man, how, from the very first moment of our meeting, his expressive eyes, his frank, brusque, manners, his awkward shyness in dealing with me, awakened in me a longing to see more of him, to explore the essence of his nature. I find it difficult to describe the interest he aroused in me. All I know is that each day it grew stronger, and that at no time did it even occur to me to resist the love that I refused to acknowledge to myself until the very moment I heard my voice raised in acknowledging it to him.

Jules was obligated to return to his studies in Paris early in the autumn, and by that time he and Aurore had convinced themselves they had achieved a grand passion unequalled in France since the time of those chivalric lovers, Abelard and Héloïse, whose letters they quoted to each other in long, flowery exchanges. They believed their love would make them immortal; years would pass before it dawned on an embittered Jules Sandeau that he would achieve some measure of reflected glory only because he was the first of George Sand's major lovers.

Having experienced an illicit love briefly with Stéphane, Aurore had no intention of pursuing a platonic relationship with her adorable Jules. They consummated their love in a little summerhouse located deep in Nohant's remaining woods, and returned there daily before Jules went off to Paris. These naive innocents were astonished when La Châtre began to gossip about their affair, and the word spread throughout Berry. It did not occur to them that the servants, among them Casimir's mistresses, would watch them closely and report all of their activities to anyone who would listen.

After Jules' departure Aurore returned to her stultifying existence. She supervised her children, gave Casimir a home he failed to appreciate, and spent six to eight hours every night working on her manuscripts. Beyond all else, she pined for the light of her life, little Jules. For three months her urge to pursue a career, her need to be free of Casimir, and her desire to be reunited with Jules compelled her to take steps she had previously avoided.

So she formed a plan that was daring, original, and extraordinary. She would go off to Paris, set up a residence of her own there, and try to advance her career as an author. But she would spend only half of each year in the city, and would return to Nohant for the other six months. In this way she would maintain the façade of a stable marriage and normal home life that the socially conservative Casimir found necessary for his own peace of mind.

Under no circumstances would Aurore give up her children for the six months of each year she would spend in Paris. As soon as she found a suitable flat and established a home for herself there, she would return to Berry for Solange, and thereafter would keep her daughter with her at all times. Maurice's situation was somewhat different: in another year or two the boy would be old enough to attend a boarding school in Paris, and would be near enough to spend part of every weekend with her. Until then, while he continued to study with a tutor, Aurore was willing to let him remain with his father at Nohant during her six months' absence, provided that he was sent to her several days every month.

The new arrangements would be costly, of course, but Aurore was so anxious to put them into effect that she made Casimir an offer she knew he would find attractive. She would not interfere in his management of her estates, and allowed him to dispose of the income as he pleased. In return she asked for an allowance of only three thousand gold francs per year.

A startled Casimir temporarily stopped drinking when Aurore presented her scheme to him in the closing days of 1830. It was his duty, he felt, to point out that even now at home she spent a great deal more than three thousand francs a year. It would be impossible for her to survive in Paris on such a pittance.

The determined Aurore was ready to counter any argument. Never having known want, she admitted that she could not live for six months away from home on three thousand francs. She knew that most people subsisted on a small fraction of that sum, and knew she could not change her own standards so drastically. It was possible, she conceded, that she might need time to establish herself as an author, and until then she would have to find some other way to augment her income. She told Casimir she had already found that way: she intended to earn additional money by painting flowers and other decorations on snuff boxes.

The idea was absurd, but she would not listen to her husband, and she laughed at Hippolyte and Émilie when Casimir called them in to stand by him. The fear of scandal was far more important to Casimir than his concern for her welfare, but she would not be budged from her decision. The desire to lead her own life in her own way had made her adamant. Overnight, the emotional, domestic young gentlewoman was transformed into a new person, one whose disregard for all convention would soon shock the civilized world. Nothing, Aurore declared, would dissuade her from carrying out her plan, and when Casimir saw that she meant it, he was forced to capitulate.

On January 4, 1831, Aurore Dupin Dudevant, wife, mother, and heiress, left her family and ancestral home to set out for Paris and a dubious existence as a would-be author, a decorator of snuff boxes, the mistress of a charming, untried young man totally lacking in emotional or intellectual maturity. But she was free to do as she pleased, and therefore had accomplished a miracle. Other marvels, she felt certain, soon would follow.

Paris in 1831 was a city of ferment, and although the political upheavals of the previous year had ended in victory for middle-class moderation, new frontiers were being explored. An ugly little man named Buloz, who soon demonstrated a remarkable ability to persuade authors to do their best work for him, assumed the editorship of a magazine called the *Revue des Deux Mondes*, which under his leadership, would become the most renowned literary journal in the world. Alexandre Dumas the elder had just completed a new play, *Antony*, which not only condoned adultery but made it respectable. The most incandescent actress of the era, Marie Dorval, created a sensation in the starring role. Victor Hugo's masterpiece, *Notre Dame de Paris*, was published, and was not only hailed as the greatest literary work of the century, but immediately Set some new styles in architecture. The indefatigable Honoré de Balzac brought out three new books, all of them so candid and explicit in their treatment of sexuality that a shocked public bought edition after edition as rapidly as they were printed.

Public dining came into favor, and many of the coffee houses that had been popular since the days of Voltaire a century earlier expanded to become fine restaurants. The English aristocracy discovered Paris, and so many visitors of distinction crossed the Channel that new hotels had to be opened to accommodate them.

This was the world that awaited Aurore Dudevant, in search of all the excitement and adventure Paris could offer. Hippolyte and Émilie were allowing her to borrow their small flat until she could afford to rent a place of her own, and she immediately made herself at home there. Jules Sandeau danced attendance on her, and every evening she went out with him and his friends, among them young lawyers who had just been admitted to the bar, neophyte journalists, and would-be actors.

Overnight Aurore became the center of their circle, and as Sandeau later wrote with great bitterness, almost all of them imagined themselves in love with her. Most were younger than Aurore by several years, but she did not care; they were helping her to capture the youth she had never known. And, long starved for affection, she relished the attention they lavished on her.

She and her new friends quickly discovered that limited funds created problems for ladies. Most of the new restaurants limited their clientele to men, and those that opened their doors to women were either shockingly expensive or tawdry places that admitted streetwalkers. More than thirty legitimate theaters offered plays, most houses changing their fare every week or two, and the young intellectuals attended them nightly. Seats in the sections that admitted ladies were beyond the reach of those who were forced to count their copper coins, and no women were permitted in the pit, where riots occurred when audiences disapproved of a play and became unruly.

Aurore quickly found what she considered a sensible solution: she would dress as a man, which would enable her to accompany her new friends to inexpensive restaurants and the theater. She scrubbed all traces of cosmetics from her face, concealed her long, dark hair beneath a soft-crowned, broad-brimmed hat, and hid her obviously feminine figure under a long, smock-like shirt, trousers, and riding boots. At home she had sometimes gone out riding this way. As additional protection she appeared in a great coat that fell almost to her ankles. Her disguise was effective — at theaters, cafés, and restaurants in every part of Paris she was mistaken for a man.

The lark not only amused her, but Sandeau and his friends approved of her daring, which gave her even greater stature in their eyes. None of them had ever known a woman who displayed such bravado, and she could always excuse her masquerade on the grounds that she was saving money on the wardrobe that Paris otherwise would have made necessary.

These were Aurore's golden days, as she later called them in her autobiography, and she savored each of them. She could walk with young men on the boulevards of Paris, and no one would bother to glance in her direction. How different it was from Berry, where gossips went wild if she halted her carriage in the streets of La Châtre to converse for a moment or two with a male.

She still had problems, to be sure. Hippolyte's business affairs required him to make frequent trips to Paris, and he was less than appreciative when he found his flat crowded with young Bohemians who spent the entire night solving the world's most pressing questions enspirited with cheap wine. It was obvious that Aurore would have to find a place of her own before she dissipated her half-brother's generosity. She visited libraries, hoping to do research for a novel with a historical background, in the manner of Sir Walter Scott, but she found the heating so inadequate that she had to fee from each of three libraries in turn. As to the idea of decorating snuff boxes, she soon discovered her foolishness; artisans could produce a score in the time it took her to paint the lid of one box.

Through a friend in La Châtre she obtained a letter of introduction to one of the more prominent literary figures of the day, Henri de Latouche, who had been Balzac's mentor until they had quarrelled. Himself the author of several moderately successful books, Latouche was the proprietor and publisher of the small newspaper, *Le Figaro*, which he had recently purchased and was transforming into a satirical journal. He knew everyone who was anyone in Paris publishing, and had acquired a deserved reputation as a literary critic of stature.

Aurore was graciously received at his apartment, and she became elated when he agreed to listen to a reading of her novel, *Aimée*, which she had recently completed. As she read, his face was expressionless, and he made no comment until she had finished. Her letter of introduction had indicated she had a husband and children in Berry; he heartily advised her to return to her family without delay. Her novel was amateurish trash; no publisher would print it.

Aurore was so incensed that she stamped out of his flat. But the following day she returned to apologize for her bad manners — and to retrieve her manuscript. Latouche was amused by her fiery display of independence, and offered her a trial, at a token salary, as a junior editor on *Figaro*. Aurore accepted, and went to work that same day.

Henri de Latouche proved to be a devilish fiend. Nothing she put on paper satisfied him; he forced her to rewrite and polish, revise and begin again. Often she was ready to give up in despair, but it gradually dawned on her over a period of weeks that discipline was the key to any success that she might achieve as a writer. She began to absorb the essence of the profession.

Latouche rewarded her efforts in March by giving her a small increase in wages, and Aurore found the courage to suggest that Jules Sandeau be given a trial on the staff. Jules submitted several samples of his work, and his sense of humor proved similar to Latouche's, so he was hired. The happy lovers, both gainfully employed, worked at adjoining desks in the crowded *Figaro* office, and for a short time Aurore was content.

But her burning ambition would not permit her to rest, though she was the only member of her sex employed on the staff of any publication in France. One door had been opened, and through it she could pry others ajar. At her instigation she and Jules collaborated on several articles, which they submitted to their employer under the signature of 'J. Sandeau', and he accepted three of these pieces, paying a hundred francs for each.

Aurore promptly set her sights a little higher. A weekly publication, the *Revue de Paris*, boasted such contributors as the critic Sainte-Beuve, as well as the literary lions of the period — Hugo, Balzac, Dumas, Théophile Gautier, Alfred de Vigny, and the industrious Eugène Sue, whose popularity outstripped that of most of his contemporaries. The *Revue* printed articles on many subjects, as well as fiction, poetry, and literary criticism, and took pride in the quality of all it published. An author whose work appeared in its pages had reason to believe he had joined the elite. Aurore saw no reason why the joint efforts of 'J. Sandeau' should not grace the pages of the *Revue*.

She spurred Jules, who was showing the first signs of occasional intellectual laziness, and together they wrote two short articles in which substance was subordinate to style. The *Revue* bought both, and Aurore had reason to believe she was making solid progress in her chosen profession.

The additional income made it possible for the couple to rent a two-room attic apartment on the fifth floor of an old building on the Place Saint-Michel. It was inferior to any dwelling Aurore had ever known, even her mother's flat. But she was enchanted with the view of Notre Dame, and when she grew tired of looking out at the great cathedral, she could study the jumbled rooftops, with their infinite assortment of chimneypots, which she always found fascinating.

Aurore invested in a small, charcoal-burning stove so she could prepare meals. Cooking still interested her, though her work at *Figaro* and her collaborative efforts with Jules left little time to think of meals. Food was expensive, too, so she seldom used the stove, and more often than not she and Jules dined on bread, cheese, and inexpensive wine. An occasional cold cutlet, she noted in her *Intimate Journal*, was a treat.

It was Aurore's open defiance of convention. Still a married woman who had agreed to spend a part of each year with her husband, she made no attempt to conceal the fact that she was living with her young lover. She had no hesitation in setting up housekeeping with Jules, though neither advertised the arrangement in letters to friends in La Châtre. Aurore barely observed the proprieties; in brief communications sent to Casimir, she noted in cleverly imprecise words that Jules had taken lodging in the same building.

She had taken her long stride, in her own personal life, toward the goal she would later advocate with such consistency in her writing — that women should have the same sexual freedom that men could enjoy with such impunity. She knew she was subjecting herself to condemnation by every class of people, but nothing else mattered in her new life. The vigor of her defense through the years when she was attacked, together with her insistence that she was a woman of high moral standards, indicates that she was not immune to social opinion, as some of her early biographers suggested. She lived in accordance with her own principles, and was willing to give up the respect of those who failed to understand them.

In this part of her independent life she must have suffered occasional doubts; her life with Jules Sandeau was far from ideal. Jules' neurotic manners created never-ending problems for his loving mistress. He was jealous of her social success, sulking when his friends paid too much attention to her. He resented being teased about Aurore as partner of 'J. Sandeau', and took pains to assert that his was the major contribution. Aurore controlled her own vanity, and when in his company always saw to it that he received the lion's share of praise.

In spite of his youth, Jules was already a confirmed hypochondriac; two or three days each week he remained in bed, complaining of various ailments. Aurore not only nursed him, pampered him, and catered to his supposed illness, but enjoyed the experience. For the rest of her life she would repeat this pattern of behavior with all of her most enduring loves. Her cheerfulness under stress, her refusal to complain, and the relish with which she performed her nursing chores enabled her to dominate every sickly partner. Though she herself had been ill on numerous occasions since her marriage, she enjoyed a miraculous recovery after she established her own, independent life, and never again suffered a major ailment.

Contrary to the views of those who proclaimed her licentiousness, she lived a surprisingly chaste life, treating Jules more as a son than a lover. Sexual relations, as such, meant nothing to her, it seemed, although in *Lélia* and later works she revealed how disturbed she was by the realization that Sandeau was unable to give her any greater satisfaction than she had received from either Casimir or Stéphane.

Aurore's children remained her greatest concern; she dreamed of the day when she would be able to move into a larger flat and bring them to Paris to live with her. Her separation from them became increasingly unbearable, and in April she returned to Nohant for a month and a half, leaving Jules behind in Paris. She slipped back into her old routines immediately, spending her days with the children and writing at night; she worked in her garden, made jams, and, when in the mood, paid calls on old friends in La Châtre and elsewhere in the neighborhood.

By now she and Casimir were strangers who were living under the same roof. They seldom saw each other; when they happened to meet, he no longer bothered with the civilities, but became openly abusive in his language. A letter she wrote to her mother late in May, 1831, reveals the essence of their relationship:

> My husband does exactly what he likes. Whether he has mistresses or does not have mistresses rests entirely with him. He can drink wine or water, as the fancy takes him, and is free to save or spend money. He can build, plant, sell, buy, run the house and the estate exactly as he sees fit. I have washed my hands of his concerns.

But it is only fair that he grant me the same liberty that he enjoys. If he did not, then I would think him odious and contemptible — and he would hate that to happen. He values my good opinion of him, although he speaks to me in the language of the gutter to hide his true feelings. He does not interfere with my life, and I ask for nothing more from him.

Consequently I am completely independent here. I go to bed when he gets up. I visit La Châtre and other places as I please. I come home at midnight or at six a.m., as my own fancy dictates. All that is my business, and no one else's. When a husband is free to do as he wishes, a wife is entitled to the same prerogatives!

Early in June Aurore returned to Paris, and Jules Sandeau immediately rented a single room on the floor beneath their apartment. Her correspondence with Hippolyte and Émilie suggests that they had lectured her on the subject of appearances, and had hinted that Casimir might exclude her from custody of the children if she persisted in advertising her precious freedom. The possibility frightened her, so Jules moved to the separate room whenever relatives or friends from Berry came to the city. At other times, the couple abandoned pretense and continued to live together openly.

On a warm summer evening, she and Jules, together with several other young *Figaro* editors, were dining with Latouche at a small restaurant frequented by writers. Honoré de Balzac happened to be sitting at an adjoining table, and at Aurore's request Latouche presented her to him. Her instinct told her not to exercise her talents as a flirt with him. Balzac's interest was aroused only by very pretty women, and she knew she was far from beautiful. Instead she made certain to him that she was familiar with almost all of his work and admired it.

Balzac was flattered. Her eagerness to learn more about methods of writing impressed him. He seemed also to enjoy

Jules' company, finding the same charm that Aurore did behind the young man's sullen mask. A few nights later he called on the couple, gasping for breath as he hauled his huge body up five steep flights of stairs. With that, a lifelong friendship was born.

Balzac was convivial only when he consumed food and drink in quantity. Discovering that the attic cupboard was more or less bare, he began to bring groceries and wine with him. Soon he appeared every other night, carrying bags of food. Aurore prepared a three- or four-course meal, with Balzac her willing assistant, and in return for her efforts at the stove, he answered her countless questions in meticulous detail.

Over a period of months Aurore received the benefit of all the wisdom of authorship in that creative age. She was sincere when, a decade later, she wrote to Balzac, 'Your guidance has made possible whatever success I have found. You showed me how to bring people to life and how to manipulate them in the world they inhabit.'

Jules Sandeau contributed little to these conversations, but Aurore and Balzac assumed he was listening. Sometimes he dozed, which amused them. Both treated him as indulgently as a child. He was their audience, which made him happy, so all three enjoyed the friendship.

It would be difficult to exaggerate the influence of Balzac on the writing of the young woman who became his disciple. She lacked his grasp of the world of their day, his sensitivity to people of every kind. But he taught her to create moods in words and drilled her in the fundamentals of story-telling. She learned dramatic essentials, the building of plot, and how to touch on the subtleties of character. George Sand's more ardent admirers have claimed that she was endowed with natural talents as a novelist, but it was Balzac who made it possible for her to use them fully.

As they became friendlier and she lost her awe of him, she began to show him chapters of the books on which she was working. Balzac, who was frequently jealous of colleagues more popular than he was, helped her as he would never have helped another man. The generosity was not one-sided; Aurore was a mature young woman who had acquired her own insights and understanding of human nature, too. In spite of his international renown, she knew that Balzac was a shy, lonely man who desperately needed the companionship she so willingly gave him.

Both wanted love, and both spent their lives seeking it, but it did not occur to either that they might find some measure of happiness together. Both were strong-willed and demanding, and both took lovers who were soft, yielding, and rather selfless. It well may be that Balzac's celebrated imagination was playing tricks on him, some years later, when he wrote that George Sand offered herself to him. She described him as physically repulsive in her letters and *Intimate Journal*. Every man with whom she is known to have had an affair was handsome; she had no reason to make an exception in his case.

Balzac's personal reaction to Aurore is worth noting because so many others felt as he did, but were incapable of expressing their feelings with his precision:

> When I dine with George Sand or spend an evening in her company, I forget she is a woman. She is so forthright, so lacking in artifice, never stooping to employ the little tricks that are the basic nature of most women, that I find myself treating her as I would another man. The aura that surrounds her is that of a man. Yet I have seen her transform herself into the most feminine of women when she is in the presence

of a man with whom she might wish to become intimate. Her eyelids flutter, she sighs without reason, her smile is mysterious and beguiling, and she makes herself appear to be the most helpless of creatures. I have never met a member of her sex who is more self-reliant, so I have reason to rejoice that she and I are drawn to each other only as friends and colleagues.

The encouragement Balzac gave his ambitious friend in the formative stages of her career was priceless. She would never acquire stature or much money as a journalist, he told her, and urged her to try her hand at a long novel. So Aurore went back to her desk, again working with the compliant Jules, and turned out several hundred pages of a romantic work of fiction that would be called *Rose et Blanche*. With the help of Latouche and Balzac, who cordially despised each other but cooperated for the sake of helping young friends, they persuaded a Paris publisher, Renault, to accept the book. He agreed to pay an advance royalty of one hundred and fifty francs for each of five volumes, and an additional seven hundred and fifty francs when the book was finished. The payment was quite respectable, and Aurore celebrated by taking a larger flat in the same building, buying several pieces of badly needed furniture, and bringing Solange, her daughter, to live with her.

Feeling she could afford to gamble, she cut her working time at *Figaro* to a minimum and concentrated on the book. It is difficult, as it always is in a collaborative effort, to determine the extent of her contribution and how much Sandeau wrote, but the many similarities in her later work indicate that Aurore was the senior partner in the enterprise.

In the early autumn of 1831 she returned to Nohant for a stay of several months, and the docile Jules followed, taking up residence with his family in La Châtre. Aurore saw no need to change their work habits, so he came to her house every evening, and shocked the good citizens of Berry by spending most of the night there. Jules was bored by small town living, and as soon as work on the book was completed, he returned to the city, expecting Aurore to follow him.

But she intended to live up to her agreement with Casimir, remaining at Nohant for another two to three months. Consequently she missed the excitement of the publication of *Rose et Blanche*, which appeared late in the autumn under the joint pseudonym 'Jules Sand'.

Influenced by Balzac, Aurore thought the novel realistic, but Latouche came closer to the mark when he called it unabashedly romantic. The critics, who treated it gently in spite of implausible characters, and a plot sometimes absurdly melodramatic and stiff agreed with him. The public overlooked the obvious faults and the book sold well, earning the collaborators an additional eight, hundred francs.

Aurore was anxious to bring out another book on the heels of this modest success, but Jules told her he would expire if forced to return to the stultifying provincial atmosphere of Berry any longer. He would be waiting for her whenever she decided to return to Paris.

Aurore had no intention of postponing another book until they were reunited, and set to work alone in her Nohant bedroom. Casimir, to whom the publication of *Rose et Blanche* had meant nothing, was alarmed by the thought that the good name of Dudevant would be sullied if it appeared on a novel, though Aurore revealed in her autobiography that she had no intention of bringing out the book under her own name. She knew all too well that the public in France was not yet ready to buy a novel written by a woman, so she assured Casimir that the name of Dudevant would be protected.

Suddenly, all that she had wanted was within reach. Renault encouraged her to write the new book as rapidly as possible, Latouche wrote her a long letter assuring her she could earn a considerable sum if she struck the right note, and, Balzac sent her a series of notes in which he urged her to waste no time.

Aurore settled into the most disciplined regimen she had ever subjected herself to, and was delighted to discover she could work far more rapidly and efficiently alone than when collaborating with Jules. The words flowed with ease, as they had in her earliest, amateur efforts, but now she knew what she was doing, conscious of the effects she wanted to achieve. Each day she wrote at least twenty pages, and often she counted twice that number before she fell into bed for a few hours of sleep.

Driving herself without pause, she completed the novel before the end of 1831, and called it *Indiana*. After a brief period of hesitation, she decided to use the pen name George Sand.

V

The author of *Indiana* thought of her book as realistic, and it was similarly regarded by Balzac, whose work was establishing new standards of realism in the literature of many lands. Both would have been surprised to know that later generations would judge the partly autobiographical novel romantic and sloppily sentimental. Certainly *Indiana* as an enduring work of art is dubious; it has survived largely because it was the first of many books to bear the name of George Sand.

But the young lady from Nohant, with almost no professional experience, knew intuitively what the reading public wanted. As she proved repeatedly during the next half-century, she struck the popular note of any given moment, attracting large numbers of people to her current work. Of all her contemporaries, only Victor Hugo achieved a better sales record, and the comparison is unfair because no author in history has ever equalled what Hugo accomplished. Some books by Dumas the elder, Balzac, and Sue sold more copies than any single novel by George Sand, but no one could match her consistency. All of the others occasionally produced a financial failure; not one of the forty to fifty books George Sand wrote was unsuccessful.

She achieved fame overnight. Her pseudonym, used for the first time, won her instant recognition. She wisely made no attempt to hide her real identity, as the gossip mongers who wrote for more than a score of cheap Paris newspapers lost no time telling the world that George Sand was an aristocratic housewife and mother from provincial Berry. Public curiosity increased the sales of *Indiana*; within the first two years of its initial publication it earned the respectable sum of more than five thousand francs.

Book reviewers hailed George Sand as superior to Mme de Staël, the author whose person and work Napoleon had banned from France because he was afraid that her liberal ideas endangered his regime. Now it appeared, France had been awaiting the arrival of another talented woman, and *Indiana* was praised excessively, far beyond its actual worth.

Aurore returned to the city, bringing her three-year-old daughter with her, and was hailed as a celebrity. She could afford to move to quite a large apartment in the building on the Place Saint-Michel, no longer being concerned about money matters. She accepted an advance payment from her publisher of two thousand francs for her next novel, which she was calling *Valentine,* and the editors of the powerful journals and other magazines inundated her with offers, most of them granting her the freedom to write articles for them on any subject she might choose. Such influential men as Gustave Planche, the critic, and Buloz, regarded as the foremost magazine editor of the day, called on her before she had a chance to buy furniture for her new flat, and a dozen others who had just learned of her existence paid court to her, too.

Aurore's sudden fame immediately created complications in her relationship with Jules Sandeau. On the surface nothing was changed; he continued to live in the same building, ate all of his meals with her, and, more often than not, slept with her. But the dramatic change in her standing created strains for Jules' paranoid nature. He accused Aurore of patronizing him, laughing at him behind his back, and told her new literary friends she was awaiting an opportune moment to be rid of him. Her denials temporarily allayed his suspicions, but they flared again whenever the couple disagreed.

One of the obvious bones of contention was vocational. The independent success of George Sand ruled out future collaboration, and Jules was too undisciplined, too lazy, to turn out a book by himself. His share of the royalties earned by *Rose et Blanche* paid for only a fraction of his living expenses, so he took the easiest road and permitted his mistress to support him. At the same time he hated his own weakness, and tried to rid himself of his guilt by lashing out at her.

Soon Jules was spending most of his waking hours taking care of Solange. They made innumerable trips to the new zoo, took boat rides on the Seine, and visited many places that a little girl found fascinating. Jules' fondness for the child whom he called his daughter was sincere, but it was disturbing to realize that, while he was baby-sitting, his mistress and former writing partner was busily conferring with some of the most prominent men in the publishing business about future projects from which he would necessarily be excluded.

Aurore's meetings, interviews with the press, and other activities made it impossible for her to write during the day. She locked herself into her small sitting room at night, and permitted nothing to interfere with her writing. Not only did *Valentine* take shape, but she wrote a number of other stories, most of them somewhat longer than usual for magazines, for which she was paid handsome fees.

Her productivity was a never-ending embarrassment to Jules, and her busy schedule interfered with their sex life, which further embittered him. As usual, he took refuge in illness, but she cheerfully nursed him, somehow finding the time to minister to him while neglecting none of her other duties. There was no pettiness in her nature, and she tried to encourage Sandeau, telling him that he could achieve even more than she accomplished. But he was honest enough to recognize his limitations. In the late spring of 1832 he wrote her a pathetic letter that summarized his situation:

> You want me to work. I, too, want it, but I cannot! I was not born, as you were, with a small steel spring in my mind. You press a button, and your imagination goes to work for you. I try, but when I sit before a blank sheet of paper on my desk, my mind remains as blank as that paper.

The affair eventually assumed the predictable overtones of tragedy. Jules began to question his mistress about meetings that took her away from her flat for hours at a time, and Aurore was quick to resent any attempt on his part to curtail her freedom. After one angry quarrel early in the summer of 1832, she wrote him a brief note that succinctly expressed the basic principle of life she now led: 'I go where I please, when I please, and I am accountable to no one for what I do!'

A number of new developments in the summer of 1832 hastened the collapse of the affair. Aurore went off with Solange for a visit to Nohant, and when she returned to Paris, she did not go back to the Place Saint-Michel. Latouche had decided to leave Paris and take up permanent residence in the country, so he offered Aurore his magnificent apartment on the Quai Malaquais. It was a place worthy of a prominent author, with a large, carpeted salon, a paneled library, a huge dining room and kitchen, and, best of all, four bedrooms. Aurore could now bring her son to the city for prolonged visits.

Valentine was published soon after Aurore moved, and its success was even greater than that of *Indiana*. It, too, had autobiographical roots, the story of an aristocratic young woman trapped in a loveless marriage to a man of her own class. The scene was similar to that of her beloved Berry, and she described the countryside in lyrical detail which gave the work a genuine literary quality. Again the critics applauded, and she was hailed as a professional author whose second book had surpassed her first, making her a figure of unassailable stature.

The schism between her and Jules grew wider, and she added insult to injury by taking her children to visit her mentor, Latouche, at his new country home. Jules not only believed they were lovers, but tried to win the sympathy of friends by charging her with infidelity. Balzac, for one, accepted his word, and wrote to a number of mutual acquaintances that Aurore and Latouche were engaging in an affair, but their correspondence fails to indicate that they were intimate, and no evidence has ever been unearthed to substantiate Jules' suspicions.

It was another person whom Sandeau failed to recognize as the competitor for his mistress' affections who placed their love in jeopardy. It did not cross his mind that she might develop a romantic interest in another woman, who was herself notorious for her intimacies with men.

Marie Dorval was the leading feminine star of the Paris stage, so popular that her mere presence in a play guaranteed its success. Approximately Aurore's age, she deserved her reputation as the loveliest woman in France. Marie's long, blue-black hair, her striking brown eyes, and her figure would have been considered breath-taking in any age. A guttersnipe at birth, she had clawed her way to the top in the theater, and at eighteen had married a leading actor of the day, Allan Dorval. Four years later, as she was giving birth to their third child, he dropped dead on stage.

In 1829 Marie had married the managing director of the Théâtre Porte-Saint-Martin, Jean-Toussaint Merle, in what both recognized as a business partnership. Two years later she became the mistress of Comte Alfred de Vigny, poet, playwright, and a leading member of Victor Hugo's literary circle. De Vigny, a stiff, humorless man wildly jealous of Marie, wrote a number of the plays in which Merle presented her, so all three enjoyed the benefits of the intricate relationship.

Theater-goers of the next century would have rejected the excesses of emotion in which Marie indulged on stage, but the public that filled the Porte Saint-Martin in her own time thought her incomparable. No one applauded her with greater enthusiasm than Aurore, who thought her Lady Macbeth was a masterpiece and wrote her a letter of congratulations. In it she expressed the hope that their paths might cross, and as her own name would have no meaning, she used the pen name that was making her famous.

Posterity is indebted to Jules Sandeau for an account of the next scene in the drama. He revealed in a letter to Balzac that he and Aurore were eating a late breakfast one morning when a tap sounded at the front door of the apartment. Aurore answered the summons, and an excited Marie Dorval swept into the flat, saying, 'Well, here I am.'

Each of the women recognized a kindred spirit. They became so engrossed in their conversation that Sandeau was forgotten, even though he remained close at hand for the duration of the visit. The author and the actress chatted for an hour, and as Marie departed she invited her new friend — and Jules — to dine at the Merle apartment the following night.

Marie's husband was on hand for the occasion, and so was de Vigny, who wrote his impressions in his *Journal*. George Sand, he declared, elected to appear in a spectacular version of man's attire, which consisted of a close-fitting shirt, snug trousers which were tucked into tasseled boots, and a high-crowned beaver hat. 'She looks and talks like a man,' he said, 'and has the voice and forthrightness of one. I cannot, as yet, altogether place this woman.'

Aurore, in her autobiography, treated de Vigny with equal candor and greater justice: 'I don't at all like M. de Vigny's person, but when our minds meet I feel quite differently.'

De Vigny lacked the sophistication to pinpoint the danger, but he had ample cause for uneasiness. His beautiful mistress and the unorthodox novelist quickly developed a close friendship, and soon were inseparable, spending several hours together every day. There can be little doubt that they became lovers, as an entry in George Sand's *Intimate Journal* reveals:

> The dawn is here. Come, angel of the morning, the dew is falling and you will feel the penetrating cold. Have you no fear of cold or of clinging mist? Come, the windows are open. My room is prepared for you with flowers. I am waiting for you.
>
> It is the hour for slumber. If you do not come soon, I shall fall asleep.
>
> At last you are here! Blessed art thou, heavenly one, give me your forehead to kiss, let your black hair fall over me, your glorious hair a cubit long!
>
> Oh, but an angel with floating hair is beautiful in the morning! Why is it that men do not have long, floating hair?
>
> Come, unnameable one, sit at my bedside. You speak no language, you do not try to reveal yourself in words. That is why I love you, that is why I understand you so well.
>
> Silent angel, put your cool hand on my shoulder. No man has ever touched it with his lips.
>
> What flowers are those upon your forehead? Unknown flowers, flowers more beautiful than any woman has ever worn. Their perfumes are intoxicating, my angel, shower them upon me, tear the leaves from your dewy crown and strew them over me.

It is enough. I am dying. I want to live for another dawn in which to see you again. Farewell. The light breaks. Go quickly, my treasure, so that no one will see you, for they would steal you from me, and then I should have to give my love to men.

Farewell, let me kiss your snowy neck and your forehead, where shines a star. Give me a feather from your wing, that I may keep it as proof that you have been with me. It will be a souvenir of happiness.

Why do not men have wings with which to come at night and fly away in the morning?

I prefer thistledown to a man. You blow on it, and it is lost in the air. Man never sublimates himself and never dissolves into spirit.

Go now, angel of the morning. I am falling asleep; kiss me on my forehead and make my soul as beautiful as yours.

Marie Dorval had no talent for poetic words, but her feelings were no less intense, and one day she wrote a hasty note: 'A. has made such a scene that I cannot join you as planned. But know that, until we meet, I cover you with a thousand kisses, as you shall cover me with them when I come to you.'

It was George Sand who replied, Aurore Dudevant having vanished into the psyche of her other, stronger self: 'Not a thousand kisses, dear one! Ten thousand!'

Perhaps to posterity the greatest significance of the relationship is that George Sand herself understood its essence in a time long before the era of psychiatry. She believed herself gauche, homely, and cold, emotionally and physically unable to respond to the love of men, while Marie was lovely, charming, and warm, all that she herself had ever wanted to be. In *Questions d'Art et de Littérature*, she describes her relationship with Marie in terms that strip it of mystery and romance:

Only those who know how differently we were made can realize how utterly I was in thrall to her. She had been given by God the power to express what she felt. She was beautiful, and she was simple. She had never been taught anything, but there was nothing she did not know by instinct.

I can find no words to describe how cold and incomplete my own nature is. I can express nothing. There must be a paralysis of a sort in my brain which prevents what I feel from ever finding a form through which it can achieve communication.

She aroused me from a lethargy I had known all of my life. When she appeared, with her drooping figure, her listless gait, her sad and penetrating glance, I can say only that it was as though I were looking at an embodied spirit.

When de Vigny discovered the true nature of the friendship, he redoubled his efforts to prevent the women from seeing each other. In at least four or five pungent notes he ordered his mistress to see no more of 'that damned Lesbian'.

Marie pretended to obey, but continued to see George Sand secretly, and the relationship long outlasted her affair with de Vigny. The two women remained close through the tragic years of Marie's declining fortunes, when she was forced to appear with second-rate provincial theatrical companies. After her death she was forgotten by everyone but George Sand, who assumed financial responsibility for her children, not only supporting them but giving them the best education available.

Jules Sandeau, who was unable to comprehend either the nature or depth of his mistress' friendship with Marie Dorval, lacked the strength to fight for his own rights, and helplessly watched his affair disintegrate. Had he been courageous he would have called a halt, but he complained, pouted, and again took refuge in pretended illness. It did not occur to him that he had already outlived his usefulness to an energetic, self-confident George Sand, who had not required his help in the achievement of fortune and personal triumph.

In the early autumn of 1832 George Sand shed her newly acquired cloak of fame, and returning to Nohant with Solange, donned the lace apron of a gentlewoman as she assumed the role of Mme Dudevant. Sandeau did not accompany her. From his letters it appears that she told him to wait until she sent for him, but the summons failed to materialize, and she was 'too busy' to answer his requests for her attention. Within a very short time, he was reduced to writing all of their mutual friends in La Châtre, begging them to send him scraps of information regarding her activities.

Thanks to Jules' complaints to anyone who would listen, George Sand was criticized by many of her contemporaries for her ruthless treatment of a lover she no longer wanted. Even their closest associates, among them Balzac, knew only his side of the story. Her friendship with Marie Dorval was irrelevant to their romance, and represented a side of her nature that she did not allow to interfere with her heterosexual relationships. Now, as earlier, she thought of herself as a normal woman whose principal interest was men.

The truth of the matter was that she could no longer feel any respect for Jules. After moving into her own sumptuous apartment she had rented a small, comfortable flat for him, and supplied him with enough money to pay for his meals, clothes, and entertainment. She was still keeping him.

Jules, who was convinced that she was unfaithful, repaid her generosity by engaging in affairs with several working-class girls, and one afternoon in the summer of 1832 George Sand found him in his flat with one of them. She made an ugly scene, Jules wept, and she finally forgave him, but he waited only a few days before he began to bring other girls there.

Jules, it seemed, was far from the mind of Aurore-George during her sojourn at Nohant. She had arrived in time for the harvest, and busied herself preserving fruit and vegetables. She visited old friends, usually accompanied by Maurice, who worshipped her, and by Solange. She avoided Casimir, who took care to stay out of her path when he was sober, but who pounded on her door and cursed her when he was drunk. She could shut out the sound of his voice when she was working, and it was a relief to know she no longer needed his financial assistance, though it grieved her to see the deterioration of the old estate that she loved. Some day, before he completely ruined Nohant, she would have to take steps to preserve it.

Early in the winter of 1832 a rested George Sand returned to her Paris apartment, taking Solange with her, and made an attempt to resume her relationship with Jules, who continued to accept her money and made no pretense of trying to work. She quickly discovered it was impossible to breathe new life into an affair that had died, and reacting with decisiveness was determined to be rid of him.

A change of scene would not only remove him but would help him forget her, so she bought him a new wardrobe and gave him funds for a journey to Italy. To make sure that he actually departed, she accompanied him to the stagecoach and saw him off.

Most of their friends were sympathetic to Jules. Balzac felt so sorry for him that, when Sandeau returned from Italy, he took him under his own roof, intending to employ him as collaborator on some of his own books. For a year and a half Balzac's relations with George Sand were strained, and they did not resume their friendship until he learned what she already knew, that Jules would happily accept financial support while giving nothing in return.

The change in Sandeau from the time George Sand rid herself of him until Balzac cast him onto his feet was remarkable. He almost doubled his weight, lost most of his hair, and, within a period of two years, came to look middle-aged. Forced to earn his own way in the world at last, he tried both acting and writing, and finally through George Sand he gained a tiny measure of immortality. All but forgotten, he told the story of their affair in a novel entitled *Marianna*, which enjoyed an extensive sale because of her fame. Not surprisingly, it was a scathing portrait, in which she was depicted as a human leech who tried to obtain pleasure through others, but was incapable of finding satisfaction in life.

There were times when her opinion of herself was equally unflattering, much to the distress of a new and influential friend, Charles Augustin Sainte-Beuve, one of the most curious figures in nineteenth-century French literature. Although he was only twenty-nine in 1832, which was George Sand's age, he had already established himself as the foremost literary critic and had achieved something of a reputation as a poet. Something of a spinster by nature, Sainte-Beuve had complicated his own life by engaging in a surreptitious affair with Adele, the wife of his best friend, Victor Hugo, who had broken relations with him after learning of the situation. Hugo, always the gentleman, had taken care to protect his wife's reputation, so Sainte-Beuve's good name remained untarnished.

The public accepted his evaluations without question, so Sainte-Beuve was courted by most authors, but he remained aloof, impervious to blandishments. He was not as remote as he appeared, and obtained some measure of vicarious satisfaction in quietly meddling in the lives of those he considered his friends. One of those closest to him over a period of many years was George Sand.

They had met soon after he had written a review hailing the appearance of *Indiana*, and thereafter their relationship had developed slowly. There was a strong feminine streak in Sainte-Beuve, who was firm and aggressive only in his writing, and during the period that George Sand was terminating her affair with Jules, she began to use the critic as a confidant. Sainte-Beuve could have enjoyed nothing more, and in the winter of 1832-33 he was a frequent dinner guest at her apartment.

There was no physical attraction on either side. Though George Sand recognized him as spiteful and weak, she was also aware of the force of his intellect. So she used him as a literary sounding board during the preparation of a new novel, the most ambitious project she had yet attempted, and Sainte-Beuve helped her to attain greater objectivity in her work. His interference and advice concerning her private life caused new snarls in her already complicated existence.

George read him portions of the new book, *Lélia*, and Sainte-Beuve was fascinated by the theme and her shockingly candid interpretation of it. He knew the market, understanding what the French reading public wanted, and believed that the balance of frankness and good taste she achieved would win her greater fortune and enduring renown. There can be little question that he deserves a degree of credit for the success of *Lélia*, as George Sand freely admitted that she wrote more boldly than she would have done without his encouragement. But he was not as influential a puppet-master as he tried to appear; even he eventually realized that his initial claims were exaggerated, and he toned them down.

In effect, *Lélia* was the disguised autobiography of a woman who was incapable of finding physical or emotional satisfaction in her relations with men. Its theme was sounded by one of its male characters, who declared, 'Lélia is not a complete human being. What is she, then? — a shadow, a dream, perhaps only an idea. Where love is absent, there can be no woman.'

The novel tells of a woman who goes from one lover to another, always seeking gratification but finding that it escapes her. Lélia is maternal, ever the aggressor in her physical relations, yet she secretly longs to be the passive partner. Occasionally she tries to subdue her own impulses, but finds she obtains even less satisfaction with a strong lover than with one whom she can control and manipulate.

Displaying a candor that no author of the period except Balzac had matched, George Sand wrote in detail about the erotic hunger that no affair could satisfy. In scene after scene she depicted a frenzied Lélia wearing out a lover and exhausting herself, yet failing to satiate the burning desire that still consumed her and caused her to indulge in wild flights of imagination.

In all probability it was Marie Dorval, rather than Sainte-Beuve, who made it possible for George Sand to write such painful, self-revealing prose. During the long winter and early spring of 1833, when she was spending hours every night pouring her innermost secrets onto paper, George spent at least a portion of each afternoon with Marie, who appears in the book as Lélia's sister, a courtesan who freely gains pleasure from men because she gives pleasure so unstintingly.

When the two friends were separated for as long as twenty-four hours, George wrote letters revealing more than she intended: 'You, my dear, have so much in your life, while I have nothing — except you. I cover you with a thousand kisses.'

Marie replied infrequently, and the few notes she sent to her friend were brief, crisp, and so discreet they conveyed an impersonal tone. De Vigny was keeping her under close observation, and she tailored her communications accordingly.

Sainte-Beuve, the eternal busybody, made it his business to help the unhappy young woman who had made him her confidant. In the late winter of 1833 he initiated a bizarre campaign. What she needed, he told her in person and in a series of astonishing letters, was a lover so virile that he would smash the mental and emotional barriers she had created. The idea sounded reasonable, and George Sand — who was now calling herself only by that name — was willing to make the experiment, provided she fell in love with the man. Under no circumstances would she take a lover for any other reason.

After due consideration Sainte-Beuve proposed a candidate. Théodore Jouffroy was a distinguished professor of philosophy at the Sorbonne, a man of such intellect that he could more than hold his own with the author whose sharp mind made many men uneasy in her presence. Jouffroy was a huge bear, and in spite of his profession had never lost some of the crude personal traits that had been part of his makeup since his childhood in the slums. He, of all men, could give the real-life Lélia the erotic gratification she sought.

George listened to the persuasive Sainte-Beuve, and so did Jouffroy. The two principals in the mating game had already met briefly at the theater one evening, and although neither had been particularly impressed, both were somewhat amused and intrigued by Sainte-Beuve's protestations that they would make the perfect couple.

Before the critic could arrange a meeting, however, George backed off. The scheme was so cold-blooded that she found it distasteful. As it happened, Professor Jouffroy shared her sentiments, and acting without her knowledge, he also declined. The plan collapsed.

It may or may not have been coincidental that another strong-minded, aggressive man with a bull-like body appeared in George's life at just this time, and that he, too, was a friend of Sainte-Beuve. No correspondence has ever been unearthed to prove that the critic was responsible, but the possibility cannot be discounted. In any event, Prosper Mérimée was a fellow author who ate in the same restaurants and attended the same plays, so it may be that he developed an interest in George on his own initiative, without prodding from Sainte-Beuve.

Mérimée was rapidly becoming one of the major literary figures of the period, writing Romantic books but refusing to align himself with Hugo and other advocates of the Romantic movement. It was one of his proudest boasts that he 'walked alone', and he frequently went out of his way to treat other writers, as well as editors and publishers, with extreme discourtesy. Passionately interested in history, archaeology, and politics, he had held an important government post after the Revolution of 1830, and although only a year older than George, had travelled extensively throughout Europe at the time of their meeting in the winter of 1833.

Glorying in his cynicism, Mérimée was an iconoclast who rejected — or professed to reject — the institutions and values that others held dear. He was opposed to marriage, and believed an affair should be conducted for its own sake, simply because both partners found pleasure in it. He had acquired a reputation as a rake, but not one of the many beautiful women who had been his mistresses could claim he had lulled her with false promises of marriage. Any woman who slept with him knew his principles, or his lack of them.

The gossips had cause to whisper, in the early spring of 1833, when Mérimée and George Sand began to be seen together at the theater. Solange always accompanied them, and as the little girl inevitably fell asleep during the performance, Mérimée carried her to a waiting carriage after the final curtain descended. The wits of Paris insisted that such conduct was ruining his reputation as a roué.

Was it possible that the man who sought the company of the most attractive feminine women of Paris was to be found engaging the least feminine member of her sex? Whispers grew louder even when the two principals took pains to set the record straight. George told everyone she knew that she and Prosper were not lovers. She offered him her 'loving friendship', she said, but she had not fallen in love with him. Mérimée was even more candid: the only reason they were not sleeping together was that she rejected his advances, and he assured his friends that the day would come when he would win her.

The café-watchers agreed, placing their wagers accordingly, while those who knew the strength of George's will were certain she would hold out. They were mistaken. The writing of *Lélia* was a torture, and the end of her relationship with Jules made her more vulnerable than she had ever been. Mérimée was the sort of man with whom she had no experience. He countered her arguments, laughed at her introspection, and made her feel like a foolish young girl.

By the late spring she succumbed to him, and their tempestuous affair lasted for one week. Mérimée used his superior physical strength to master George in bed, but she submitted to him with ill grace, and found the experience distasteful. Contrary to the theories expounded by Sainte-Beuve, her new lover left her colder than ever. And when they were not engaging in a wrestling match, they quarrelled. Many years later, describing the affair in a letter to her good friend, Gustave Flaubert, George wrote, 'Mérimée and I shouted and cursed at each other as the wives of fishmongers would if they possessed larger, more imaginative vocabularies. We devoted ourselves exclusively to insults and hurtful remarks, and not once in the entire week did either of us address a civil comment to the other.'

They parted on such bad terms that they went out of their way to snub each other when they happened to meet at a restaurant or theater, and hostesses knew it would be catastrophic to invite them to the same dinner party. Not until both grew older, mellowed by fame and the changing fortunes of life, was it possible for them to exchange surface pleasantries when they met. Late in middle age their paths crossed frequently on social occasions, and both made the effort to behave in a manner befitting two of the world's most famous authors. But Alexandre Dumas the younger, who had a number of opportunities to observe them during this period, said that neither relaxed in the presence of the other. They remained wary; they kept up their guards.

At the end of June, 1833, George wrote the final pages of *Lélia* and sent the manuscript off to her publishers. Too weary to make a journey to Nohant, she sent for Maurice. For two weeks the exhausted author spent her days with her children and her nights in long, deep sleep. She did not know it, but she was shaking off the trauma that the writing of the intimately autobiographical book had induced.

Sainte-Beuve proved a better literary seer than he had been a prophet of Love. *Lélia* created a sensation. It was a foregone conclusion that Sainte-Beuve would praise it, and the other critics were equally laudatory. The book was universally regarded as a masterpiece. Posterity has not chosen to confirm such a judgement, but in George Sand's own time the novel catapulted her to international renown. It was translated into German, Italian, Swedish, Dutch, Spanish — and ultimately into English. The daring theme, the knowledge that the author was actually a woman, and her delicacy in handling her subject made *Lélia* the outstanding financial success of the year.

Overnight, George Sand became independently wealthy, but there were other repercussions. Ladies of standing did not write about the nature and degree of their erotic responses to men, and a shocked French society closed its doors to her — while avidly reading every word of the book. Casimir Dudevant, who had not bothered to glance at any of his wife's previous literary efforts, heard the uproar she had caused, and stayed sober long enough to read and convince himself that she had disgraced him and their children.

The disapproval of upper-class Paris and the stunned reaction of Berry aristocrats meant nothing to George Sand. She had already excluded bluebloods from her life. Her friends were all either literary or theatrical, and she enjoyed the company of Delacroix and several other rising artists who were held in even lower esteem than those in publishing or the theater.

But the possibility that Casimir might go to court to obtain complete, permanent custody of the children was another matter. She discounted this in discussions with her friends by reminding them that Nohant was her property; if a legal battle developed, she could drive her husband from her estate and deprive him of his income.

Men with some knowledge of the world were less sanguine. Buloz, Gustave Blanche, and others advised her to observe greater caution, urging her not to advertise her love life so blatantly.

Even Sainte-Beuve joined the chorus. It was all well and good, he wrote to her, that she demand the prerogatives of a man in her private life, and he would be the last to deny her such rights. At the same time, he told her that it would be wiser to conduct herself as men did, and to be quiet about her affairs. George replied with some heat that most men of her acquaintance were anything but discreet, boasting of their latest conquests to anyone who would listen.

In spite of her brave words, she became concerned. Maurice and Solange meant more to her than her independence or her career, or so she convinced herself. Less than twenty-four hours after sending her angry letter to Sainte-Beuve, she wrote to him again, this time in a far more subdued tone. She was grateful for his advice and appreciated his concern. He was right, and she would exercise great care to prevent gossip about her private life. But she could not resist reminding him that, for the present, there was no cause for concern. She was in love with no one, and knew no man who might interest her.

George Sand was more than discreet when she wrote Sainte-Beuve. She was already involved in the first stages of a romance — with Alfred de Musset — that would develop into one of the most tempestuous and scandalous affairs of her life.

VI

'Musset is so beautiful that, if he were a woman, I could fall in love with him myself,' Honoré de Balzac wrote with heavy-handed humor as he observed George Sand's new romance from a distance.

Certainly no one who saw Musset could deny he was extraordinarily handsome in a delicate, brittle way. Six years younger than George Sand, he was a genius, a child prodigy who had first gained attention for his poetry, plays, and novels while still in his teens. Before he had reached the age of twenty he had been accepted as an equal by Victor Hugo, at whose house he had become friendly with de Vigny, Sainte-Beuve, Dumas the Elder, and many other prominent literary figures of the century.

A lyric poet and romanticist, Musset was also a satirist whose self-irony led him to mock the values he himself most admired, and this duality confused many of his contemporaries, who failed to recognize or understand his extraordinary talents. His colleagues, saluting his accomplishments, also realized he had achieved too much too soon, and was the victim of an emotional instability that led him to behave wildly, even irrationally. His conduct was controlled when he remained under the influence of his brother, Paul; his friends, all of them older, did what they could to curb his drinking and keep him from irresponsible women.

According to tradition it was Hugo who said, 'If Musset isn't killed by drink or loose women, he will some day become a member of the Academy.' In actuality, it was George Sand who first made the observation in a letter to Sainte-Beuve, written soon after she met the young poet, late in the spring of 1833.

She was twenty-nine, just completing the novel that would make her the best-known woman in Europe. Musset was twenty-three, the author of a recently-produced play that was the rage of Paris. She was suffering from a depression, Musset was high-spirited, seeking adventure, chafing under the restriction of his watchdog brother.

Inevitably, George Sand and Alfred de Musset should have fallen madly in love once their paths crossed. What makes their romance fascinating is the time they took to recognize their mutual fulfilment. Musset was artistic and intellectual, he was slender, unbelievably handsome, and almost effeminate — the 'Sandeau type' George Sand could not resist. She was earthy, possessed of a mind equal to his, but was almost overbearingly maternal, a quality that unfailingly dazzled him when he encountered it in an older woman. He, too, was recovering from an unhappy affair.

A word in passing, a letter George sent to Gustave Planche soon after her first meeting with Musset at a dinner party indicates her consciousness, from the outset, that the poet was a weak man, in spite of his intellectual brilliance. And the novel Paul de Musset subsequently wrote about the relationship, *Lui et elle*, the answer to George's own novel, *Elle et lui*, is the authority for the assertion that Alfred de Musset was from the beginning aware of her strength.

Yet these two, whose affair created a scandal across Europe for the better part of two years, remained casual acquaintances. Their paths crossed on a number of occasions before Musset casually accepted George's equally offhand invitation to drop in for a reading of a new play by a mutual acquaintance. Thereafter the pace remained leisurely. Alfred, accompanied by his brother, drank tea at George Sand's apartment, romped with Solange, and told stories to Maurice. The couple met by accident at the theater, and at Alfred's informal invitation, supped together. Destiny was beckoning, but both were impervious to its signals.

Then, in July, 1833, George sent Musset a set of the page proofs of *Lélia*, which had just been set in type, and invited his comments. Her gesture was in no way unusual, since copies had just been made available to her, and she was anxious to obtain opinions from a variety of sources. No one replied with greater enthusiasm than Musset, and no one else seemed as sensitive to her theme.

All the same, she told Sainte-Beuve, this devilishly handsome young man who dressed in the latest, most rakish styles, made her uneasy. He was known to have had at least a dozen affairs, and it was said he regarded all women as witches, allowing himself to fall under one's spell only so he could demonstrate his own ability to break her hold over him. Perhaps her own reputation was no longer as pristine as she might have wished, but Musset was said to be a debauched philanderer, in spite of his youth, and common sense told her to avoid him.

By now, however, the die was cast, and at the end of July he sent her another, more personal letter:

> My Dear George: I have something stupid and ridiculous to say to you. You will laugh in my lace, and hold that, in all I have said to you so far, I was a mere maker of phrases. You will show me the door, and you will believe that I am lying.
>
> I am in love with you.
>
> I have been in love with you ever since the day when I came to see you for the first time. I thought I could cure myself by continuing with you on a level of friendship. There is much in your character that might bring about a cure, and I

have tried hard to persuade myself of this; but I pay too high a price for the moments I spend with you.

And now, George, you will say, 'Just another importunate bore!' (to use your own words): I know precisely how you regard me, and, in speaking as I have done, delude myself with no false hopes. The only result will be that I shall lose a dear companion. But, in very truth, I lack the strength of mind to keep silent.

No one knows or will ever know how George Sand felt when she received Musset's letter. She neither replied to it nor commented on it to anyone else, and her silence is open to a variety of interpretations. Was she reluctant to enter into another relationship with a handsome, younger man when she had not yet completely recovered from her disappointment with Jules? Is it possible, as some biographers have indicated, that Musset's wild reputation frightened the countrywoman from Berry who was, in essence, a simple, straightforward person?

Certainly she knew that Musset was no Sandeau. The young genius might willingly allow a woman to dominate him for a time, and she had heard he was unable to resist temptations, but his intellectual independence was as firmly rooted as her own. So she may have realized that the union of two such strong, clashing minds could cause nothing but trouble for both.

For whatever reasons, George hesitated. Alfred's instinct prompted him to write her a second, much longer letter, and this time he threw aside all restraint. He loved her as a man loves a woman, as a child loves its mother.

It was this last phrase that destroyed George Sand's defenses, so she admitted with startling candor in *Elle et lui*. She was unable to identify the cause of her own emotions, and knew only that his desire to have her love him like a mother made him irresistible to her. In spite of her feelings, she continued to hold him at bay, making no reply to his second letter.

Finally, in mid-August, a haggard Musset presented himself at George Sand's apartment, and both of them must have enjoyed the melodramatic scene in which they were the principal players. He declared his love for her, and she turned away from him; he threatened to kill himself, and she laughed. He tried to use force, but her physical strength was greater than his, and it was a simple matter to hold him at arm's length. At last, all else having failed, Musset wept, and George's resistance promptly crumbled.

They became lovers that day, and the following afternoon he moved into the apartment on the Quai Malaquais.

Literary Paris was duly affronted by their affair. Gustave Planche was furious. Balzac, who had become Jules Sandeau's champion, called George a she-wolf who devoured young men. Even Sainte-Beuve, who tried to maintain a philosophical attitude, made it plain that he disapproved. Alfred de Vigny, who hoped — in vain — that the correspondence with Marie Dorval would cease, let it be known that he thought Musset's great talent would be stifled. Victor Hugo refused to express an opinion, but his eyes, according to Delacroix, indicated his disgust. Paul de Musset told everyone who would listen to him that the voracious George Sand had kidnapped his brother and was holding him prisoner against his will. The happy 'prisoner' could be seen escorting George to the theater every night and dining with her in restaurants, but the myth persisted.

In fact, none of the many scandals that subsequently upset George Sand's life damaged her reputation as severely as did the furor caused by Musset's move into her apartment. Men who had regarded themselves as his protector were annoyed, and others were afraid that George Sand's stronger will and dominating personality would make it impossible for him to write.

The lovers happily ignored the outbursts, and Musset's proximity provided George with a cushion that eased the notoriety of *Lélia*. She made no secret of her attachment, sending letters to various friends to inform them that she and Musset were deeply in love.

Soon she no longer cared what anyone was saying about her, and Delacroix, who was a frequent visitor, said she looked ten years younger. She spent several hours every evening working on a new book, and the words flowed effortlessly. Musset was doing no writing, but filled a number of sketchbooks with his drawings, and Delacroix, who thought his work as an artist showed great promise, wrote that Alfred was inspired.

Musset was a prankster, and George, who was too shy to make jokes in the presence of outsiders, was delighted when he played crude little tricks on various dinner guests. One of his favorite games was to pretend that he was a butler or housemaid, and he dressed accordingly, serving dinner to a group of assembled guests. Inevitably an 'accident' occurred, and George laughed until she wept when a pitcher of water or a bottle of wine was spilled over the head and shoulders of a helpless guest.

But she believed there was a time to work as well as a time to play, and her own schedule did not change. It disturbed her when Musset repeatedly postponed his labors on a new book of poetry, and finally she treated him as a mother might handle a bright but wayward child. They would not entertain, dine in a restaurant, or attend the theater, she said, unless Alfred produced his quota of work.

The chastened young man made the attempt to follow her instructions, and his own writing instincts were sufficiently strong to insure some progress. But his work progressed fitfully, and on his unproductive days he complained it was too much to expect a poet to force his inspiration. On other days, when he was able to work more easily, he wrote her brief notes thanking her for her disciplinary influence.

George found one aspect of Musset's personality startling, but failed to pay as much attention to it as common sense dictated. When he was subjected to severe strains or mental pressures, he sometimes became the victim of a form of delirium. During these spells, which lasted from a few minutes to an hour or longer, he suffered from hallucinations and insisted on conversing with spirits invisible to anyone else. It should, have been apparent to George that Musset's mental balance was delicate, and that he might be living close to the border of madness. But it was enough that she could take him in her arms and soothe him after a spell had passed. If trouble loomed ahead, she was too happy to think in such terms.

The stares and whispers that followed the lovers in public irritated them, and by the late autumn of 1833 they decided it would be wise to leave Paris for a time. It had become fashionable for authors and artists to visit some of the Italian states, so they decided they would make a long trip to Genoa, Florence, and Venice. They would be together, but would avoid the limelight; and, as George was quick to point out, they would have ample time to work.

There were some cumbersome, uncomfortable details to be settled before they could make their plans. Not the least of these was that George, a married woman, required her husband's permission to travel abroad. She wrote a carefully worded letter to Casimir, who replied cheerfully that he would be delighted if she travelled for her 'instruction and pleasure'. Whether he was seeking evidence he could use against her in court or was merely relieved that her name would no longer appear in the gossip columns of Paris newspapers is impossible to determine.

He voluntarily offered to take charge of the children at Nohant for as long a period as she wished to remain abroad. If he had ulterior motives, in her eagerness to travel with Alfred she did not suspect them.

Musset's problem was equally serious. He and his brother still made their home with their mother, a formidable old lady with a strong sense of propriety. Alfred had spent most of his royalties, squandering his money as rapidly as he earned it, and would not consider permitting George to pay for his share of the holiday. Therefore he had to depend on his mother for the funds, but he was afraid to confront her for the purpose.

George Sand did not hesitate, and immediately went to the town house of the Comtesse de Musset for an interview. Too little has been written about this meeting, and George herself barely mentions it in her autobiography. What the old lady thought of her son's mistress, how she received the younger woman, and whether George elected to wear a dress that day instead of trousers and boots are all questions that will continue to tantalize posterity.

The facts that emerged from the conference are sufficiently amazing. George managed to convince Alfred's mother that she would look after the young man, protect him, and see to it that no harm came to him. The Comtesse was convinced of her sincerity, and proved it by handing her a purse containing fifteen hundred francs, which she urged George to dole out to Alfred in small sums, as he was incapable of handling large quantities of money.

All necessary blessings duly bestowed, the lovers set out on their journey in December, 1833, with George startling their fellow passengers on the stagecoach by traveling in man's attire. A fellow passenger during a portion of the journey was Stendhal, then an unknown author. They chatted with him at length, and George was so impressed by his concepts of life and literature that, years later, when Balzac befriended him and helped him achieve the renown that had so long been overdue, she also came to his support.

Musset complained that the ruts and the potholes in the long road that ran from Paris to Marseilles by way of Lyons caused the carriage to jolt so badly that he suffered raging headaches. But George felt no discomfort, and took careful notice of the changing countryside. The weather in Marseilles was miserable, and the couple did not linger there, but immediately took the best quarters available on a small packet boat bound for Genoa. Their cabin was tiny, cramped, and suffused with the odors of unwashed humanity. Musset was offended, but George found the experience interesting.

No sooner did the little ship put out to sea than the Mediterranean erupted in a storm, and Musset promptly became seasick. For a day and a night he was unable to rise from his bunk, and later described the ailment as the most agonizing he had ever known. George, however, was not affected by the elements, and spent most of her time on deck, watching the vessel pitch and roll as it inched eastward in the high seas. The following day Musset wrapped himself in his heaviest cloak and staggered up to the deck to join his mistress. He discovered her standing in the prow, her hands jammed into the pockets of her trousers, her feet spread so she could balance herself, with a lighted cigarette protruding from one corner of her mouth.

Smoking had just become popular in French artistic circles, from which the habit would spread, first to the aristocracy and then to the working classes, with only the bourgeoisie abstaining. Even the writers and artists who adopted this custom, imported from Turkey by way of Vienna, considered smoking an exclusively masculine pleasure. Playwrights and portrait painters smoked, an occasional lawyer or member of the bar could be seen with a cigarette, and dashing officers of cavalry regiments were picking up the habit. But it was believed to be beneath the dignity of a woman to smoke; Parisian actresses carefully abstained, both in public and private, and not even the inmates of the notorious brothels near the Pont Neuf cared to subject themselves to the criticism of men by allowing themselves to be seen with cigarettes in their hands.

George Sand was unable and unwilling to accept even a symbol of masculine superiority without protesting, so she, too, began to smoke, probably acquiring the habit early in 1833. No affair, no wild adventure, not even her adoption of man's attire brought her greater notoriety, and she was not only the first woman in France who dared to smoke, but no member of her sex emulated her until her prominence in the Revolution of 1848 caused a few daring women to follow her example.

Although she adopted the habit as an act of defiance, it soon became a necessity, and for the rest of her life she smoked regularly, sometimes incessantly. Coupled with her need for tobacco, however, was a deep-rooted fear of fire, perhaps caused by some incident in her childhood that she was unable to recall. This phobia caused her to take extraordinary precautions, particularly when she smoked indoors. Regardless of whether she was in her own dwelling, a restaurant, or the home of a friend, she insisted on keeping a bowl half-filled with water beside her, and carefully dropped lighted butts into it. Anyone who invited her to a dinner party was forced to accept her idiosyncrasy.

On the deck of the bobbing packet ship that struggled along the Mediterranean coast toward Genoa, Musset claimed that the odor of cigarette smoke made him feel queasy again. George's solicitude for his welfare was responsible for one of the more amusing incidents in the couple's ill-starred relationship. She immediately threw her cigarette overboard, to Musset's infinite relief. Then, a few moments later, she took a cigar from a leather case, explaining that its heavier smoke would not blow in her lover's direction, and consequently would cause him no harm. A single whiff was enough to send Musset hurrying back to their cabin, and George wondered how any man could be so delicate.

It was raining in Genoa when the couple arrived there, and Musset complained of the cold, but George insisted they see the sights of the city and the surrounding countryside. They spent a day or two visiting churches, museums, and palaces. As there were relatively few places to visit, Alfred balked when, attempting to drive beyond the confines of the city, the wheels of their carriage became mired in mud.

Musset, a born holiday maker, wanted them to spend the better part of their time drinking, eating exotic foods, and making love, but the provincial, convent-bred George was too sensible to accept such a regimen. She enjoyed a little wine with her meals, but had made an experiment or two, and had made up her mind that she would never become intoxicated and lose her self-control. She had been reared on the simple dishes of Berry, and although she liked a rich, unusual dish on occasion, she far preferred a regular diet of plain fare that included fresh vegetables and fruit. As for sex, it was but one aspect of love, and she had no intention of spending hours in bed every day. Only trollops behaved that way.

There were far more important things to do, she reminded Musset. Like most authors of note in every period of literature, George Sand was compulsively driven to put words onto paper. When she was working on a book — and only rarely did she pause for a short time between manuscripts — she allowed nothing to interfere with her work. She set herself a quota, and would not stop until she had written at least fifteen pages each day; she preferred to turn out twenty, but was willing to stop after doing fifteen, if it should be necessary.

These labors occupied her full attention for some five hours a day, and frequently she required seven or eight hours. She believed she did her best work at night, but was malleable if other arrangements interfered. She could willingly spend an afternoon at her desk instead of waiting until she had eaten dinner. Under no circumstances could she write in the morning, maintaining that she needed to be awake for a number of hours before her mind functioned as it should.

When working on a manuscript, George Sand always retired behind the closed door of a private room, and even when traveling with Musset she rented quarters accordingly, making certain there was a separate bedroom or a sitting room in which she could write. Musset, younger, playful, and less driven, tried to solve the problem of her daily disappearance in his own way by interrupting her at her desk and insisting she pay attention to him. He could not understand that it was impossible for her to relax and enjoy herself if the ghost of unwritten pages hovered over her head, so she had to take matters into her own hands, and when she vanished, she took care to lock the door behind her.

George was not only conscientious in her own work, but played her maternal role to the hilt and suggested ideas she thought would be of interest to Alfred. Whether she actually inspired some of his later efforts, as she subsequently claimed, has never been verified. One thing is certain: Musset resented her attempts to force him to work, and told her he was no slave, even though she was a slave driver. It was inevitable that the bored Alfred and the irritated George began to quarrel. Fortunately for posterity, both aired their grievances fully in long, explicit letters to others.

Musset was the first to resort to name-calling. He told her that she was a 'prim nun who should have remained in the convent that nurtured you'. He called her a dreamer, an idiot, a woman who knew nothing of life, and insisted she was 'the ultimate representative of boredom incarnate'.

Then, descending to the gutter, he took advantage of what he had learned in his reading of *Lélia* to tell her, 'You have never known how to provide the joys of love because you have never experienced them, yourself.'

Deeply wounded, George could only reply that her concept of love was 'more exalted' than Musset's. And the most forceful retort she could muster was dignified but feeble: 'I am content to know that the joys to which you object have been more austere and less obvious than those you find elsewhere! At least, when you are making love with other women, no memories of me will spoil your ecstasies!'

All might have been well again, at least for a time, if George had not succumbed to a case of the ague, an ailment known to later generations as a severe head cold. She was running a fever, so she fell into bed, and for the moment had no interest in romance.

This gave Musset the opportunity to strike back at her, and after announcing, 'The artist is not a slave, now or ever,' he stalked out of her sickroom. For the next few days he drank far too much and sampled the night life of Genoa. One of the world's busiest seaports, it boasted a brothel district known to every seafaring man, and Musset visited every type, from the elegant, expensive establishments that catered to ship owners to the cheap cribs that functioned for the benefit of common seamen. Had he been content to use his rebellion to work off his resentment, George might have been able to tolerate his infidelity, but he insisted on returning to her sickroom while still intoxicated, and goaded her with accounts of his exploits.

Certainly she was aware of his immaturity, and, like a loving mother, she forgave his transgressions. But the rose of immortal love had lost something of its bloom, and the couple should have separated. Instead they went on to Florence, where George, after a longer and more thorough round of sightseeing, settled back into her usual routine of writing each day. The quarrels became worse, and Musset flatly refused to contemplate a new project of his own. He was enjoying a holiday, he said, and began to overindulge in her presence.

For reasons George never defined, but probably because she needed to cling to something, she pinned her hopes on the magic of Venice, which would revive their love and restore its wonders. They engaged a suite at the Hôtel Danieli, the finest in the colorful city, and for a few hours after their arrival there George believed she had been right. They wandered on foot together, crossing bridges, looking at St Mark's and the Doge's Palace in the moonlight, and Musset appeared fresh, eager and revitalized.

Then, when they returned to their suite, he dropped the totally unexpected bombshell, saying, 'George, I was completely wrong about my feelings, and I can only hope you will forgive me for what was never a deliberate deception. But the truth of the matter is that I don't love you — and never have.'

The unexpected blow stunned her. Unable to speak, she retreated to her own room and closed the door. George's pride urged her to abandon him without delay and return to Paris, but her conscience would not permit her to leave. Musset was a wild, irresponsible boy, even though of age and presumably responsible for his actions; she had promised his mother she would protect him, so she could not break her word. She could not admit to herself that she still loved him, which created the same, unfortunate dilemma.

So she stayed, and the tensions that grew out of the strange new relationship became unbearable. The couple spent a portion of each day together, sometimes walking, sometimes sightseeing, sometimes trying to chat about literature, art, and the history of Venice over a cup of thick Turkish coffee. More often than not they dined together, usually at their hotel, and then, while George retired to her writing desk for an evening of work on her manuscript, Alfred went out on the town. Before long, as he himself later admitted, he knew every bar and every prostitute in Venice.

The situation overwhelmed George. She could not drop off to sleep until she heard Alfred stumble into his room at dawn every morning, and she concluded their relationship was beyond repair. She convinced herself that his conduct had relieved her of her promise to his mother, but she lingered in Venice for yet another reason. The drinking water of the city had given her a severe case of dysentery, and the young physician called in by the hotel ordered her not to travel. Dr Pietro Pagello, an earnest, plump young man in his mid-twenties, apparently knew his business, even though he was obviously nervous in the presence of the celebrated author, and was very firm in his insistence that she remain in Venice.

George's health improved gradually over a period of many days, and the end of George's nightmare appeared to be within sight. In a week, perhaps less, she could go home. To the best of her belief she could feel only pity for Musset, and could scarcely wait until she was rid of him.

Then, one morning a few days before she planned to leave, he tapped at her door after returning from his night's revels. His face was smeared with blood, but he was too drunk to answer her questions coherently, so she cleaned him and put him to bed.

Whether Alfred de Musset suffered a concussion in a fight in the slums of Venice is unknown. He appeared somewhat irrational to George when he awakened after several hours of sleep, but he was still capable of tormenting her, and producing a jug of cheap brandy, began to drink from it. Her protests were useless and goaded him into finishing off the jug.

Modern physicians who have debated the matter at length have been unable to determine whether Musset's chronic mental condition, his fight, or his excess consumption of liquor — perhaps a combination of these factors — was responsible for the madness that suddenly afflicted him.

He saw demons appearing before him, and screaming in terror, tried to hide beneath the sheets. His sudden deterioration frightened George, and she summoned Dr Pagello, who administered strong sedatives. Musset became somewhat calmer, but was still delirious, and with the physician in almost constant attendance, George took up a vigil at the bedside of her former lover.

The care lavished on Musset over the next few days and nights gradually restored his senses and health. But his recovery was slow, and sometimes suffering relapses, he went out of his mind again, seeing apparitions and babbling incomprehensibly. Occasionally he behaved like a lunatic for hours at a time, yet, thanks to George and the physician, he completely recovered from his malady.

George Sand's conduct during the period of Musset's convalescence has been the subject of heated controversy ever since it occurred, yet no one can say with certainty why she behaved as she did. A number of influences were at work, and one or more of them may have been responsible. Her own physical condition had been weakened, and the hours she spent nursing Alfred had made her light-headed, distorting her sense of values. She was a woman who had been scorned and abused, and her ego, more demanding than that of most people, was desperately in need of balm.

When Musset was lucid, he felt no remorse over the way he had treated her. He was not the first or last man to deal with a wife or mistress in such a high-handed manner. Yet he dared to embarrass her by claiming — perhaps when only semi-lucid — that she was flirting with Dr Pagello. It was his right to sleep with anyone he pleased, he believed, yet he demanded she remain faithful to him. This reversion to the double standard, coupled with his insistence that he no longer loved her, denied everything George Sand was trying to prove in her way of life, and infuriated her beyond measure. Her precious principles of feminine equality were at stake, and she must have felt obliged to put Musset in his place.

She may have been motivated, too, by something basic and non-intellectual. Alfred had hurt and humiliated her, and she wanted to retaliate. So the explanation could be very simple.

In any event, and for whatever reason, she came to think herself in love with Dr Pagello. While Musset dozed, she and the physician went to bed together in the adjoining room.

Later, when the new affair became known, and the air was filled with charges and counter-charges, Musset made a number of extraordinary claims. He had awakened from naps, he said, to see George and Dr Pagello indulging in intimate embraces in his sickroom a few feet from his bed. His description of these scenes was imaginative, lurid, and detailed.

Many people accepted all this at face value as the literal truth, and condemned George Sand as an immoral woman completely lacking in sensitivity. Throughout the long harangues she refused to dignify Musset's charges by either confirming or denying them. Under ordinary circumstances she would have been far too reserved and shy to exchange intimacies with a new lover in the presence of the old, even when the latter was unconscious, but it does lie within the realm of the possible that she was so eager for revenge that she waited until Musset was awake before encouraging Pagello to kiss and fondle her.

Whatever the circumstances, the situation became worse as Musset recovered. By this time, he was aware of the budding romance, and in his paranoid state he decided that George and the doctor were conspiring against him. It was their intention, he declared — and later repeated — to put him out of the way by sending him to a madhouse and confining him there for an indefinite period. This claim, which George also did not bother to deny, could not have been true. She was under no obligation to nurse Alfred back to good health, and could have left him at any time she wished, so she was under no pressure to remove him from her life by sending him to a lunatic asylum.

The unhappy farce ended at the beginning of March, when Musset moved out of the hotel into other quarters. Whatever he may have imagined, the subsequent correspondence of George Sand and Alfred de Musset, which was remarkably verbose, makes one point very clear. Before Alfred departed for his new lodgings, George could not deny herself the sweet pleasure of informing him she was in love with Dr Pagello. Musset demanded to know whether that love had been consummated, and she obtained her ultimate revenge by refusing to answer the question. Musset was tortured, but George, unexpectedly demure, merely informed him that her private life was no longer any of his business.

Late in March Musset returned to Paris, and the scandal burst into the open on his arrival. Meanwhile, apparently unconcerned, George Sand moved into Pagello's small apartment with him, displacing his bewildered young Venetian mistress, whom he was forced to dismiss. Of all the figures in the sorry farce, the almost forgotten Pietro Pagello is the most pathetic. An ambitious, conscientious young man, he was overwhelmed by a force beyond his control, a determined human whirlwind who called herself George Sand. He accepted the famous author as his mistress because she gave him no choice, and thereafter he appears as a puppet she manipulated at will.

Pagello's seeming lack of character may be deceptive; his side of the story was never told. A number of George's friends who later met him in Paris wrote that he was a young man of integrity, humor, and courage, somewhat dazzled by the experience, yet determined not to permit his own life to be ruined. People who met him in later years in Venice reported that he had become a distinguished, highly successful physician, happily married, and that two of his sons also became physicians.

His situation must have seemed insecure, however, at the time George Sand moved in with him. If he expected her to behave like a passionate mistress, he must have been disappointed, because she plunged into her work with unprecedented zeal. First, she finished the manuscript of her long novel, *Jacques*, and sent it off to Buloz for publication. It was one of the least consequential of her books, the story of an unhappy wife who gave up marriage to an intelligent, substantial husband and tried in vain to find happiness with her lover, a gadfly whose interest in his wardrobe was reminiscent of Alfred de Musset.

George Sand was still the darling of the critics, who were reluctant to admit she could write a second-rate novel, but they found it difficult to read significance into *Jacques* and damned it with faint praise. *Lélia* had guaranteed her a large audience, however, no matter what she wrote, and the Musset scandal, which remained the talk of Paris, also helped sales. The new novel earned more money than anything she had written previously.

Not pausing for breath, she continued to work in the little Venetian flat. She turned out the first volume of what would become one of her more ambitious works, *Lettres d'un Voyageur*, and made extensive notes for a book of short stories with an Italian background. She also found the time to teach Pagello something about the blessings of domesticity. The young physician was too poor to afford a servant, so the indefatigable George, who refused to embarrass him by paying for Servants out of her own purse, did the marketing, cooked their meals, and cleaned the apartment. She also made a complete set of slipcovers for his furniture, and proudly wrote to Sainte-Beuve that her handiwork had been superb; the covers-would last for many years.

Her correspondence increased with everyone she knew, particularly showing concern about Maurice, now attending a boarding school in Paris. She was informed that enemies, among them Jules Sandeau, were damning her unmercifully, regarding her treatment of Musset as disgusting, but she refused to reply to any specific charges.

Her most astonishing letters were with Alfred de Musset — four or five each week. George was warm, friendly, and considerate; she remained calm when Alfred became hysterical, and she soothed him, humored him, and offered him sound advice. Occasionally she indicated that she was happy with Pagello, but she exercised the restraint expected of a provincial lady, and discussed no details of her new affair.

Musset, on the other hand, wallowed in excited self-pity. No matter where he went in Paris, he was reminded of his once-beloved George. He visited her apartment one day, and burst into uncontrollable tears when he saw a cigarette butt she had left in an ash tray. The wicked, cruel remarks that were being made about her filled him with horror and anger, and he had decided to issue a rebuttal of his own. In fact, he intended to tell the true story in the form of a novel, but he needed her help. He had kept all of her letters to him, but needed the letters he had written to her. He would be the first to understand if she were reluctant to part with them, but he would be forever grateful to her, his dearest friend, if she could find a little time to copy them for him.

The tone of George Sand's letters indicates that, at this time, she would have been willing to drop Alfred de Musset from her life. It was obvious, however, that he could not bring himself to make a clean break with her, so she kept up the correspondence, partly out of habit, partly out of pity, partly because it was good to know that he still wanted and needed her.

By the end of June, 1834, George knew the time had come to end her Venetian sojourn and return to Paris. Buloz had become lax in forwarding royalties to her, and Casimir Dudevant had completely 'forgotten' to send her the allowance he owed her. Even more important, she had not seen her children for almost eight months. She knew that Maurice would be awarded several prizes at his school in July and could allow nothing to prevent her from attending that event.

Dr Pagello posed something of a problem. If she abandoned him, walking out of his life, she would become the heartless creature, the man-eater, whom her enemies in French literary circles were painting in such lurid colors. The obvious solution was to ask the good physician to accompany her.

Pietro agreed. He had always wanted to see Paris, he was very fond of George, and he knew, as his correspondence with members of his family later revealed, that the curtain was rising on the last act of the drama in which he would be a player. He was still embarrassed by lack of funds, but George, who thought of everything, took care of that problem. At her instigation he brought with him a number of ordinary paintings that he owned. When they reached Paris, she pretended to sell them, presenting him the supposed proceeds, fifteen hundred francs, which made him financially independent.

George also made certain that he would not follow her around Paris like a satellite. In order to give his visit meaning, she quietly arranged meetings for him with a number of prominent French physicians, and he spent part of each day inspecting the city's leading hospitals. In all, Pagello made a pleasant impression on almost everyone who met him. Those who expected to find him either a satyr or a dashing nobleman were disappointed when he proved to be unassuming, quiet, and dedicated to his profession.

The impression he created, however, did not lessen the damage that George Sand had done to her own reputation. She quickly discovered that Gustave Planche had turned against her. Saint-Beuve, in a visit to her apartment, delivered a long lecture, telling her she would destroy herself unless she mended her ways. Some said she had the affairs with the two men concurrently, that she had become so disreputable nobody would continue to read her books. Even Buloz was worried; the concern of the hard-headed publisher made George uneasy.

Alfred de Musset chose just this time to re-enter her life with a flourish. He wrote her to the effect that their previous troubles had been caused by misunderstanding, compounded by their illnesses. He felt certain all would be well if they met again, and he was eager to see her. At the same time, however, he expressed great apprehension. If she saw him and rejected him, he did not know whether he could stand the strain.

George's reply was less than truthful. She was happy, she wrote, with Pietro and there was nothing to be gained by another meeting with her former lover.

Pagello happened to see one of Musset's love-letters, and the usually placid physician suddenly became jealous. He, too, had rights, he insisted, and he demanded that George remain faithful to him. In an attempt to calm the young doctor she invited him to Nohant, hoping the tranquil atmosphere of Berry would soothe him. In an effort to persuade him to come there with her she even managed to persuade Casimir to send him an invitation. Pagello drew the line; marriage was sacred. He refused to come between Mme Dudevant and her husband.

The mad comedy soon became wilder. Musset wrote yet another hysterical, nearly incoherent letter. He knew at last that George wanted nothing more to do with him. His heart was broken, and he doubted his survival. He was leaving France on a journey to a 'distant place' where he would try to regain his health and composure.

Before leaving, he wrote, he requested a final favor. Their love had been immortal, and they would be remembered as lovers throughout all recorded history. Like Romeo and Juliet, like Abelard and Héloïse, their names would be linked together through all eternity. Therefore it was not too much to beg that she see him once more, so he could bid her a final farewell, so he could kiss her for one last time.

George sensibly refused to see him, and Musset's friends, spurred by his brother, cited this rejection as conclusive proof that she was ruthless, rejecting the limp bodies of men after drinking their blood.

On August 24, 1854, Dr Pietro Pagello returned to Venice. He reproached George bitterly and at length before he left, accused her of having lost interest in him and swore he would renew her love for him. For several months he wrote her long, plodding letters, trying to convince her to come back to Venice and resume her life in his small apartment there. George wrote him a few brief notes and never saw him again.

On August 25, 1834, Alfred de Musset left Paris, and it was revealed that his 'distant' journey was taking him to the watering resort of Baden, across the German border. He continued to inundate his former mistress with passionate letters, some of which, thanks to the foresight of his brother, who copied them, were quoted at length by friends in Paris as proof of his sincerity and devotion. Only his intensity and the effect of his letters on their recipient, not noted for objectivity in her personal life, prevent these absurdly distorted avowals of undying love from being regarded as a monstrous joke.

On August 29, 1834, George left Paris for her beloved Nohant. She was accompanied by her mother, of all people, the two women having surprised themselves by achieving something of a rapport. George's tribulations were broadening her outlook, making it easier for her to tolerate the older woman, while Sophie, who was growing softer as she aged, was impressed by her daughter's international reputation and an income believed to reach twenty thousand francs a year. Sophie spent two weeks at the estate, and not once did she and her daughter quarrel.

At Nohant George Sand became Aurore Dudevant again, and made strenuous attempts to reorder her life. Casimir was drinking less, but went out of his way to avoid her, and she made no attempt to seek his company. Her woods and flower beds were unchanged, the river and the pasture lands were the same, and she spent hours each day wandering in the open as she tried to unravel her personal dilemma. For the first time in several years she made no attempt to work on a manuscript, but spent most of her nights reading.

Her favorite subject, as she admitted in *Lettres d'un Voyageur*, was suicide, and she claimed in her correspondence with Musset that she was thinking of doing away with herself. Her intent may have been serious or she may have been indulging in the melodrama of her recent life.

In any event, the proximity of her two children sobered her. Maurice and Solange were so delighted to see her that they followed her everywhere, accompanying her on her walks, remaining awake long past their usual bedtime to read as they sat beside her, and even eating all of their meals with her, not the custom of nineteenth-century aristocrats. She realized how much the children needed her, and only that, she wrote Musset, prevented her from killing herself, Dr Pagello's reproachful, pedestrian letters quickly-cooled what had been, at best, a tepid love. He had lost faith in her, George reported to a number of friends in her correspondence, which meant he no longer loved her. Love could exist only if it was reciprocal, which meant she no longer loved him, either.

The pragmatic Pagello appears to have been going through polite motions that were expected of him. Having already informed his family that his relationship with George Sand was ended, he resumed his liaison with his former mistress, increased his medical practice, and, in the following year, met the young lady who would become his faithful, lifelong wife. He made his exit from George's life slowly, gracefully, and not once did he make a false move or say anything that would cause her new complications.

With Pagello no longer a contender for her heart, she became romantically philosophical, and in several long letters to Musset tried to probe the nature and meaning of true love:

> Is there, really, anywhere, such a thing as a love that moves upon the heights, and has absolute trust in the beloved? Am I fated to die without ever meeting it? I am weary of finding that what I clasp is only a ghost, that those I pursue are merely shadows!

Her excess emotionalism revealed that the wild events and strains of the past year had exhausted and confused her. It has even been suggested by observers who have not been charitably inclined toward her that she was imagining her own love life in terms suitable only for the heroine of a romantic George Sand novel.

In mid-September, only three weeks after Musset left for Baden, he precipitated a new crisis by writing to George that he was returning to Paris immediately. He could no longer live without her, he declared, and if she refused to meet him in the city, he threatened to storm the gates of Nohant.

The possibility created an embarrassing predicament. Casimir Dudevant's indifference had made it possible for his wife to live her own life as she pleased, without interference or criticism. If she chose to behave scandalously in Paris or Venice, that was her business. But he had achieved a solid reputation of sorts as a Berry squire, he had inherited his father's title, and when his stepmother died, he would become wealthy in his own right. Certainly he would react violently if a melodramatic young poet dressed in high fashion suddenly camped on his doorstep with hysterical scenes in the making. Casimir could not afford to be a laughingstock in his own bailiwick, and George knew he was capable of causing her serious problems when aroused.

The return of Maurice to his Paris boarding school for the new term gave her the chance to solve her dilemma without appearing to accept Musset's terms. Obviously she was weakening, although she may not have realized it, but she could say she was going to the city to deliver Maurice to his school. She wanted to confer with her publishers and had no desire to be separated from her daughter again, so she took Solange with her.

George reached her apartment on the Quai Malaquais on the last day of September. Musset learned of her arrival the following morning, and carefully timing his arrival so he would not appear before Solange's bedtime, he waited until late that evening before presenting himself at George's door. The former lovers promptly and blissfully fell into each other's arms, and Musset stayed for the night.

The self-styled Romeo and Juliet not only rediscovered that the course of true love does not run smoothly, but also learned the impossibility of turning back the clock. Some of George Sand's supporters have written that Musset was again deranged. At the very least, however, his behavior was strongly influenced by powerful neuroses, while her conduct was foolish and ultimately became hysterical. Rarely have two supposedly responsible adults acted and reacted to each other with such a total lack of wisdom, dignity, and poise, and it is difficult to excuse their game-playing on the grounds of their genius. The modern observer can only conclude they thoroughly enjoyed their self-indulgences, no matter how absurd their charade became.

Alfred de Musset's passion was almost frightening in its intensity, and for a few days his ardor disposed of all problems. Then, as his erotic desires cooled, his neuroses took possession of him. He began to question George in infinite detail about her affair with Dr Pagello. He wanted — eventually demanded — to know everything about that relationship. What bothered him most was his fear that George had obtained greater physical satisfaction in her relations with the physician than she did with him.

George could have ended the distasteful discussions by telling him what he wanted to hear and soothing him, but her pride — and, perhaps, a touch of sadism — made her obstinate. She refused to answer any of his questions, and would not discuss the matter.

So they began to quarrel again, far more violently than they had in Italy. They made dreadful, inexcusable scenes, were reconciled tenderly, and then fought again. George would not be budged from the position she had taken, and the thwarted Alfred was forced to use his ultimate weapon, illness. He went off to his mother's house, and soon worked himself into an alarming condition.

The old Comtesse de Musset swallowed her pride and begged George's help. So George went to the Musset home, disguised in the Uniform of her own parlor maid, and spent several days there nursing Alfred back to health. Meanwhile, for the sake of appearances, his mother pretended to be unaware of the other woman's identity.

As soon as Musset fully recovered his health he returned to the apartment on the Quai Malaquais, but too much dirty water had flowed under the bridge by now, and it was impossible for the lovers to achieve a tranquil relationship, They snarled and clawed, begged for forgiveness, spent a day or two serenely, and then began the wearying process again.

How long Musset would have been willing to go on in this manner is questionable because George Sand was the first to break down. They could neither live together nor live apart, and she wrote Musset a note of her desperation:

> We are playing a game, you and I, but our lives and our hearts are the stakes, and it is not quite so amusing a pastime as it seems. Do you not think it would be best if... we blow out our brains? It would be by far the quickest way of reaching a solution.

She had no intention of killing herself, however, and instead went off with Solange on a hurried trip to Nohant. She felt certain Alfred would write another of his passionate letters, begging her to return. For a short time she would punish him by remaining aloof, but eventually she would forgive him, and then, perhaps, all would be well.

Musset astonished George by ignoring her script and following his own. Making no attempt to get in touch with her, he silently vanished from her life. Within a few days she received a number of letters from busybodies who took relish in telling her that a lively', happy Musset was attending the theater and was seen in restaurants with ravishingly beautiful young ladies.

Never has the perversity of human nature been more evident: the indignant, wounded George Sand promptly rushed back to Paris, again taking Solange with her. Only her genuine concern for her daughter was admirable as she and Musset played out their pathetic farce. Now it was she who sought a renewal of the relationship, and she besieged him, walking past his mother's house several times daily, going to the restaurants she knew he frequented, bombarding him with letters.

Alfred's brother and friends knew the affair would drive him out of his mind unless a permanent halt could be called, and they surrounded him, sometimes using persuasion and occasionally resorting to physical force as they prevented him from seeing his mistress or replying to her letters.

George tried a new stratagem. She wrote freely in her *Intimate Journal*, relating the agony and despair of her longing for Musset. Then she sent him the diary, but still there was no reply.

Buloz, the publisher, was afraid she would destroy her own health and that he would lose a lucrative author, so he made a new suggestion. Eugène Delacroix, the painter, was her friend, so perhaps she could persuade him to do a portrait of her so luminous that it would melt Musset's reserve. She leaped at the idea, Delacroix agreed, and, beginning in November, she went to the artist's studio daily for a sitting. She conceived the idea of a portrait after the manner of Goya, because she knew of

Musset's great fondness for the work of the Spanish master, but Delacroix demurred. He would work only in the style of Eugène Delacroix.

The sittings were a torture. According to George's *Intimate Journal*, Delacroix passed much of the time chatting with her about Musset's sketches and his potential as a painter. It seemed to her that he talked only about Alfred. Delacroix, on the other hand, revealed in his correspondence that George was obsessed by the subject of love, and delivered long monologues in which she tried to dissect, analyze, and understand the essence of the emotion.

In December she made another hurried journey to Nohant, but the ruse was no more effective than the earlier effort had been, and again she returned to Paris. Then, in late December, she received a letter from Musset.

Whether it was his own work or had been prompted by his friends, it was in his handwriting, an extraordinary document. He apologized to her for the many scenes he had made, for his unkindness and lack of consideration. He was ashamed of having used illness in attempts to win her sympathy. But all that was in the past. Their relationship was ended now, and he hoped both of them could find tranquility as they went their separate ways.

The finality of his letter was more than George Sand could bear. In a gesture dictated by cunning as well as hysteria, she cut off her dark, waist-long hair and sent it to Musset. This act has been interpreted as that of a woman crazed by love, but the modern observer must draw other conclusions. George knew Musset loved her hair, which had never before been cut, and that the receipt of it might spur him, as nothing else could, to break through the barriers that he and others had erected.

Having performed the deed, George made certain it would be immortalized by going off to Delacroix' study for a sitting. It is not accidental that this portrait, the most renowned of her many contemporary paintings, shows her with hair cut as short as a man's. Inasmuch as she had sometimes complained that her long hair made it difficult for her to wear a man's hat and spoiled the effect of her male costume, it is difficult to suspect that there was not a double motive in her grand gesture. Her act, she knew, would exert a strong influence on Musset's highly inflammable feelings; consciously or otherwise, she found the perfect gesture to gain for herself the masquerade of a man.

It produced the desired effect. Musset wept uncontrollably when he opened the package and saw George's long hair. Overwrought, he went to bed for forty-eight hours, and immediately thereafter hurried to her apartment for another glorious reconciliation.

Everyone who cared about either of them was worried, and within a short time the worst fears of the pessimists were confirmed. The fights became brutal; one night Alfred became so incensed he chased George into the street, brandishing a large kitchen knife, and threatened to kill her.

Sainte-Beuve, the most moderate and controlled of George's friends, decided the time had come for him to intervene, and told her that for her own sake as well as Alfred's it was essential they part. When she replied that they loved each other, Sainte-Beuve said forthrightly, 'Love does not become genuine until lovers part, and then their tears become the true expression of their love.'

Even Honoré de Balzac, whose sympathies for George had been reawakened by his own problems with Jules Sandeau, sent her a brief note. His novels on obsessions were already recognized as classics, and he appeared to understand the dilemma that robbed her of her free will. He sent her a curt note: 'If you hope to survive, go your own way. If you remain in thrall, you will perish.'

George appreciated the concern of her friends for her welfare, but refused their advice. Her love was unlike any emotion they had ever experienced, so they could not know how much Musset meant to her. No-matter how high the cost or how great her suffering, she could not give him up.

The intolerable situation dragged on through January and February of 1833, and even the cheap newspapers that thrived on gossip no longer bothered to print items about the private war being waged on the Quai Malaquais. George lost weight, deep smudges appeared beneath her eyes, and her restless, ever-present energy gave way to an almost dream-like lethargy. Musset was equally disturbed, and became so thin, so distraught, that his brother felt certain he would not survive the spring.

Sainte-Beuve happened to be present at George's apartment when a new fight, similar to scores of others, broke out on the evening of March 5th. He was the first outsider to witness one of the frightful scenes in its entirety, and, a civilized man dedicated to the principles of moderation in all things, he was appalled. Displaying a greater physical courage than anyone would have suspected of him, he managed to separate the combatants and, himself outraged, ordered Musset to leave the apartment without delay. Alfred was so ashamed that he departed.

Proving his friendship, Sainte-Beuve talked to George for a long time. A small cloud of mystery hangs over the conversation, since neither of the participants ever revealed the scene. But the general outlines are clear. Sainte-Beuve viewed the ridiculous situation realistically and gave George common-sense advice. Undoubtedly he emphasized something he had mentioned briefly in several of his notes to her, that she had done no writing of consequence since her return from Italy the previous summer. He must have pointed out to her that, unless she gave up Musset without delay, she would be sacrificing her career, and with it, all of her future.

George had reached the limit of her endurance, and not only listened, but promised to take Sainte-Beuve's advice. She was awake early in the morning, and through friends made hasty plans. Maurice had joined her at the apartment a few days earlier, suffering from a cough, and Solange was now infected, too, so she was afraid to travel with the children, as their condition might grow worse on the road. Therefore she would leave them in Paris for the present, and would either send for them in a few days, when their health improved, or would return for them.

She, however, could not remain in Paris for another day. She would go to Nohant, and felt certain that Casimir's presence there would deter Musset from following her unless he received an invitation. So, she believed, her home was the only place she would be safe from him.

George departed the same day, leaving her children at the apartment with friends and servants, arranging to receive daily bulletins on their health. She was afraid Alfred would reappear before she could go, and was in something of a frenzy to pack a few belongings before she might see him again.

Musset, as it happened, chose to sulk until March 9th, when he finally presented himself at the flat on the Quai Malaquais. There, to his astonishment, he learned that George had disappeared, that Maurice was returning to his boarding school that same day, and that Solange was being taken to Nohant, presumably for a visit with her father, that same afternoon. No one could give him any information on George's whereabouts.

Alfred spent the rest of the day writing frantic letters to George's friends, begging them to tell him whether she had gone to Nohant or had travelled elsewhere. He thought it probable that she had retreated to her ancestral home, and wrote to her there. When George received it, she had the sense to destroy it without having read it.

As it happened, she was busy on March 9th, too. She wrote letters to a number of friends in Paris, telling them that the affair with Musset was finally ended, and that she would allow nothing to weaken her stand. Her only concern for him was his health, and she hoped he was well. If he had taken refuge in illness again, however, there was nothing she could do to help him, and he would have to regain his health and balance without her assistance.

One brief paragraph that appeared in several of her letters indicated that she was cured of the madness that had warped her life for the past two years. 'I am very calm,' she wrote. 'I have done what it was necessary for me to do, and I feel no regrets. I will not turn again in the opposite direction, I am certain, just as I know I will not love in that way again.'

Ordinarily George would have awaited the arrival of her daughter at Nohant, but this was a special occasion, so she planned to ride to Châteauroux late in the evening and engage a hotel room for the night. Then she would be on hand when the stagecoach from Paris arrived late the next morning.

George reached Châteauroux somewhat earlier than she had anticipated, but slept very little that night. Nothing better indicates her new frame of mind than the fact that she sat down at the little desk in her cramped hotel room, and quietly wrote page after page of a new novel she began that night.

VII

The recovery of George Sand and of Alfred de Musset was rapid, complete, and, in the light of the intense passions they had displayed, rather remarkable. When Musset learned that George intended to have no more to do with him, he abandoned his attempts to get in touch with her, and began to lead a far quieter life. Before long he was writing poetry, novels, and plays again, and a number of years later his place in letters was recognized when he was elected to a coveted seat in the French Academy. His private life became somewhat more serene, although he enjoyed a number of affairs, the last of them with an attractive and literate actress, lasting for many years. His general health improved, though he suffered from occasional spells of hallucination to the end of his days. His death in middle age, which many regarded as premature, may have been caused, at least in part, by the dissipations of his early years.

The changes in George Sand were more profound, and, over a period of years, caused her to reexamine her concepts of human nature and of love, as well as her beliefs in the relationship of God and man. That she matured is obvious, yet the change was fascinating. Her feelings may have become more cautious, but her basic personality, no matter how much greater her serenity, remained unaltered.

Certainly she achieved a far greater awareness of her own faults. She had been too proud, she wrote to Sainte-Beuve, just as she had expected too much of a lover. She admitted that she had endowed love itself with mysterious elements that actually played no part in it. She was wise enough now to know that the day well might come when she would love again, but she believed that under no circumstances would her relations with another person become the reason for her existence.

Her new serenity was tested, late in 1835, when Musset published, as a novel, his version of their romance, calling it *Confession d'un Enfant du Siècle*. It was a surprisingly honest work, in which he made no attempt to excuse his own conduct or to rationalize at the expense of his former mistress. It was also a sensitive work in which he indicated a deeper understanding of George than she had believed possible. Later she wrote that she wept herself into a state of exhaustion after reading the book, and that she had then sent Musset a brief letter. In it, she said, she told him she had loved him very much, that she had forgiven him any harm he had done her, and that, above all, she wanted no more to do with him.

Both took care to avoid restaurants to which they had gone together, and hostesses followed the lead of Delphine Girardin, the wife of the most prominent magazine publisher in France, who said she would give up entertaining before she would ever invite George and Musset to the same dinner party. So the couple did not meet again for five years.

In 1840, their paths crossed in the lobby of a theater. George looked through her former lover, and there was no change in her expression, no flicker of recognition in her eyes. Neither then nor at any later time did she mention the brief encounter to anyone. She had put Alfred out of her life, and did not readmit him, even in her confidences to others. Musset, however, was badly shaken by the chance meeting, and that night he wrote one of his most famous poems, *Souvenir*, in which he lamented the passing of love. Thereafter he made it his business to describe George's appearance to everyone he saw, and emphasized his belief that, miracle of miracles, she had not aged a day since he had first seen her.

She learned her lessons more thoroughly than Musset did; if anyone was the winner in their feud, it was George.

Once she put Alfred out of her thoughts in the late winter of 1835, another problem intruded. She hoped to remain at Nohant for several months, knowing no balm more soothing than the serenity she found there. All of her visits had been short in recent years because of the conflicts that arose with Casimir when she stayed for any length of time, and she resented his intrusions on her privacy. In fact, his very presence was becoming abhorrent to her. He displayed an occasional spark of interest in Maurice, but was totally indifferent to Solange, a beautiful, mischievous child, and he made George feel like a stranger in her own home. In her autobiography she relates that she sometimes found it difficult to remember that Nohant was *her* property.

In La Châtre George sought the advice of an attorney who had been a lifelong friend, and then discussed the situation with Casimir. It was the first time in years they had engaged in more than a surface chat, and she may have been as surprised as she was pleased to learn he had grown tired of life as a country squire and found it boring. For all practical purposes he was a bachelor, yet everyone in the area knew he was legally married, and no woman of his own class was willing to flout convention by associating with him. So he had no companionship other than that of the serving maids with whom he had his crude affairs. A few hours of conversation revealed that he would far prefer to live in Paris, where he would enjoy infinitely greater freedom.

The greatest stumbling block was his continuing financial dependence on his wife, whose funds he needed until his stepmother died and he came into his inheritance. So George worked out a deal with him whereby Nohant and its income would revert to her direct control, and he would leave the estate. In return she agreed to give him, until such time as he received his inheritance, the income from her Paris properties. Although rents fluctuated somewhat, Casimir would be guaranteed some seven thousand gold francs per year, a considerable sum, out of which he would pay the cost of their son's education. George would accept full financial responsibility for their daughter.

The agreement was reached, and both principals signed the necessary documents, but Casimir immediately suffered regrets and tried to back out. He had been too generous to an undeserving wife, he said, and began to pose as a martyr who had been cheated out of his rights by a conniving woman.

Had no one else been involved, George would have ignored his complaints. But Casimir knew the children were her great weakness, and he deliberately played on their sympathies. George was horrified when they appeared to listen to him, and was afraid she might lose their love and respect. They were too young to realize that Casimir was using them as weapons in his own campaign, and George became frantic.

The local lawyer believed she needed legal help more potent than he could provide, and recommended that she go to Bourges and engage the attorney with the best reputation in the entire area. He was Louis-Chrysostom Michel, known throughout France as Michael de Bourges. Although still in his thirties, he had achieved renown in politics as well as in the law. An ardent Republican, he represented the district in the National Assembly, where he was the leader of the forces opposed to King Louis-Philippe. His followers had wholehearted faith in him, the moderates thought of him as a liberal, while the monarchists called him the most dangerous of radicals.

A man of unprepossessing appearance, Michel de Bourges had a large head and spindly body, wore thick eyeglasses, and, because he suffered from poor circulation, always wore heavy clothing to ward off the cold he felt at all seasons. Born and reared as a peasant, he was self-educated, and according to the newspapers of the period, no public speaker was more effective than he. His voice was deep and resonant, which, with all his brilliance, prompted Louis-Philippe to call him 'the most articulate Beelzebub of our century'.

In April, 1835, George Sand went to Bourges for a consultation, and was dazzled by Michel's intellectual pyrotechnics. He agreed to take her case, then spent hours trying to convert her to his brand of socialism. She was flattered that he had read and admired all of her books and considered *Lélia*, in particular, to be a masterpiece. Within days the woman who had been emotionally exhausted by her relationship with Musset was immersed in a new romance, bewildered by what was happening. Michel was short and ugly, while mentally he was domineering; she could not counter his arguments.

By May both were in Paris, and George found herself developing a strong interest in politics. Until now she had been mildly Bonapartist in her sympathies, conducting a desultory correspondence with the Emperor's exiled nephew, Charles Louis Napoleon Bonaparte, an admirer of her work, who was destined to make history himself as Napoleon III. She was humanitarian in her views, what might have been considered as liberal in a later age. Under the influence of Michel de Bourges, she became a passionate convert to the cause of Republicanism. She discovered that a fellow author, Lamartine, was equally devoted to the cause, as was Louis Blanc, one of Hugo's close friends. For the first time her circle of friends expanded in new directions. In due time, this would place her in the forefront of the French government.

George could not be bullied into accepting Michel's ideas. His rhetoric stunned her, but she insisted on thinking for herself, drawing her own conclusions. In her exchange of letters with him she resisted strongly, refusing to permit him to sweep her off her feet. When she gradually became a convert to the Republican cause, she took her own stand as a moderate, and at no time would accept Michel's far more revolutionary views. Over a period of many months it occurred to her that he offered no specific program. She taxed him with this, accusing him of seeking revolution for its own sake, refusing to find new means of government for those he wanted to destroy. Michel, even more stubborn than George, angrily denied her charges.

Michel was unique in George Sand's experience; none of her other lovers resembled him in temperament, intellect, or appearance. She might have found in him a new and different outlet for her masochistic tendencies, being browbeaten and called an idiot. She was fascinated by Michel's attitudes because he, in his own way, reflected the iconoclasm which had become so important in her life. In spite of their many differences they were birds of a feather who happened to live in a time of great social and economic upheaval, and for a time they travelled the same road.

Nothing in their romance paralleled George's passionate devotion to Musset. If her attitude was maternal, she managed to keep her feelings well hidden, and from first to last she maintained her independence. In Michel she found a man to whom the physical aspects of love meant as little as they did to her. She relished the excitement of developing new interests in the company of a man whose manner electrified his colleagues and won him a large, national following. Her correspondence with him was impersonal, and each tried to overwhelm the other with logical arguments, so it may be that they slept together only occasionally, because they found it convenient. Sentiment was conspicuously lacking.

Contemporaries noted this remote quality; many who believed George Sand could not live without passion felt certain she was having a more romantic affair with another man. As it happened, Franz Liszt, the great composer and piano virtuoso, was her close friend for many years, and the myth has persisted that he and George were lovers. No revealing letters, no incidents have ever substantiated this claim; on the contrary, all evidence indicates that they were never intimate.

Liszt, who had met George through Musset, was the type of man who interested her, to be sure. He was so handsome that women were known to faint during his concerts, and he, too, had acquired a reputation for libertinism. Certainly sexual attraction must have been at least partly responsible for the friendship, but George did not become Liszt's mistress at this time for the simple reason that he was madly in love with another woman.

Marie, Comtesse d'Agoult, was one of the most extraordinary and beautiful women of the century, and for a number of years also played a major role in the life of George Sand. Independently wealthy, endowed with an independent mind and great personal courage, she belied her appearance. She had haze-filled blue eyes, lovely blond hair, and a figure universally regarded as ravishing, but her temperament was as strong as George Sand's. She abandoned her husband to live with Liszt, bore him three children, and was supremely indifferent to the scandal that made her an outcast from the patrician society she had known.

Eventually she would emulate George, write books under a male pseudonym, and form her own intellectual circle. As Daniel Stern she achieved a measure of fame as a philosopher, and her tangled friendship with George was one of the most complex that either knew. They were intimate friends driven by jealousy to become bitter enemies. Their feud became the talk of Paris for years. Liszt was not the cause of that enmity; he was Marie's lover for a long time, she kept him under close surveillance, and she would not have tolerated an affair with George.

It was during the period of George's romance-of-sorts with Michel de Bourges that her friendship with Liszt and Marie d'Agoult developed. During the spring and summer of 1835 she also came under the influence of another remarkable man greatly admired by Liszt, as well as by Sainte-Beuve and a number of prominent other figures.

The Abbé Félicité de Lamennais was a living symbol of the unrest, the search that characterized the new values of the nineteenth century. An ascetic who had entered the Church at an early age, he had been disillusioned by what he considered the worldliness of popes and cardinals. Feeling called upon to reform the Church from within, he antagonized his superiors, who dismissed him from his post. But Lamennais persisted in his attempts to reconstruct the Church on a more spiritual basis. Although he spent part of each year living as a hermit in Brittany, he developed a devoted following among the intellectual rebels of Paris.

George Sand met the Abbé through Liszt, and was delighted when she learned Sainte-Beuve approved of him. Soon she was listening to his private lectures on the need for pure theological concepts, and her own Catholicism, which had become dormant since her last visit to the convent in an hour of need, became transformed. Before the end of 1835 she, too, believed that man should draw closer to God, and she agreed with Lamennais that this could be done only if one dispensed with power-loving clergymen who intervened between the individual and the Almighty.

The year may have been the most important in George Sand's life: she abandoned her views of romantic love, acquired new concepts of politics, and discarded religious beliefs that had become stale to her. Her change was not reflected overnight in either her work or her personality, but she grew from a giddy rebel to a woman of conviction.

George's domestic problems made concentration difficult. She spent more of the spring and summer of 1833 in Paris than she had planned, and was delighted to return to Nohant in July, when Maurice finished his school term. Casimir was still living there, and refused to leave, though he had signed the agreement with George. The atmosphere was tense, and one evening marital fireworks erupted in the presence of some of George's dinner guests from La Châtre and Châteauroux.

The cause of the dispute was trivial, but Casimir, who had been suffering strains of his own for months, lost self-control after drinking too much wine. He sent the children from the room in tears, threatened to beat George, and, when he went to his gun rack after announcing that he intended to kill her, had to be subdued by several of the guests.

The following day George left for Bourges, where Michel told her she had gained the upper hand and insisted she keep it. She returned to Nohant, sent Maurice back to school, and enrolled Solange in a Paris boarding school. With the children out of the line of fire, she ordered Casimir to leave without delay, threatening to cut him off financially if he refused. She gave him no choice, but he filed a suit against her before leaving for Paris.

George remained alone at Nohant with two or three servants. While she waited for the courts to hear her case and Casimir's counter-charges, she wrote an adventure novel about espionage. *Mauprat* was a tightly plotted action tale, completely lacking in literary pretensions, but served as a model for countless suspense stories that would appear during the ensuing hundred and more years.

The Dudevant case was heard by the court in La Châtre in January, 1836, and Casimir refrained from pressing his counter-charges to avoid the risk of losing the income he had been promised. It appeared that George would win a victory by default, but she went too far when she claimed her husband owed her one hundred thousand francs. Casimir could not afford to remain quiet, and encouraged by George's half-brother, Hippolyte, he drew up a petition to the court that listed, in full detail, his wife's transgressions over the past ten years, beginning with Aurélien de Sèze in 1825.

His charges created a sensation, and the little courtroom in La Châtre was crowded with visitors when the verdict was rendered in early May, 1836. The court ruling was in George's favor, and Casimir promptly appealed to the higher court in Bourges. This was a grave tactical error as it permitted Michel, who had been supervising George's case from the sidelines, to appear in person as her attorney.

Before the court of appeals in early June, he delivered such a moving address that many of the spectators wept as they contemplated the life of misery the abused Mme Dudevant had led. It was obvious that the court would decide in favor of

George, so Casimir was persuaded to withdraw his counter-suit, and Michel de Bourges worked out a private agreement on terms almost identical to those in the original deal. George became the mistress of Nohant and would receive the income from the property, ten to twelve thousand francs a year. She also received exclusive custody of Solange. Casimir would be paid the income from his wife's Paris holdings, and would pay for the education of Maurice, whose custody he would share with George.

The court officially approved the agreement, and Michel further enhanced his reputation. But the only tangible result of the long legal fight was the further blackening of George Sand's already damaged reputation, as many of the details that Casimir outlined in his petition had not been known by the general public.

Two of George's love affairs were not publicized even now. Casimir may have known of her relationship with Michel de Bourges, but made no mention of it in his petition, possibly because he had not wanted to antagonize the famous attorney. George and Michel had already moved apart. The lawyer had already persuaded George that France would prosper as a republic, but would flounder as a monarchy. His career kept him busy, and he had lost romantic interest in George at the same time she turned away from him.

George had by now found someone else, and was relieved when Casimir saved her from fresh embarrassment by making no mention of her new love. This slip was due to ignorance rather than gallantry, as very few people were as yet aware of George's latest liaison.

Charles Didier was a Swiss poet, one year younger than George, who had come to Paris soon after the Revolution of 1830. Handsome, personable, and virile, he was establishing a place for himself as one of the rising poets of the era, owing his success to Victor Hugo, who had adopted him as a protégé.

George had met him at a dinner party before her final break with Musset, and was fascinated by his candor when he told the guests of Hortense Allard, then his mistress, that he needed women in order to survive, just as other men needed food and drink. His affair with George probably began in the winter of 1836. She had been told that Casimir was keeping her apartment on the Quai Malaquais under surveillance in the hope that he would be supplied with additional ammunition to use in court, so George did not entertain Didier there. Instead, when she visited Paris for several weeks in March, 1836, she lived with the poet at his flat.

Both writers went through all of the motions of a romantic affair, yet George was not deeply involved. She needed emotional support during her court fight, and Didier made her feel wanted. In her correspondence with Liszt, Sainte-Beuve, and others, she referred to him as a friend, sometimes as an old friend, but she made no attempt to pretend that their love absorbed her.

Didier was equally realistic. In his *Diary* he called her passionate, tender, and loving, but did not reveal that they were deeply in love. She was 'an incredibly complicated creature', he wrote, and in several entries admitted he was incapable of understanding her. She demanded independence at all costs, he wrote, and deliberately went alone to Nohant when she seemed afraid that she might become too involved with him.

Didier followed her there, and they spent several happy days together before he returned to Paris, apparently convinced that they had established a lasting relationship. But George wrote him just one more letter, and then forgot him. Not only was the court case on her mind, but she was working on a revised version of *Lélia*, having decided she had been too candid in her revelations.

By the time she won her case in early summer, Didier had become a minor incident in her life. Thereafter, when she happened to meet him in Paris on occasion, he was invariably astonished by her casual, unaffected greeting. She truly thought of him as a friend, he wrote in his *Diary*, and apparently did not remember they had ever been intimate.

In August George celebrated her legal victory by making one of her more notable journeys. Liszt and Marie were enjoying a holiday in Switzerland. Both wrote to her repeatedly, urging her to join them. She was in such a light-hearted mood that she went, taking Maurice and Solange with her.

The vacationers were in high spirits. Liszt and Marie registered at hotels under the name of Fellows, and everyone referred to the lovely Marie as the Princess of Arabella. George adopted the nonsensical name of Piffoëls for herself and the children, and they refused to be called anything else. The party included a retired Swiss army major named Pictet, an old friend of Marie's who conveniently fell in love with George, even though she refused to become intimate with him. Also traveling with the group was Liszt's pupil, Hermann Cohen, whom everyone called Puzzi. A brilliant pianist, Puzzi wore male attire only when playing the piano; the rest of the time he preferred to disguise himself in women's clothing.

The group met in Geneva, then went on to Chamonix, where they went on into the foothills each day on picnics. They created sensations wherever they went because of their odd manners of dress, and neither the hotel staff nor the other guests could be certain of the sex of most members of the party. The short-haired, cigar-smoking George and her daughter wore men's clothes for the excursions, and changed into dresses only in the evening, when they went into the hotel dining room. Marie usually dressed as a woman, but sometimes it amused her to wear trousers and a shirt, too, while the languid Puzzi always indulged his transvestite tastes, and regardless of the time of day, appeared exclusively in trailing gowns and a long, blond wig. Liszt, Pictet, and Maurice sometimes wore the uniforms of lackeys and, as Musset had done, went through the motions of waiting on the others, who had to be careful that pitchers of water and bottles of wine were not emptied over their heads.

Everyone played practical jokes on everyone else, but the adults had their more serious moments, too. Liszt preached a brand of mysticism and tried to convert his companions to his way of thinking. Major Pictet was an authority in economics, geology, and archaeology, and delivered daily lectures. Marie was developing an interest in philosophy, but her views were too simple for George, who held long discussions with her on abstruse subjects.

Neither of the geniuses in the party neglected their work. No matter what else might be on the daily schedule, George found time to sit at her desk and work on her *Lettres d'un Voyageur*. Liszt allegedly composed music because no one else's work was sufficiently complicated to enable him to show off his dazzling techniques, and he either practiced several hours each day or retired behind a closed door to compose.

Before returning to Geneva the party made a trip to Fribourg so that Liszt could play the organ in St Nicholas' Church there. It was said to be the finest organ ever built, and George believed it when she heard Liszt play Mozart's *Dies Irae*. Never had she been so thrilled, she wrote at length in her *Intimate Journal*, and never had she seen ethereal beauty like that of

Marie d'Agoult, who stood motionless, leaning against a pillar as she listened to her lover playing the organ.

Soon after the party returned to Geneva, Liszt composed a *Rondo fantastique*, which he dedicated to George. She promptly returned the compliment by writing a story in verse, *Le Contrebandier*, in the spirit of the music, and dedicated it to Liszt.

When the time came for George to return to Paris, she felt refreshed in spirit and body, and arranged to meet Liszt and Marie when they returned to the city. Marie, who had been afraid that George's interest in Liszt might become too personal, no longer regarded the author as a potential rival, and for the moment thought of her as a 'sister'.

When the musician and his aristocratic mistress reached Paris two weeks after George, the two women rented a room on the ground floor of the Hôtel de France so they could open a salon there. It was the custom of the time for prominent persons in the arts and the political world to maintain salons where they could meet their friends and discuss issues. As George had never shown any desire to impress her colleagues, the idea of establishing a salon was probably Marie's. Snubbed by nobles and other wealthy patricians, the ambitious woman wanted to prove to her old friends, whom she had also offended by open defiance of convention, that she was accepted in circles she considered superior.

Thanks to George and to Liszt, the salon was a great success. Sainte-Beuve dropped in frequently, as did Balzac, who had renewed his friendship with George. Lamartine and Louis Blanc appeared, sometimes accompanied by Michel de Bourges. Victor Hugo himself occasionally graced the company with his Olympian presence.

Another regular visitor was the German-born poet, Heinrich Heine, who now lived in Paris. George was impressed by the lyric beauty of his work, and Heine, who enjoyed her company although he did not care much for her novels, paid her the compliment of announcing that he was 'in love' with her. George accepted the statement as he had intended it, and they established an intellectual friendship that lasted for the rest of the poet's short, tragic life.

The Abbé de Lamennais happened to be in the city for several weeks, so he came to the salon, bringing with him a group of his intense followers. George enjoyed listening to Lamennais, but wrote in her *Intimate Journal* that he exhausted her mind.

A seemingly harmless regular attendant was Mme Manoel Marliani, the wife of the Spanish Consul-General. An exuberant, high-spirited woman with no pretense of being an intellectual, she insinuated herself into the good graces of both George Sand and Marie d'Agoult, neither of whom appeared to realize that she was wildly jealous, a malicious gossip who could cause great harm.

At the salon George also met a very young friend of Liszt, a frail Polish composer of French descent named Frédéric Chopin. He failed to interest her as a person, but she wrote to several friends that he displayed extraordinary talents as a pianist and was 'second only to Franz as a virtuoso'. The impression George may have made on Chopin at this time, if any, is unknown.

Charles Didier embarrassed George by making frequent appearances at the salon, apparently incapable of understanding that she had lost romantic interest in him. Didier hoped Marie would intercede on his behalf and made her his confidante, thereby supplying her with priceless information that she could use to George's discredit when their great friendship fell apart.

Didier's persistence, combined with the overly social atmosphere of the salon, suddenly made Paris less appealing to George, and in early December of 1836 she suddenly left for Nohant. She had told Lamennais that country dwelling refreshed her soul, and she made her estate sound so appealing to him that the Abbé accepted her invitation to pay her a visit there.

Lamennais had just started to publish a newspaper, *Le Monde*, and was so enthusiastic in his descriptions of the good it would accomplish that George voluntarily wrote a number of articles for him and refused to accept payment, the supreme gesture of friendship that a professional writer could make. Lamennais happily accepted the articles, but did not pay another visit to Nohant. A year or two later he confided in a letter to Sainte-Beuve that George Sand's way of life was too rich for his blood. He was overwhelmed by the velvet spread on his bed, the satin cushions on the divan in the drawing room where they held their discussions, the sauces on the dishes that were served in her dining room. She thought she lived simply, the Abbé told Sainte-Beuve, but the truth of the matter was that she had been wealthy all of her life and didn't understand the true meaning of simplicity.

Soon after the Abbe's departure another visitor arrived to enjoy the refreshing wonders of the Berry countryside. Marie d'Agoult accepted George's invitation to spend several weeks at Nohant, and her journey set off waves of speculation that Marie herself was the first to recognize. In her long daily letters to Liszt she declared candidly that she knew the world regarded her visit as a sign of a relationship 'à la Marie Dorval', but she said she was afraid she had to disappoint the gossips.

If George felt Lesbian tendencies toward Marie — and there are hints in her *Intimate Journal* of such emotions when she refers repeatedly to her guest's 'blinding beauty' — they remained undeveloped. Marie was still deeply in love with Liszt, and had no personal interest in anyone else, male or female, as her *Diary* emphatically indicates. She and George went for long rides every morning and walked together every afternoon. They ate separately at noon, each retiring to her own quarters for a light meal, but dined together every evening, when George changed from her man's attire into a formal gown. They invariably parted again as soon as they left the table, George retiring to her long night of writing, while her guest wrote to Liszt, made notations in her *Diary*, and sampled the many books in her hostess' library.

Liszt, like Marie, must have been aware of George's Lesbian inclinations, but his letters express no fears that his mistress would be corrupted. George was their mutual, good friend, and he trusted her, just as Marie did. His letters give no hint that he might have entertained fears or doubts.

So, it would seem, the story that made the rounds of literary and artistic circles of Paris after George Sand and Marie d'Agoult fell out were false. According to these rumors, the two women had been Lesbian lovers, but quarrelled because Marie refused to leave her beloved Franz for George, and thereafter they became bitter enemies. The two women did become enemies, each writing at length about the other's faults, real and imagined, but no evidence has ever been uncovered that sex was a cause.

George brought both of her children to Nohant with her, hiring tutors for them. Maurice and Solange were old enough to become aware of adult relationships, and they dined with the ladies every evening. George wanted to keep the respect of her children, and would have done nothing to jeopardize their good opinion of her.

Actually, Marie was surprised to discover that George was already involved in an affair, which she was taking great pains not to publicize. She and Michel de Bourges had come together again after meeting at the Paris salon. George felt unfulfilled when there was no man in her life. She well may have been less in love than desirous of being in love. She needed an outlet for the abundant emotionalism in her makeup.

She corresponded regularly with Michel, and they no longer wrote about politics, but accused each other of indifference and infidelity, both indulging in long, rhetorical diatribes. In Paris they had been able to enjoy the anonymity that a large city afforded them, and had been able to sleep together where they pleased, without fear of consequences. But it was impossible for Michel to visit Nohant, and George could not go to him in Bourges. Michel had married early in life, and his wife had all the failings as well as the virtues of the peasant class. She was loud, strident, and suspicious; she demanded the absolute fidelity she gave, and she would not have hesitated to destroy her husband's political career if she could prove he was having an affair.

Michel was forced to exercise extraordinary caution in his relations with George, and could arrange to meet her only for a few hours at a time, usually on short notice. They met in Châteauroux, where they conspicuously failed in their attempts to fool the hotel management by taking a room together under assumed names. Even these fleeting sessions were difficult to arrange: George sometimes received a message in mid-afternoon that Michel would meet her late that evening, so she saddled a horse and rode off alone after dinner, returning soon after dawn the following morning. These sessions were uncomfortable, satisfied neither, and created new tensions.

An entry in Marie d'Agoult's *Mémoires*, written under her pen name of Daniel Stern and published many years later, is significant because of observations that shed light on the mercurial nature of a woman whose temperamental needs remained unfulfilled:

> All evening George has acted as though she were numbed into a state of brooding non-existence. Poor great woman! The sacred flame which God has instilled and kindled in her can find nothing beyond the confines of her own being to grasp, and that flame is consuming what faith and hope and youth she still retains. Charity, love, desire, those three goals of one's soul and one's heart and one's senses, are all of them, in George, too ardent, too extreme, in a nature clearly marked for too high a destiny. They have been thrust headlong onto the rocks of doubt, disappointment and satiety, so she has been driven back within herself, and in depths that no outsider can fathom, she makes a martyrdom of her life.
>
> Too often I have seen her leap to the other extreme, when the mere contemplation of a meeting with a loved one causes her to scale the heights of ecstasy. Alas! these moods are fleeting, and the ever-moving pendulum hurls her once more into the darkest pit of despair. The greatest of God's boons, serenity, is unknown to her, and I am afraid she will never become acquainted with it. She knows only the highest peaks and lowest valleys, and cannot be content to dwell on a plateau, even one of her own making. She condemns herself to a life of torment from which there is no escape.

George was well aware of her own personality traits. In the spring, long after Marie had returned to Liszt in Paris and her own relationship with Michel had become even stormier, she made a painful entry in her *Intimate journal*. As she always did when her insights made her uncomfortable, she tried to inject a note of humor into her writing by referring to herself as Dr Piffoël. She wrote:

> My dear Piffoël, the sooner you learn the truth about life, the better. When next you set about writing a novel, try to gain a little deeper understanding of the human heart. Do not take as your ideal of womanhood someone who is strong of mind, objective, courageous and lacking in artifice. The public will be sure to boo her from the stage, and will call her by the hateful name of *Lélia the impotent*.
>
> Impotent, indeed! Yes, impotent where servility is concerned, impotent in adulation, impotent in baseness, impotent in fear of you, *Man the Stupid*, who lacks the courage to kill without the support of laws which punish murder with murder, who can take your vengeance only by employing calumny and defamation! But when you can find a female who can do without you, then your power is vain: it turns to fury, and your fury is punished by a smile, by a farewell, by eternal forgetfulness…
>
> Were it not for my pride, I could dissemble. I could pretend to be a helpless creature overwhelmed by the crumbs of love a man might wish to throw in my direction. But I cannot, I will not! I know I am the equal of man, and my own nature forces me to live accordingly, even though I know his vanity will be hurt and he will withdraw the crumbs he has dropped at his feet for me.
>
> Reflect, my dear Piffoël, on the fact that woman, not man, is to blame for this sorry state. If all women were honest and dealt candidly with men, instead of hiding their true feelings beneath feminine trickery that is unworthy of our sex, men would learn soon enough to deal with us as equals. But you, Piffoël, will not live to see the day when candor reigns, when women as well as men find happiness in love. An honest Rome cannot be built in one generation, or in ten.

George's fierce pride made it increasingly impossible for her to engage in a backstairs relationship with any man. The approach of her thirty-third birthday in 1837 helped restore her dignity and gave her new courage. Thirty-three, in George's time, supposedly marked a woman's transition from youth to middle age. George felt no older and looked no older, but she felt that approaching maturity forced her to take a dignified stand for the principles in which she believed. Her opportunity came on June 7th when she received a note from Michel, asking her to meet him the next night in Châteauroux. She rebelled, and sent him a brief note:

> I am ill. I cannot go galloping off tomorrow night in this frightful heat. I do not even feel strong enough to start off. I should arrive in an exhausted condition, and I do not imagine it would be much pleasure for you to hold me in your arms at the Inn when I was in such a condition.
>
> I shall sleep until you can find the time and the desire to visit *me*. *Here*. Until then, goodbye.

As she anticipated, Michel took umbrage and did not reply. That ended the affair, and four nights later George made an ironic entry in her *Intimate Journal*:

> Hail, Piffoël, full of Grace. Wisdom is thine. Thou hast been chosen from among all dupes. The fruit of thy suffering has ripened at last. Blessed weariness, mother of rest, descend upon us, poor dreamers, now and in the hour of death. Amen.

The following day the atmosphere at Nohant improved considerably when Liszt and Marie arrived for a visit, accompanied by several friends, among them an actor and playwright, both of whom tried to persuade George to try her hand in the theater. One night the hostess felt compelled to defend Victor Hugo when disparaging remarks were made about the great man. George launched a furious assault on the actor when he further dared to call Marie Dorval depraved. Apparently he was unaware of her friendship with the actress.

The next week, unexpected and uninvited, Didier came to Nohant. George was surprised, and firmly rejected the advice of Marie d'Agoult, who had been acting as Didier's advocate. George was too polite to create a scene by asking the poet to leave, instead handling him in her own way by flirting with the actor while maintaining a reserve in her relationship with Didier himself.

The poet poured out his troubled heart to the lovely Marie d'Agoult, who might have encountered romantic difficulties of her own with him had she been less adroit. Didier could neither eat nor sleep, and within a few days the situation became so intolerable for him that he departed. He intended to sneak away, but George happened to see him as he was leaving, and bade him such a casual, impersonal farewell that he became completely disillusioned, and thereafter did not try to enter her life again.

Liszt and Marie remained at Nohant until the latter part of July, and George changed her writing schedule so she could listen to the great composer-virtuoso play the piano after dinner every evening. She was the first to admit that her understanding of music was limited, but felt soothed by it.

In any event, she had become more tranquil than she had been in a long time. She began the writing of a new novel, *Les Maîtres Mosaistes*, soon after terminating her affair with Michel. In early August, a scant eight weeks later, it was completed. A romantic story set in Venice, it was one of the most sensitive and successful of her novels.

By the time the guests departed, the friendship of George and Marie d'Agoult was wearing thin. Paris for a long time gossiped that this was another of George Sand's Lesbian affairs; probably George feared the loss of Liszt's respect. But in a letter to Sainte-Beuve, George confided that she thought Marie was an essentially shallow woman who should have been content to live her life as a great beauty, but instead elected to pose as an intellectual. She lacked the qualities of real intellect, however, and when she relied on ideas and phrases supplied by others, she made herself look ridiculous.

Marie d'Agoult was even less flattering in her opinion of George, as expressed in her *Mémoires*. George, she declared, was illogical and could not be consistent in her thinking, which shifted with the winds. She was audacious, to be sure, but that audacity was assumed in order to conceal the basic weakness of her character that she herself secretly recognized. Worst of all, she was a badly spoiled, undisciplined child who demanded attention, reached out for whatever she wanted in life, and made scenes when it eluded her grasp.

The charges were malicious and exaggerated, but there was a measure of truth in them. George was one of those people who could be disciplined only by life itself.

VIII

An inevitable tragedy, perhaps the worst blow George Sand ever received, made her miserable in late August of 1837 and speeded the process of her maturation. She received word that her mother was ill and hurried to Paris, arriving a scant twenty-four hours before Sophie Dupin died. George, who was holding her hand when the end came, tried to think of their relationship in the best possible light, yet she knew she would never be granted the maternal approval she had sought, and the knowledge tortured her.

In a letter to an old friend in La Châtre, she called her mother 'sensitive, generous, intelligent and artistic', all of them qualities which Sophie had failed to display to the world. 'She caused me much suffering,' George admitted, 'and the worst things that have happened to me were due to her.'

Then, in the next breath, she tried to argue that they had enjoyed a good relationship: 'But, of late, she more than made up for the deficiencies of the past, and I had the satisfaction of knowing she had, at last, come to a complete understanding of my character, and that her attitude to me was one of equity and justice. It is a consolation for me to know that I did everything for her demanded by duty.'

Unable to believe her own protestations, George admitted in letters to many of her friends that nothing in life would compensate for her loss and that she found it impossible to stop weeping. Almost overnight she became more sober, less inclined to participate in irresponsible adventures, but it could be argued that her thirst for love, already unquenchable, became still greater.

The trauma of her mother's death was complicated by yet another problem. While George was in Paris, she received word from a friend to the effect that Casimir had been seen in the vicinity of Nohant, and she jumped to the conclusion that her husband had appeared for the purpose of carrying off their son. Correspondence with Maurice's tutor, Félicien Mallefille, a would-be author who had been recommended by Liszt and Marie, revealed that the boy was safe at home and that all was well.

But the fears prompted by George's intuition soon proved valid. Casimir's stepmother had died, and he had at long last inherited his father's property in Gascony. Baron Dudevant, the master of his own realm, had gone off to live on his own estate. George, who understood his temperament, was afraid he would try to express his new independence by taking custody of their son, which was his right under their separation agreement, and would dare her to defy the court.

Her guess proved to be fairly accurate, but years of hard drinking had warped Casimir's judgement. It was true that he had returned to Berry for the purpose of striking a blow at his wife. Knowing that his wife was far more concerned for the welfare of their daughter, and instead of taking Maurice, he 'kidnapped' Solange and took her off to Gascony. The court had granted him no such rights and no privileges in relation to the girl.

When George learned what had happened, she left Paris at once, hiring a succession of private carriages to avoid wasting time at overnight stagecoach stops. Traveling night and day without rest, she reached the Dudevant castle only sixty hours after Casimir and Solange had arrived there. Casimir had declared war, and George was ready to do battle, giving no quarter. She carried a court order requiring Casimir to relinquish custody of Solange forthwith, an attorney accompanied her, and, taking no chances, she insisted that police surround the castle.

Casimir knew when he was beaten. According to his own correspondence, as well as the letters George wrote to various friends, he surrendered graciously by escorting Solange to the ancient drawbridge at the castle entrance. Playing the role of host to perfection, he invited George to accompany him into the castle for a cup of tea. The lawyer was offered something stronger, but was denied the refreshments when George refused to set foot on her husband's land.

There was a brief but vicious flareup before the estranged couple parted. Casimir reminded his wife that he had been given custody of Maurice, and threatened court action in order to obtain his rights. George dared her husband to do his worst, and promised she would fight him in every law court in the land if he tried to take Maurice from her.

There the matter rested, and George wrote to a friend in La Châtre, 'We parted, mutually charmed.'

The winter that followed was one of the most tranquil periods George had ever known. She remained at Nohant with her children, working on the manuscripts of new books, while they studied under their respective tutors. Maurice, who was developing talents as an artist, spent much of his spare time drawing sketches. The break with Casimir became complete, and although the children bore the name of Dudevant — and Maurice would inherit his father's title — they now called themselves Maurice and Solange Sand. That was how George referred to them in her correspondence, as she tried to remove any connection with Casimir from her life.

According to rumors that have never been substantiated or disproved, George also had an affair that winter with Félicien

Mallefille. In her correspondence with Liszt and Marie d'Agoult, who were traveling in Italy, she made several admiring references to Mallefille, but these comments are open to a number of interpretations. It was enough that she had acquired a notorious reputation and that the tutor was a personable, talented bachelor. The gossips of Paris had been known to create juicy stories based on far less factual data.

One visitor who came to Nohant that winter saw nothing romantic in George's relationship with the tutor, and there was little of significance that escaped his professional eye. Honoré de Balzac happily responded to George's invitation to come to Nohant in late February, 1838, and spent several days renewing his old friendship with her.

Balzac subsequently wrote about the visit in great detail, and related with relish how George had received him in man's attire, smoking a cigar. At no time, he stressed, did he feel he was in the presence of a woman, but enjoyed their talks as though George were another man. Far more discerning than most of his contemporaries, Balzac peered beneath the surface of her masquerade, and understood the character behind the escapades that had made her notorious. In a comment to his future wife, Mme Evelina Hanska, that has been quoted many times, he declared, 'She is an excellent mother, and is adored by her children... In the matter of morals, she is like a young man of twenty, fundamentally chaste, decidedly prudish and surprisingly shy. She is the artist only in externals. The true artistic temperament is indifferent to the rules of society, and therefore creates its own. But society's laws are 'important to George Sand, and she defies them only for the purpose of shocking public opinion. If she did not feel the need to rebel, I am sure she would prefer to live chastely.'

The hostess and her guest vied with each other in damning the lazy Jules Sandeau, and when he no longer served as a topic of conversation, the gluttonous Balzac stuffed himself on Nohant's large meals and fine wines. George, who was fascinated by the relationship of Liszt and Marie, who were complaining to her separately about their deteriorating affair, had been wrestling with the temptation of writing a novel about them. She resisted, knowing her friendship with both was so close that neither would forgive her. But she hated to see a first-rate story go to waste, so she told it to Balzac, filling in all the details she knew, and offered it to him as a subject.

The gift delighted Balzac, and he wrote the story the following year in one of his great novels, entitling it *Béatrix*. George appeared in it, thinly disguised, and no colleague ever painted a more flattering portrait of her. Balzac called her a genius, and said that her exceptional existence could not be judged by ordinary standards. She was one of those unique people who was so talented, so unlike the common herd, that she had to be regarded only on her own, extraordinary level.

When *Béatrix* was published in 1839, George wrote Balzac several long, heartfelt letters of thanks. Her one fear was that she would lose the friendship of Liszt and Marie, but her fellow author quietly took care of the matter by sending her, at her request, a letter of his own in which he declared he had heard his leading characters resembled the musician and his mistress. This, he said, was sheer coincidence; he admired Liszt as a man and an artist, so anyone who saw a resemblance was insulting him as well as the piano virtuoso. George saw to it that both Liszt and Marie read the letter, and neither ever learned of the role she had played in the creation of *Béatrix*. The portrait of Marie was far from flattering, and this gave

George additional pleasure, as her friendship with the patrician beauty was growing increasingly sour.

By 1838 George was developing an interest in the remarkable young man she had met at her salon in Paris. Of all her love affairs, that with Frédéric Chopin is the most famous. He was seven years her junior, a slender aristocrat with dark blond hair, brown eyes, and impeccable manners. Everyone who met him recognized his genius, and there were many who said he would surpass Liszt in the years ahead. Unlike Liszt in temperament, however, he was a moody introvert, usually shy in the presence of women, and he found his concerts and other public appearances a torture he preferred to avoid.

George extended him several casual invitations to visit Nohant after she returned there in 1837, and he declined with polite indifference. They knew many of the same people, and George apparently thought he would be a welcome addition to the Nohant circle, but at this time she had felt no real personal interest in him. Chopin, after his visit to her salon at the Hôtel de France, thought her a caricature, and told several friends it was difficult to believe that she and Marie Wodzinska, the girl in Warsaw to whom he was betrothed, were members of the same sex.

By the spring of 1838 the situation began to change. Chopin's engagement had been broken, and on a number of occasions he met George, on her brief visits to Paris, at the home of Mme Marliani, the busybody wife of the Spanish Consul-General. Chopin was usually accompanied by his friend, Count Albert Grzymala, who soon established a hearty rapport with George, and may have been influential in softening the young pianist's attitude.

On a number of occasions Chopin was induced to play the piano, and George listened in quiet appreciation. By late spring he was paying visits alone to the apartment on the Quai Malaquais and playing for her alone. Heinrich Heine, who was close to both of them during this critical period, observed that George was superbly sympathetic and Chopin was abnormally sensitive. She was instantly aware of any tiny nuance of change in his moods and attitudes, and had the knack of drawing him out, listening intently and without interruption, and then making the reply that invariably soothed him.

According to a persisting legend, George was a man-eating dragon who deliberately devoured Chopin, but those who watched the couple drift into a romance — including Grzymala, Heine, Sainte-Beuve, and even Mme Marliani, who was habitually jealous of anyone else's happiness — thought otherwise. By the early summer of 1838 there could be no doubt that Frédéric was in love with George. Her name was ever-present in his conversations, he sulked when she was at Nohant, and he came alive only when she returned to Paris.

His physical similarity to Musset and Sandeau was marked, his unmistakable genius strongly appealed to her, and he was the type of young man she could mother, dominate, control. George fully recognized the dangers of her own situation, and held herself emotionally aloof until she learned precisely where she stood. Frédéric had already become too emotionally involved to discuss matters rationally with her, so she retired to Nohant and opened a correspondence with Count Grzymala.

What bothered her was Chopin's relationship with the young lady in Warsaw whose miniature still stood on the piano in the drawing room of his apartment. Was he still intending to marry Marie Wodzinska? Did she love him? Would she be a good wife for him, bringing out his genius and shielding him from the world? Obviously George had no intention of complicating her own existence, and intended to step aside if Marie was still a factor in Frédéric's life.

Grzymala appreciated her candor and was equally blunt. He himself was confused because he thought Chopin was confused, but he would endeavor to find out the truth. He did know the engagement had been broken, but he had no idea whether the girl and Chopin still cared for each other.

In mid-summer of 1838 the Count sent George a second letter, which subsequently disappeared from her files, but his message is known: Chopin had lost all interest in Marie, and now thought only of George Sand.

That was all George needed, and she lost no time returning to Paris. The affair began at once, and both were ecstatically, peacefully happy. George worked at her manuscripts regularly, without interruption, and Chopin worked equally hard, publishing a collection of *Études*. But he was taking great pains to insure that the world did not learn of his relationship with George, and to her astonishment — as well as that of the friends who knew of the affair — he dedicated the volume to Marie d'Agoult. Perhaps he was being modest, as Grzymala maintained, but Heine's deduction may have been more accurate when he observed that Chopin had a passion for secrecy that grew out of his shyness. He literally could not tolerate the idea of advertising to the world, on his own initiative, the fact that he and George had become intimate.

Then, too, he was a member of a strait-laced, pious family, and knew his relatives would be horrified if he engaged in a 'public' affair. George, for reasons of her own, agreed that they should avoid publicity. She was tired of notoriety, and knew that if they remained in Paris they would be buffeted by gales of gossip that would cause the exceptionally sensitive Frédéric to shrivel. It would be far better if they went off somewhere together, preferably to a remote place where their fame meant nothing.

Chopin was suffering from a persisting cough, and Maurice was making a very slow recovery from a severe case of ague that had sent him to bed for several weeks, so George thought it would be wise if they spent the winter in a warm, sunny place. Marliani, the Spanish Consul-General, convinced her the perfect place would be Majorca, then a virtually unknown island.

George closed the manor house at Nohant for the winter, and accompanied by her children, set out for the south of France. Chopin, who had been reluctant to leave Paris with her, met her in Perpignan, and they travelled together to Barcelona, where they took passage on a ship to Palma, the principal town of Majorca.

Their first reactions to the place were wide-eyed. George wrote to friends that flowers were in bloom everywhere, and ripe citrus were hanging from the trees in great clusters, waiting to be picked. Chopin was naively happy, as his own correspondence indicated. He loved the palm trees, the blue skies, the warm breezes, and he remarked at length on the singing he heard in the streets, usually to the accompaniment of a guitar. For about a month after their arrival in November, love and the climate conquered all.

All too soon it became apparent, however, that Palma was not Paradise. George and Frédéric paid an exorbitant rent for a small, cramped house in bad repair, and the Majorcans they hired to replace broken window glass or install doors that closed either failed to appear or did sloppy, ineffective work. The furniture was primitive, and even the poorest French peasants would have rejected the straw mattresses that served as beds. Worst of all, the odors of garlic and olive oil permeated the house, and nothing would get rid of them. The delicately attuned Chopin complained, the children imitated him, and even the hardy George had to admit she often felt queasy. It was almost impossible to buy meat at any price, and the local fare consisted almost exclusively of oranges and a variety of fish, all of which were fried in olive oil and heavily seasoned with garlic.

George was undismayed, and displaying her usual energy, found a larger house in the foothills outside the city. No sooner did the lovers and the two children move into it, however, than the rainy season began. Torrents of water fell every day, and it soon became evident why the rented house had been vacant for years. Water permeated the place, crumbling plaster everywhere, and the ceilings in two rooms resembled sieves. It was possible to keep warm and dry only by lighting charcoal fires in the little stoves, and the ever-present, smoke made Chopin's cough much worse.

He became so ill that George had to call in a Palma physician, who diagnosed the ailment as consumption and announced that no cure was known. The landlord promptly demanded that the tenants vacate the premises before the contagious disease 'soaked into the walls' and made the house uninhabitable in the future.

Had Chopin's health permitted, the party would have returned without delay to France, but he was far too sick to make the long journey, and George was afraid to take the risk. They had to find another dwelling without delay, but no one else would rent them quarters. A Majorcan priest took pity on them and told them that nothing would prevent them from occupying an abandoned monastery called the Charterhouse of Valdemosa, which stood high on a cliff overlooking the sea. Only part of the monastery was completely man-made; the rest consisted of natural caves that had been somewhat enlarged to serve as monks' cells.

The superstitious Majorcans had been giving the place a wide berth since the monks had moved out two years earlier, leaving most of their furniture behind, and the only occupant was a political refugee who was vacating the premises and agreed to sell his own furniture for a nominal sum.

The monastery was bleak and forbidding, but with no place else to go, George agreed to pay the Church a nominal rent. On the rainiest day of the year, in late December, she moved in with Frédéric and the children. Three women who lived in a nearby village and had worked for the monks agreed to come in daily to cook, clean, and take care of other chores. Maurice and Solange were enchanted by the caves, and soon were exploring other caves in the cliff.

But Chopin, who was still ill, hated the new 'house', and George was busier than she had ever been. Frédéric could not eat the fish prepared by the local women, so George not only cooked his meals herself, but made several trips by donkey into Palma each week to search the markets for edible food. She was required to nurse Chopin, often spending most of the night at his bedside when his coughing spells gave him no rest. The children needed attention, and depended on their mother to supervise their studies. To further complicate George's life, the hired women were so inefficient she had to do the daily chores herself.

Somehow she found the strength, energy, and time to maintain her regular quota of writing. Buloz was demanding the manuscript of a new romantic novel, *Spiridion*, and she needed the advance royalties he was doling out to her as she mailed him portions of the book. She was also continuing to revise *Lélia*, a task that showed slow progress, as she was unaccustomed to making revisions.

Then, out of necessity, George declared war on the Spanish bureaucracy of Majorca. Chopin's piano, which had been shipped to the island, had been locked away for weeks in a customs warehouse, and the officials had refused to release it. Unable to persuade or bludgeon them into giving her the instrument, and tired of discussions that led nowhere, she went to the military governor of the island. Insisting that his aides admit her, she made such an angry scene that the piano was delivered the following day by a squad of soldiers. Hoisting the piano up the cliff proved a major project, but George directed the operation, and after several hours the soldiers succeeded in carrying it into the room Chopin would use as a study when his health improved. Now, George reasoned, he would have greater incentive to feel better.

When the rain clouds vanished for a few hours, the weather was balmy, and the view from the cliff, by day or by night, was breath-taking. But the rains were almost unceasing, the winds howled around the old Charterhouse of Valdemosa, and the sea beat against the rocks below. A heavy fog sometimes settled over the cliff and did not dissipate for days at a time. Small birds made their nests in several of the cells, and George soon discovered there was no way she could keep eagles out of the monks' refectory, which she was using as a drawing room.

The lack of social life simplified her existence somewhat. The villagers were scandalized because the foreigners did not attend church, and George was criticized because she wore men's attire and dressed Solange as a boy. The village fathers would have nothing to do with the strangers, who had to depend on their own resources, and every night after dinner,

Frédéric's health permitting, George took her children for a long walk, no matter what the weather.

Maurice and Solange, neither of whom had even been in more robust health, thrived on the simple fare and rough living. George herself was impervious to such living conditions, and Chopin, under her ministrations, began to improve. He gained weight, his cough subsided, and he was able to sleep nearly through the night. Eventually he, too, returned to work, and during the rest of the stay on Majorca he composed a number of *Préludes* and *Ballades*, among them some of his most inspired works.

Chopin nevertheless loathed the island, hated the monastery, and despised the semi-civilized living conditions. He remained depressed, even when it became obvious that he had weathered the crisis of his illness, and his thoughts often turned to death. His morbidity became so intense, George wrote, that he often wept when she and the children returned from their nightly walks, having convinced himself they had been blinded by the fog or rain and had fallen from the cliff into the sea far below.

George was indefatigable, and worked ceaselessly to cheer Frédéric, but she was incapable of performing miracles, and by the end of February she admitted defeat. Chopin's spirit, she said in a letter, resembled a crumpled rose leaf. His physical condition made it possible to leave Majorca at last, so she took passage on the first available ship. Very few passengers travelled to and from the island in winter, and the best she could manage were three tiny cabins on a commercial sailing ship.

The nightmare was not yet ended. The vessel carried a cargo of live pigs, and the stench was unbearable; then a furious, late winter storm swept across the Mediterranean, and the ship almost foundered before it limped into Barcelona. Chopin, who had been violently seasick, had aggravated his cough, and had lost so much blood he had to be carried onto the dock.

A French passenger vessel happened to be in port, and George immediately engaged cabins for the voyage to Marseilles, the ship's physician attending Frédéric on board. His relapse was so severe that a return to Paris before he recovered was out of the question, so George took a suite at the Hôtel Beauvau. Residents of the seaport seldom saw celebrities; celebrity hunters and music lovers flocked to the hotel in great numbers. The management was forced to post guards in the corridors to prevent them from invading George's privacy and forcing their way into Frédéric's sickroom.

The children required more attention, too. They had grown accustomed to the wild life of the Charterhouse and chafed under the restrictions of hotel dwelling, so George had to give them increased loads of schoolwork in order to keep them occupied. In spite of all distractions, however, she completed the manuscript of *Spiridion*, and sent it off to Buloz, who had arranged for its initial publication as a serial in the *Revue des Deux Mondes*.

A romantic novel with a mystical theme, the book was unlike any of her previous works. In essence it outlined the change of her own thinking about religion; it explored facets of Judaism, Catholicism, and Protestantism, showing the eventual spiritual triumph of the protagonist, who ultimately turned away from all organized faiths and became a Christian Deist. Much of the metaphysical content was derived from the ideas of the Abbé de Lamennais, and she was also indebted to Pierre Leroux, a leader of the Republican party, who advocated the principle that the individual should work out his own relationship with God.

Buloz was horrified when he read the manuscript, and begged George to write more of the love stories for which her reader-ship clamored. But she insisted in a series of fiery letters that she had achieved new heights in *Spiridion*, and she expressed a certainty that the world would appreciate her literary and religious aspirations. She immediately began to write another book with the same theme, *Les Sept Cordes de la Lyre*, and stubbornly refused to abandon the project when *Spiridion* became her most abject failure. The critics ridiculed her, the public refused to buy the book, and Mme Marliani took a busybody's delight in repeating Marie d'Agoult's reaction to everyone she knew in literary Paris: 'I couldn't understand a single word.'

Marseilles was not Paris, however, and George was untouched by the ridicule and scorn. Chopin recovered slowly, which was of paramount concern to her, and by the end of April was sufficiently strong to make a journey with her to Genoa, where they went because, she said, they owed themselves a holiday. The setback Frédéric suffered because of this unnecessary travel was relatively mild, and by late May George decided he was strong enough to leave Marseilles permanently. They made the journey to Nohant by easy stages, halting at inns for several days and nights of rest after each day of travel.

Franz Liszt and Marie d'Agoult were traveling in Italy, and had just invited George and Frédéric to join them, a prospect that pleased Chopin, but George refused the invitation on the grounds that his health was too delicate. This was truth enough, but stronger reasons prevailed. Mme Marliani was taking malicious delight in repeating about George the unkind remarks she received in letters from Marie d'Agoult. When George replied in kind, although with less virulence, her comments were passed along to Marie. Thanks to the interfering wife of the Spanish Consul-General in Paris, who enjoyed her place in the eye of a storm, a feud of consequence was in the making.

George was so happy to be home again that nothing else seemed to matter, though she soon discovered that even at Nohant, where life was ordered and an efficient staff took care of everyone's comfort, Chopin required constant attention. He refused to exert himself physically in any way, and had to be coaxed to take a brief daily stroll in the garden.

Above all he craved human companionship, and was content when the children were in the room with him, chatting or playing games. He established a particularly close rapport with ten-year-old Solange, and when George found them together, usually declaiming doggerel or playing another foolish game, she called them 'my three children'.

Maurice and Solange spent little of their time indoors, especially during the summer, when they were relieved of their school work. Chopin complained bitterly and at length when left alone, demanding that George join him, so she spent many hours by his side each day. His frequent interruptions made it difficult for her to read and impossible for her to write, so she took up sewing, a hobby she had long neglected.

A mercurial, restless woman endowed with energies far greater than those of most people might have been expected to resent the unfortunate predicament. But George's letters to various friends written during this period show no annoyance, no impatience, no hostility. It did not occur to her that, although she felt a need to be the dominant partner in a romantic relationship, Chopin was using his illness, real and imagined, to control her. Her strong maternal feelings included the need to sacrifice for the sake of the beloved. Only by giving in to Frédéric's time-consuming demands while simultaneously living up to all of her other obligations could George prove her strength. So she shirked none of her duties, including those imposed upon her by a petulant, badly spoiled young genius whose emotional level was far less mature than her own.

The affair of George Sand and Frédéric Chopin has become renowned as one of the great romances of the nineteenth century, but it was curiously lacking in one of the elements usually ascribed to such a passionate liaison, sexual desire. As George has made clear in *Lélia* and elsewhere, she considered sex one of the least important aspects of a relationship. Sentiment was significant to her as such, and an affair succeeded when a man and woman, leaning heavily on each other, lived together in quiet domesticity as though they had been married for years.

Her life with Frédéric satisfied her, even though he imposed on her relentlessly, demanding that she give far more than he had any right to expect. For the better part of a century it was fashionable for biographers to view Chopin as George's helpless 'victim', a prisoner of a ruthless huntress, but this view is false, too.

Chopin's loving family would have welcomed him had he chosen to return to Warsaw, and in Paris loyal friends were waiting for him. He could have joined Liszt in Italy, and the Austrians would have lionized him in music-conscious Vienna. He could earn his own living, and did not need the support that George Sand provided him. He stayed with her for the simple reason that she was as important to him as he was to her. No one else pampered him so extravagantly, feeding his vanity, gratifying his whims, and giving him the tender care that made the indulgence of his physical handicaps such a luxury. He needed George and kept himself in seeming bondage to her, but it was he who used illness and temperament to dominate the relationship.

In the eyes of the world, as well as in her own opinion, George was the master as well as the mistress of Nohant, so she was content. She stopped trying to persuade Frédéric to go for a canter through the fields, swim in the river, or hike through the woods. As he became stronger in the summer of 1839, it was enough that he spent more of his time each day at the piano.

They enjoyed remarkably tranquil relations, and Frédéric composed a number of mazurkas, his second nocturne, and the immortal *Sonata in B Flat Minor*. George was the eager audience of one, always ready to drop whatever she might be doing to listen to a new work, and before the summer ended she was able to change her own habits so she could turn out page after page of a manuscript while listening to Frédéric at the piano. Few visitors came to Nohant; they needed no outsiders to augment their idyllic existence.

Good food, rest, country air, and, above all, George's loving attentions made a stronger person of Chopin, and by the autumn of 1839 he enjoyed better health than he had known in years. The pains in his chest vanished, he stopped coughing and rarely lost his breath. His appetite was good, he needed no sedatives to help him sleep, and he himself recognized the surging new vitality that had transformed him. But he was still a hypochondriac, convinced beyond reason that his health was declining, and there was no real improvement in his melancholy. A single notation in his *Journal*, made in mid-October, 1839, is enough to reveal his state of mind:

They tell me I am better... But I feel that deep down in myself, something is wrong. Aurore's eyes are misted: they shine only when I play, and only then is the world full of light and beauty... I fear she knows something about my condition she cruelly keeps from me in the mistaken belief she is sparing me new pain.

By the latter part of the autumn he was sufficiently well, in spite of his conviction to the contrary, to insist they return to Paris. Like other composer-virtuosos of the period, Chopin earned most of his income by giving piano lessons, and, too proud to depend on his mistress for his living, he made plans to go back to his pupils in the city.

George would have preferred to stay at Nohant, and tried to argue that the autumn was the loveliest time of the year there, but Frédéric would not listen, so she dutifully agreed to accompany him. Apparently she found the need to save face, because she wrote to a number of friends that she could not afford to keep Nohant open throughout the year, and swore that living in Paris saved her thousands of francs annually.

She had given up the flat on the Quai Malaquais before going off to Majorca, and friends offered to find a new place for her, but she preferred to look for her own. She soon located a house in Montmartre, at 16 Rue Pigalle, that was perfect for her needs. It had ten rooms and a large, interior garden. Chopin could use it as a short-cut from the apartment they rented for him around the corner, and could reach the house in two or three minutes.

The children were sent off to school as day students, servants were hired, and George, who was supposedly saving money, spent a small fortune on furniture and decorations. Within days a basic change was made in the arrangements: Frédéric disliked walking to the house from his apartment, so he moved in with George and the children, happily disregarding appearances. There they remained for three years, moving in November, 1842, to the Place d'Orléans, where they took adjoining apartments and, for all practical purposes, continued to live together.

Chopin, George, and the children arose early every morning, and piano pupils began to arrive soon after the children went off to school. George slept until mid-afternoon, and could be awakened only in the event of an emergency. Frédéric played the piano for her while she ate breakfast, and both spent an hour or two with the children after school hours. George attended to routine business matters for a time, and then the 'family' always dined together.

Before long friends formed the habit of dropping in for an evening of conversation, a custom that was continued after the move to the Place d'Orléans. Balzac came regularly, as did Heine, Pierre Leroux, and Eugène Delacroix, who shared an interest with Chopin in the latest male fashions. Both were outshone by Eugène Sue, currently the most popular author in France, who was always accompanied by one of the beautiful courtesans with whom he was having affairs. A sprinkling of theatrical people usually made an appearance, including actors, stage directors, playwrights, and theater owners. None was more faithful than Marie Dorval, who had terminated her affair with Alfred de Vigny, and being unattached, was free to come and go as she pleased. On weekends, when guests chatted until the small hours of the morning, she sometimes stayed for the night. No one thought it out of the ordinary when she stayed behind, and there was no gossip about her and George. Their friends were either ignorant of their relationship or took it for granted.

There were few who exerted a greater influence on George than a neighbor, Louis Viardot, who wrote editorials for various Republican newspapers and magazines and who fanned the flame of her interest in politics. It was Viardot, even more than Leroux, who was responsible for her continuing loyalty to the Republican cause, and when Lamartine sometimes dropped in for a brief visit, he made it clear he thought the friendship was beneficial to George because she maintained an awareness of the world around her.

Several of Chopin's friends were frequent visitors, too, among them high-ranking Polish nobles, Count Grmyzala, Baron James de Rothschild and his wife, and a volatile Polish poet in exile named Mickiewicz. He and Heine competed in attempts to dominate the conversation, but when Balzac arrived, they fell silent in the presence of a master who told countless stories, all allegedly true but containing no more than a faint resemblance to fact.

Most members of the company were extroverts, and conversation flourished, but the host and hostess rarely participated in the talk. When Chopin could be persuaded to play the piano, he became the center of attention, but at other times he sat quietly in a corner, usually within reach of George, who smiled at him from time to time and patted his hand.

No one spoke less on these occasions than George herself. Still shy in the presence of her peers, even though she enjoyed a reputation as great as that of any artist who attended the salon, she listened intently to everything that was said. She was carefully included in every conversation, however, and when an argument arose, it was usually she who was asked to arbitrate. She was inclined to render her decisions succinctly, and rarely allowed herself to be drawn into a discussion.

'George gives the impression,' Balzac wrote in a letter to Mme Hanska, 'of being a piece of mental blotting paper who sops up every idea that is presented to the company under her roof. She not only absorbs, but analyzes — after the manner of men. I am sometimes accused of using the conversations of my friends in the pages of my novels, and I will admit that thoughts I have heard presented at a dining table or in a salon have sometimes been the basis of enlargements that grow out of my imagination. But George, who is far more literal, will commit a statement to memory, and it sometimes reappears, verbatim, five years later in the pages of a Sand novel.'

The friendship of Chopin and Delacroix became closer, and Frédéric allowed the painter to tease him, a privilege which his sensitivity denied everyone else, George and her children excepted. Maurice Dudevant-Sand was rapidly approaching manhood, and was displaying sufficient talents as an artist for Delacroix to take a professional interest in him. George was delighted when the painter offered to become Maurice's art tutor, and the youth went off to the painter's studio for several hours of intensive study and practice every afternoon.

The majority of those who gathered under George's roof were rebels and iconoclasts, people who deliberately flouted convention or were indifferent to the rules of society that most French men and women held dear. Victor Hugo also entertained regularly during this same period, and one night George was prevailed upon to explain the difference between her salon and his.

'Those who go to Hugo's house,' she said, 'are statesmen, distinguished citizens and members of the Academy, men who make the laws and decree the customs. My friends would like to become statesmen, but cannot govern themselves. They are too disreputable to win election to the Academy. In fact, it is they who delight in breaking the laws that Hugo's friends make.'

The comment was regarded as one of George's infrequent witticisms, and there were few who understood its deeper significance: even now, as she approached the age of forty, having reached the height of her powers and fortune, she was still a rebel, even within the ranks of her own profession. It is small wonder, then, that although she and Chopin seldom slept together, she lost no opportunity to flaunt their affair before the world.

IX

If Marie d'Agoult did not originate the false story that a helplessly ill Frédéric Chopin spent the years from 1840 to 1845 as the virtual prisoner of a predatory, dictatorial George Sand, she did her enthusiastic best to spread the rumor. The tale not only was imaginative, but seemed to be based on truth, and there were many in theatrical, literary, and musical circles who, disliking George, kept the canard in circulation. It was accepted as fact by so many people that Robert and Elizabeth Barrett Browning were surprised, when paying a visit to Nohant during this period, to discover that the entire story had been invented out of whole cloth.

Unfortunately, the passage of time and the presentation of concrete evidence to the contrary have not set the record straight. The image of a vampire-like older woman tyrannizing and enslaving a dying young genius unable to escape is so powerful and dramatic that it has remained alive, permanently stamping George Sand's reputation.

The story was invented by friends and enemies, and is without evidence. Chopin and George lived together in Paris because that was what they wanted, and they spent long summers at Nohant for the same, simple reason. Chopin was free to come and go as he wished, and on a number of occasions he and George were separated because of his travels, although usually for brief periods.

The correspondence of his close friends, as well as his own letters, all tell the same story: Chopin lived with George Sand because he loved her. She also cared for him, although her own correspondence indicates she regarded him more as a son than as a lover, and it must be remembered that the maternal was always present in George's major romances. She fussed over him when they were together, and she made endless, detailed plans for his health and comfort when they were separated, always writing ahead to others to make certain he would be given the foods he liked, that there were enough blankets on his bed, and that someone would attend to his laundry.

It may be that the false picture of the Chopin-Sand relationship has persisted because sex played such a minor part in their affair. George, always frank, let it be known in her letters to good friends that she and Frédéric rarely slept together. By now she well knew that no man could satisfy her erotic cravings, and Chopin, absorbed in his music, appears to have required only infrequent sexual encounters in order to obtain gratification.

In the main, the years George and Frédéric spent together were happy, and there can be no question that her constant care was beneficial to his health. During these years his consumption was kept under control, he suffered no major setbacks and rarely was confined to his bed. All the same, George was required to supervise his physical regimen at all times.

It is obvious that she enjoyed the need to take care of him, but it is far more difficult to understand the patience she showed when he indulged in his temperamental outbursts. When he was bored, displeased, or unhappy, he could display arrogance, childish rudeness, and petulance, all beyond the normal bounds of taste and manners. The rough, exuberant humor of George's theatrical friends invariably annoyed him, and he usually responded to their jokes and horseplay by stalking from the room, retiring to his own quarters, and remaining there until the next day. He also found George's half-brother, Hippolyte, an insufferable boor, an opinion shared by a number of others, but Frédéric carried his dislike for the man to new heights, on more than one occasion refusing to sit down at the Nohant dining table with him, retiring to his room, and demanding that a complete meal be served to him there.

George not only tolerated his exhibitions of temper, but learned to cope with them. When Chopin became upset, he was capable of harping on the cause for hours, but George changed the subject, and no matter how vehement his protests would continue to talk about something else until he grew calmer.

Chopin remained on excellent terms with both of George's children. Maurice, who might have shown jealousy because the musician had partly usurped his place, always treated him with the camaraderie reserved for members of the immediate family. Solange was even closer to Frédéric, confided her adolescent secrets to him in long, whispered conversations, and told her mother's friends that she regarded Chopin, rather than Maurice, as her 'true brother'. Although no one knew it at the time, their friendship was destined to cause the immediate break between her mother and Chopin.

It was Chopin who was responsible for an innovation at Nohant that gave George Sand some of her greatest pleasure for the rest of her life. It was his custom to play the piano after dinner every evening in the grand salon, and when he was in a light-hearted mood, he sometimes stopped playing and delivered monologues in a number of remarkably authentic accents. Apparently he had a perfect ear for speech as well as for music, and could imitate anyone, including foreign guests like the Brownings, who might happen to be present.

Out of his mimicry grew performances of impromptu amateur theatricals, and Chopin, strongly supported by Solange, campaigned for the transformation of the salon into an actual theater. George was reluctant to make any major architectural changes in her beloved home, but eventually she gave in to her lover and her daughter, and a permanent stage was erected at one end of the room.

George herself rarely took part in the performances. When the games became more complicated and plots were devised for the actors, who would then improvise their roles, George frequently plotted the evening's story for the participants, then sat back as a member of the audience, and allowed herself to be entertained. The others urged her to join them on the stage, but she was far too shy, even though most performances were given only for an audience of relatives and close friends.

It was Chopin, too, who thought of using puppets on the stage, a practice George maintained for the rest of her life. She developed the hobby of creating and sewing the costumes worn by the puppets, and frequently busied herself with this pastime when she relaxed for a few hours after dinner before returning to work on a current manuscript. According to her own estimate almost a quarter of a century later, she made 'many hundreds' of such costumes over the years.

Certainly George and Frédéric spent their happiest times together at Nohant, and his health improved sufficiently for him to accompany her on the walks through the woods she had always loved and that he came to appreciate, too. The friends who visited them in the country found them devoted to each other, and on occasion, when an upset stomach forced George to remain in bed for a day, Chopin refused to leave her side.

Two former friends were conspicuous by their absence. Franz Liszt and Marie d'Agoult were no longer welcome, although George would have been happy to receive the composer without his mistress. Marie was so jealous of the more renowned author that the friendship could not have survived under any circumstances, but its termination was speeded by the meddling Mme Marliani. Encouraging Marie to write freely, Carlotta Marliani received a communication in which Marie expressed her private opinion of George Sand, and it was not a flattering portrait. Mme Marliani, in seeming innocence, passed along the letter to George, who promptly withdrew into a shell of silence.

Marie, who was unaware of the indiscretion, continued to send her usual, friendly letters to George, but received no replies until Mme Marliani, disturbed by the commotion she had created, admitted to both principals that she had broken faith. Thereafter George and Marie tried to patch up their friendship, but too much had been said that could not be retracted. Marie apologized, George accepted the apology, Liszt — who was genuinely fond of George and admired Chopin — expressed his approval in no uncertain terms, and everyone joined in damning Mme Marliani.

All through the final months of 1839 and all of 1840 George and Marie continued to see each other occasionally, but it became impossible for them to exchange confidences. George felt she had been betrayed, and no longer trusted her former friend. Gradually the two women drifted apart, and by 1841 Marie d'Agoult was writing to friends, 'Madame Sand hates me. We no longer see one another.'

The final bonds having been broken, Marie felt free to express herself as she saw fit, and thereafter lost no opportunity to denigrate her former friend. It was in 1841 and

1842 that she first referred to Chopin, in her correspondence, as George's 'prisoner', and she continued until the end of the affair to describe them in this way. The gradual deterioration of her own affair with Liszt during this time did not improve her disposition, and her jealousy of the happier couple impelled her to keep alive the lie she had created. Marie d'Agoult's principal contribution to the life of George Sand was the canard that outlived both of them.

A far stranger complication occurred in George's life during this same period. Jules Sandeau, who had failed to earn a living as an author, actor, or stage director, published a novel in 1839. Entitled *Marianna*, it was a thinly disguised version of his affair with George, and not only was responsible for a sudden surge in notoriety about her, but won Sandeau the literary and financial standing that until now had eluded him.

The theater was his first love, and in 1840 he met Marie Dorval, who had just left Alfred de Vigny after their quarrels made life unbearable for both of them. Soon thereafter Marie became Sandeau's mistress and moved into his apartment with him. She was still on intimate terms with George, and there is no reason to believe their Lesbian affair had ended. Marie often came to Nohant, and was a frequent visitor to the Sand-Chopin house in Paris when George was in residence there. As far as is known, George and Sandeau did not meet on any occasion during this time.

Through this strange circumstance, these former lovers did share the affections of the same person during the same period. Marie, like George, regarded their relationship as something apart from the norm. She thought of herself as being in love with Jules, and wrote him impassioned letters, but her relations with George were too delicate to be discussed in detail on paper. In any event, the affair with Sandeau was short-lived. He accompanied her on tour late in 1840, but returned to Paris after spending only a month or two in the provinces with her. His alleged reason was the need to work on his new book, but he neglected to answer Marie's letters, and she was forced to find what solace she could at Nohant. Then, in 1842, Sandeau married someone else, and delivered the crushing blow by sending Marie an announcement in his own handwriting. Thereafter she trusted no man, but leaned more heavily than ever on her close friend, George.

Another of George's early relationships continued to haunt her in a quite different way. Casimir, now Baron Dudevant, had become one of the first citizens of Gascony, where he lived in his ancestral castle with his housekeeper-mistress and their young daughter. He was conscious of his new status and, insisting the amenities be observed, demanded that his older children visit him regularly. Presumably George could have gone to court to fight him, but she had no desire to rake up old scandals again. Besides, the children were old enough to be curious about their father, so she agreed to permit them semi-annual visits to Gascony. Maurice, the future Baron Dudevant, regarded these journeys as disloyal to his mother, so he held them to a minimum, and at no time did he establish a real rapport with his father. But Solange, who may not have been Casimir's child, got along famously with him. The girl was already showing signs of deep-rooted rebellion, and took pleasure in recounting to her mother the joys of her visits to her father.

George showed remarkable patience and refrained from berating her. It was difficult for her to keep silent when Chopin eagerly joined in the conversation and asked for additional details of Solange's visits to Gascony. No one, down to the present day, has been able to determine whether

Chopin's interest in Solange's journeys was sincere, or whether he was following the girl's lead and finding a subtle way to torment George.

But his attempts to stray from the maternal embrace of his mistress were few, and George enjoyed a longer period of domestic tranquility with him than she had ever known with anyone else. It may have been the very serenity of her personal situation that caused her to become dissatisfied with her professional life.

Whatever her reasons, she shocked the literary world by trying to break her contract with Buloz, which had been profitable for both of them. Simultaneously her name appeared in 1841 on the masthead of a new magazine, the *Revue Indépéndante*, as co-publisher. The publisher was her old friend, Pierre Leroux, the philosopher, who had never been able to make ends meet as a publisher or editor.

Now that George had joined forces with him, however, she was certain he could succeed. After all, she intended to write for the new *Revue* herself, and the public demand for everything she wrote was insatiable. The mere fact that she elected to associate herself with Leroux created something of a sensation, since respectable people regarded him as a radical whose views were beyond the pale.

The greatest weakness in the philosophy of pudgy, myopic Leroux was his lack of any practical solutions for social problems. He wanted to improve the lot of the common man, particularly the industrial laborer, who worked the new city factories and lived in proliferating city slums. Precisely how he hoped to help the workingman was never made clear, but Leroux expressed himself with such vigorous authority that few people bothered to wonder what he really meant.

George Sand's critics have wasted their time, paper, and ink speculating on whether the influence of Leroux caused her to become a true Socialist in her thinking or whether she may have been even more radical. Some of her contemporaries called her a 'communist' at this time, but the word, which was just coming into vogue, had no practical political meaning. Many who sympathized with the laborer and peasant thought a communist as one who wanted to see an improvement in the welfare of the poor, while conservatives entertained the vague fear that a communist was one who wanted to take their wealth and distribute it to the needy.

Any attempt to define George Sand's own political philosophy at this stage of her career becomes an exercise in the straining of gnats. She considered herself a faithful disciple of Leroux, but could not have written a cohesive statement of his political position, if for no other reason than that Leroux himself found it difficult to explain where he stood.

All that can be said with certainty was that Leroux was a devout Christian, a supporter of the trade unions that had their origins in the ancient guilds of the Middle Ages, and that he tended to favor a rather mild version of Socialism. With the appearance of the *Revue Indépéndante*, he found his voice through George Sand, who also supplied some of the funds that enabled him to publish the magazine.

She wrote two pieces for the initial issue, which appeared in the autumn of 1841. One was an article on working-class poets, so lacking in distinction that Sainte-Beuve, who had intended to tease her about it, decided to remain silent.

Far more important was the first installment of a new novel, *Le Compagnon du Tour de France*, and its appearance so badly upset Buloz that he tried, in vain, to halt the publication of the new magazine. He would have been wise to save his energies.

Neither then nor later was it regarded as anything better than third-rate George Sand work. The protagonist bore a close resemblance to Leroux, who was presented as a man of such noble sentiments that he was unbelievable. The story concerned the love of a young laborer for a wealthy lady who lived in a great house suspiciously like Nohant. Some critics remarked, justifiably, that when the lady renounces her laborer because she knows she can never share his idealism, George herself seemed to be donning a hair shirt, apologizing to her readers for her own wealth.

Even though *Le Compagnon* was an inferior work, it made literary history. It was the first novel ever written in French devoted almost exclusively to a study of working-class life. Balzac, to be sure, had made similar studies in far greater depth, but he had also peopled his novels with many aristocrats and members of the middle class. George Sand was the first author in France with the courage to concentrate on a class unlikely to purchase a single copy of the book.

Le Compagnon was followed by another novel, *Horace*, which also appeared in the *Revue Indepéndante*, and it was a far superior effort, although it failed to save the foundering magazine. The hero was a member of the working class, and his principal opponent a lazy, intellectually dishonest bourgeois. What made *Horace* notable was a relatively minor character, the Vicomtesse de Chailly, and George made no attempt to hide the fact that she was writing about Marie d'Agoult. The Vicomtesse was George's reply to false friendship, and reveals a devastating cruelty that is rarely revealed elsewhere in her nature. Her portrait was sardonic, penetrating, and merciless, and the real identity of the character was apparent to everyone who knew Marie d'Agoult. George dissected her nature, mocked her better qualities as false, and even attacked her beauty as sterile.

Her summary concluded, '... her nobility was as artificial as everything else about her — teeth, bosom and heart.'

The furious Marie wanted to retaliate, but Liszt urged silence as the more dignified retort. For a time his mistress agreed, but eventually the burden became too great, and first in her correspondence, then in a number of the books she wrote as Daniel Stern, the humiliated woman struck back by attacking every aspect of George's personality, appearance, and life.

For a time the feud gave the *Revue Indépéndante* a new life, but Leroux was far too undisciplined in his personal life to edit a magazine, and George could not attend to all the details herself. The publisher's family lived in the little town of Boussac, which he preferred to Paris. He spent so little time in the capital that the *Revue Indépéndante* often appeared far behind schedule.

Finally, in the middle of 1843, a new crisis threatened. Leroux vanished from Paris and could not be found in Boussac or elsewhere. The forthcoming issue was never published, subscriptions were forfeited, and for all practical purposes the magazine's life came to an end. After a month's absence a cheerful Leroux showed up to announce that he had gone off on a fishing trip with a friend, as he had not been able to pass up the opportunity to enjoy a holiday.

George still thought he was a political genius, and immediately started raising money from her friends to enable Leroux to start a newspaper in Boussac, where he had purchased a printing plant. No sensible person could have expected this enterprise to succeed. But George Sand had convinced herself that the whole world would recognize the worth of Leroux when he found the right forum for his opinions. She badgered and browbeat everyone she knew into contributing to the cause. She even obtained the sum of one hundred francs from Chopin, whose aristocratic views were anathema to Leroux, and vice versa. One hundred francs was a small price to pay for domestic peace.

For a time Leroux did somewhat better than anyone except George had expected, which confirmed her in her judgement. But, by 1844, she had far more important matters than Pierre Leroux on her mind.

Solange reached the age of sixteen in 1844, precipitating the most violent series of personal crises George Sand had ever known. The girl was beautiful; outsiders often commented on her close resemblance to the portraits of her great-grandmother, Aurore de Saxe, which were hanging at Nohant. Spoiled and imperious, a flirt without a conscience, Solange had no understanding of discipline. This, of course, was her mother's fault, George having given her love without either demonstrating or teaching restraint.

Relations between mother and daughter had become increasingly strained, and the distracted George was almost ready to admit she was no longer capable of handling her daughter. She called in an impoverished noblewoman, Marie de Rozières, to act as a chaperone and companion for Solange, but could not have made a worse choice. Mlle de Rozières had been disappointed in love, and wanted to talk only about men, a subject that fascinated the sixteen-year-old girl. George issued a stern edict to the effect that all discussion of males was strictly forbidden, but Solange and the chaperone paid no attention to the order.

At this time a handsome young protégé of Leroux by the name of Victor Borie came to Nohant for several weeks. Leroux wanted to hire him as an editor of the newspaper, and sought George's opinion in the matter. As it happened, Chopin suffered his worst relapse in several years during this time, and was more on edge than usual. Solange, who had a genius for making mischief, saw an opportunity to cause a first-rate domestic uproar. She flirted outrageously with Borie, although never in Chopin's presence, and then reported to Chopin that George herself was behaving rather scandalously with Borie.

Chopin lost his temper, and after several domestic scenes worthy of George's affair with Alfred de Musset, the bewildered future newspaper editor took himself elsewhere. Through a fortuitous circumstance, Chopin's sister, Louise Jedrzeiewicz, arrived at Nohant just at this time for a visit. George and Louise struck an immediate rapport, and as Chopin was very fond of his sister, the domestic seas became somewhat calmer for a time. George did not learn that Solange had been responsible for the trouble until some years later.

Soon after Louise's departure, the newest of George's novels appeared, and was the cause of a fresh tempest. *Lucrezia Floriana*, a love story seemingly in her usual mold, was a thinly disguised account of her own highly complex relationship with Chopin. He recognized himself in the character that George called Prince Karol, and was outraged by a portrait of a self-centered intellectual bigot who appeals to women because of his frail health and his charm.

George denied she had written their story, and the charitably inclined might believe she had not consciously known what she had written. Chopin was rarely in a charitable mood, however, and refused to accept her explanation that he was being overly sensitive. He was too much of a gentleman to complain to anyone on the outside, however, and even as good a friend as Delacroix marveled that Chopin failed to recognize himself as Prince Karol.

In the midst of this domestic turmoil George Sand's humanitarian instincts caused her to perform an act guaranteed to estrange Solange. Through relatives on her mother's side, George learned of the serious plight of the daughter of a distant cousin, a laborer who lived with his mistress. Their illegitimate daughter, known as Augustine Brault, was several months younger than Solange, and had been educated, at George's expense, in convent schools. Now the girl was moving out into the world, and as she was exceptionally pretty, her mother made no secret of a desire to marry her off to some man who would pay the highest price.

The outraged George Sand immediately brought the girl to Nohant, and not only announced that she would stay there, but intended to adopt her. Augustine was not only attractive but sweet and docile; George responded by calling her 'my real daughter'.

Maurice, if not actually smitten with Augustine's charms, at least was strongly sympathetic and took her side in the family quarrels that soon developed. Solange, as expected, displayed violent jealousy, and when she bothered to address Augustine at all, spoke to her contemptuously.

Her own hatred not being enough, Solange attempted to influence Chopin against the intruder. If Frédéric found the girl a nuisance and complained, George would be far more inclined to send Augustine back to her own family and whatever fate might await her in Paris.

Precisely how Solange accomplished her self-appointed mission is unknown, no one having exchanged any correspondence on the subject. But the task could not have been difficult. The thin-skinned Chopin was inclined to believe that most people disliked him, and a few whispered comments from Solange to the effect that Augustine privately despised him would have been sufficient to turn him against the girl.

The feud erupted over trifles. When Chopin played the piano every evening for the impromptu theatricals, Solange and other young people sometimes took part in improvised dances on the stage. George urged Augustine to participate one evening in the summer of 1845, and the timid newcomer was persuaded to mount the stage. There, as Chopin played the first notes of music, she froze, then stumbled, and almost fell.

The composer lost his temper, screamed that he would not provide music for such a clumsy oaf, and stamped off to his room. Augustine dissolved in tears, and a grim George went off to get an apology from her lover for his unseemly conduct. Chopin stubbornly refused to apologize. George would not back down, either, and insisted that Augustine would participate in any theatricals held in the future.

An uneasy truce was established. Chopin and Augustine barely nodded to each other, and although the girl responded to George's urging and played dramatic roles on the little stage, she never again danced when Chopin sat at the piano.

By the summer of 1846 the tensions in the family were thick. Maurice may or may not have been in love with Augustine; he later claimed that their relationship had always been that of brother and sister. George, on the other hand, wrote to several friends that her son loved her 'adopted' daughter, but this may have been a form of wishful thinking.

Solange altered her tactics just enough to throw her mother and Augustine off guard. Pretending she had become reconciled to the presence of her distant cousin, she affected great friendship for the other girl. George was delighted, and Augustine must have been happy, too.

Then, with the enemy unprepared, Solange launched her thunderbolt. Making up a story out of whole cloth, she reported to Chopin that Maurice and Augustine were lovers.

By his own lights, Frédéric Chopin was extraordinarily strait-laced; it may be that he couldn't quite condone his own relationship with George, but at least they were adults. The idea of two youngsters sleeping together shocked him to the core, and he created a violent scene.

His conduct was so outrageous that George finally lost her own temper, telling him there was a limit to her patience. She hinted, even if she did not spell it out in so many words, that she alone was responsible for what transpired under her roof. In any event, she had full confidence in both Augustine and Maurice, and refused to listen to vicious lies about them.

Chopin sulked. He became petulant. He treated George with overly elaborate courtesy. He snarled at Maurice, treating him so abominably that the young man decided he would have to leave home. As for Augustine, she no longer existed in Chopin's eyes. He refused to address her, and pretended not to see her when she came into the same room.

The situation was patently intolerable, and George had to take firm steps to prevent its further deterioration. Her first move was the calming of Maurice, and she managed to convince him that under no circumstances did she want him to leave home. She also soothed Augustine, who had been making her own quiet plans to flee.

Solange retaliated by firing her heaviest artillery: she announced her betrothal to a young nobleman of the neighborhood, Fernand de Préaulx. He was wealthy, handsome, and a superb horseman, but George privately found him rather stupid and wrote to friends that he was so stiff he seemed incapable of relaxation. She wisely made no attempt to break up the romance, knowing Solange would elope just to spite her. Instead she used delaying tactics, saying that a girl of eighteen should not rush into marriage. It would be far better if Solange and Fernand waited a year before they married, she said.

Chopin unreservedly approved of the betrothal. Fernand was a blue-blood, a gentleman whose manners were perfect, and therefore would make the right husband for Solange. He secretly urged the couple to marry as soon as possible.

Disagreements over the young people had their effect on the George-Frédéric relationship. Chopin could not understand why his mistress insisted on her support of Maurice and Augustine, or why she would not permit Solange to be married at once. She was interfering in the lives of her children, he told her.

George made her reaction very clear in *Histoire de ma Vie*: 'Chopin could not bear my "interference", natural and necessary though it was. He hung his head, and muttered that I no longer loved him. What blasphemy after eight years of maternal devotion! But I really believe the poor man was so worried and upset that he did not know what he was saying.'

If George had followed her usual routine, she would have returned to Paris from Nohant in September or October. But she prolonged her stay in the country, claiming that the romantic complications in the lives of her children made it necessary to remain. The argument has been advanced that she deliberately found an excuse to avoid returning to the city, knowing that Chopin was anxious to spend the winter in Paris. She has been accused, by many biographers, of conniving to end her affair with him.

No evidence has ever been uncovered to substantiate this theory. It is true that Chopin returned to Paris in November, 1846, and equally true that he never returned to Nohant. It cannot be stressed too strongly, however, that neither of the principals realized they had come to the parting of their ways.

The return of Chopin to Nohant was prevented only by a continuing deterioration of his physical condition, which made it impossible for him to leave his Paris quarters.

His letters to various people during the autumn of 1846 and the early months of 1847 have been cited as proof that his ardor for George had cooled. He seemed to take delight in mocking her and making light of the romantic complications in her household. It is equally valid to interpret these communications as nothing more than a harmless release of his hostilities.

What provides incontrovertible evidence to the effect that he still considered himself George's lover is his own correspondence with her. He wrote her daily letters, all of them loving, all of them tender, and he took care to say as little as possible about his own health, obviously not wishing to worry her.

George and Chopin were reunited in February, 1847, when she came to Paris with Solange for the purpose of buying the girl's trousseau. George also had business to attend, but her plans were disrupted by 'a young madman, a monumental mason', as she called him.

Auguste Clésinger was a sculptor who was just beginning to win a reputation for himself. He was a man of violent exuberance and fierce independence, a former cavalry officer. He had written to her the previous spring, asking for permission to do her bust in marble, and he appeared now at her Paris house, ready to carry out the commission. One look at Solange was enough to make him change his tune, and he also asked for the right to do her likeness in marble. The flattered girl immediately consented.

George saw no need to attend these sessions in the role of chaperone, and went about her own business, much to her regret. Auguste had a strong, strange effect on Solange, and it soon became apparent to her mother that she had truly fallen in love for the first time in her life. Before George quite realized what was happening, the girl had broken her engagement to Fernand.

Hoping to avoid any possible complications with Auguste, George cut short her visit to Paris and returned to Nohant with her daughter. But Auguste showed up in La Châtre twenty-four hours later, and riding out to the estate, boisterously demanded the hand of Solange in marriage. George gave her consent, perhaps because she, too, was overwhelmed by the young man's personality.

Thereafter she made inquiries about him, and disliked what she learned. Auguste Clésinger was in debt, he was said to drink to excess, and on two occasions he had been arrested for striking young women with whom he happened to be living at the time. It proved impossible to convince Solange that there were any weaknesses in the character of her sculptor; she was so much in love that, in her eyes, he was perfect.

George knew that Chopin would object to the new arrangements, and went to great lengths to make certain he learned nothing about the end of Solange's engagement to Fernand and her new betrothal to Auguste. The condition of Frédéric's health was precarious, and any excitement would be bad for him. A letter she wrote to his friend, Grzymala, in mid-May, 1847, indicates in her own words the complicated nature of her regard for Chopin at this time:

> I do not yet know whether my daughter will be married here in a week's time, or in Paris in a fortnight. In any case, I shall be in Paris for a few days at the end of the month, and, if Chopin can be moved, shall bring him back here with me.

I think he has suffered a good deal in his solitude from knowing nothing and being unable to give any advice. But it does no good to pay any attention to anything he says when the problem to be solved deals with real life. He has never been able to face facts, nor can he even begin to understand the complex qualities of human nature. His being is all poetry and music, and he cannot abide anything that is different from his own nature.

Any influence he might exert in the concerns of my family would mean, for me, the loss of all dignity and all love in my relations with my children. Please, I beg you, speak to him, and try to make him understand, at least in a general way, that he really must stop worrying about them…

It is all very difficult and very, very delicate. I know of no way to calm and restore a sick mind, when every effort to effect a cure merely irritates the invalid. The evil which is eating away poor Chopin, both morally and physically, has been for me, over a long period of time, a form of slow death. I see him slipping away without being able to do anything in this world to help him, because it is the very uneasiness, jealousy and moodiness of his affection for me that is the principal cause of his melancholy. I find it painful and difficult to determine what is right and what is wrong in my dealings with him, but I must do what I believe right in the lives of my children.

Chopin's health made it convenient to send him no invitation to the wedding, which took place at Nohant on May 20, 1847. He would not have attended in any event, since Baron Dudevant was on hand, and spent three days as the guest of his estranged wife.

It had been necessary to invite Casimir because Solange was still a minor, and his written consent was required before a wedding ceremony could be performed. Casimir had the taste and good sense to appear without his mistress, and treated

George with convivial geniality. She was gracious to him in return, and for several days they spent most of their time together, with the father of the bride playing the part of the host in the home where he had been the master for many years.

He and George were older and presumably wiser, and the very nature of the occasion may have made a difference, too. In any event, George and her husband discovered, to their mutual surprise, that they actually enjoyed each other's company. Although they rarely met thereafter, they sometimes corresponded, and were on easy, friendly terms. Solange's marriage, if it accomplished nothing else, ended the feud between Baron Dudevant and the wife who could have used his title, but still preferred to be known as George Sand.

Among the wedding guests was a talented young painter of landscapes, Theodore Rousseau, who fell in love with Augustine. His attentions to her caused Maurice to reconsider his own position regarding the girl, and both paid court to her. Then Solange and her husband returned to Nohant after a brief honeymoon, having decided to make their temporary home there. The bride, still hating the girl who had usurped her place in her mother's affections, at least in her own opinion, promptly went into action. She told Rousseau the old lie that Augustine and Maurice were lovers, which caused the painter to leave Nohant immediately. She then tried to convince her brother that Rousseau had enjoyed an affair with Augustine.

The outraged George ordered Solange to mind her own business, and Auguste stepped in, declaring that no one could address his wife in that manner. George Sand completely lost her temper at her new son-in-law, reminded him that she was the mistress of Nohant, and commanded him to leave if he found her ways offensive.

Her language became so abusive that Auguste, who had been drinking, raised a hand to strike her. Maurice instantly came to the defense of his mother, and grappled with his brother-in-law. Solange, according to an account of the fight that George wrote to a friend, cheered her husband and her brother impartially, goading both of them.

The incensed Auguste seized a mallet, one of the tools of his sculptor's trade, and attempted to .smash his brother-in-law's skull with it. Maurice evaded him, and snatching a dress sword that had belonged to the great Maurice de Saxe from its place of honor on a wall, took off after his brother-in-law.

George intervened physically, placing herself between the combatants and ordering them to desist. The sheer force of her personality was effective, and the moment Auguste dropped his mallet to the floor, Maurice sheathed his renowned ancestor's sword. The fight was ended.

Such was the stay of Solange and Auguste Clésinger, who left Nohant for Paris early the next morning.

'I never want to see them again,' George wrote. 'Their conduct last night was without excuse, the last straw! What insults all of us have endured at their hands! Dear God, what have I ever done to deserve such a daughter!'

X

Solange Sand-Dudevant Clésinger had lost a battle in her self-declared war with her mother, but she had not yet used her most potent weapon. Now, determined to inflict the greatest possible damage, she decided to utilize it, and went to Frédéric Chopin. The lies she told him were outrageous. Her mother, she said, had been the mistress of Victor Borie for the past year or more. She had also participated in an affair with Eugène Lambert, a young painter who was a friend of Maurice's. Her brother, Solange declared, was equally depraved, and tolerated his mother's behavior because of his own affair with Augustine.

That the girl should have been so inspired by hatred to invent vicious lies out of thin air is surprising. That Frédéric Chopin should have accepted her word at face value, without demanding proof of any kind, is astonishing. Those who have maintained that Solange was responsible for the termination of her mother's nine-year romance with Chopin have failed to grasp the essentials of the situation.

The Sand-Chopin relationship had already ended, although neither of the principals as yet realized it. Frédéric was willing to believe the worst about George because he wanted an excuse to terminate the affair. Certainly George no longer thought of him as a lover. At least two years had passed since they had last enjoyed physical relations, and for a long time he had been a burden, a responsibility her conscience had not permitted her to ignore.

Now suddenly in late June, 1847, he stopped sending her daily letters. George, unaware of what Solange had done, kept up her end of the correspondence, and also wrote to several friends, wanting to know if he had suffered a severe physical relapse. They assured her they knew of no change in his health, and she became increasingly mystified.

Finally, on the morning of July 25, 1847, George received a letter from Chopin. Whether she tore it into bits or threw it into the hearth is not known; the letter has not survived. From her subsequent correspondence with Marie de Rozières and others, one can only deduce that he berated her for her supposed infidelities, citing his source of information. He preached sermons, she said, and reacted with weary disgust, saying her eyes had been opened and she would act accordingly. 'No longer,' she told Mlle de Rozières, 'shall my body and blood serve as food for ingratitude and perversity.'

Twenty-four hours later she wrote to Chopin, and her letter, long regarded as a masterpiece, has been preserved for posterity in the Bibliothèque Nationale in Paris. She said:

> Yesterday I ordered horses, and fully intended, in spite of my own ill health and this appalling weather, to set out by chaise. I planned to spend a day in Paris in order to get news of you — to such a condition of anxiety had I been reduced by your silence. Meanwhile, you had been taking time to think things over, and your reply could scarcely have been more chilly.
>
> So be it, my friend. Do as your heart tells you, and take its instinctive promptings for the language of your conscience. I assure you I understand.
>
> As to my daughter, whose ungrateful, maniacal ravings you appear to accept as pure fact. She has the bad taste to say that she needs the love of a mother whom, in fact, she hates and slanders, whose most sacred actions she sullies, whose house she fills with her own atrocious talk! You have undertaken to lend a willing — should I rather say eager? — ear to her, and perhaps you really do believe what she tells you.

I will not be a party to this kind of squabble. It fills me with horror. I would rather see you go over to the enemy than myself take arms against that same enemy who was born of my body and fed on my milk.

Take good care of her, since you seem to have decided that it is your duty to devote yourself to her. I will not hold it against you, but you will, I hope, understand me when I say I shall continue to play my role of outraged mother. To have been a dupe and a victim is enough.

I forgive you, and will not, from this day forward, address so much as a single word of reproach to you, since you have confessed frankly what is in your mind. I cannot pretend that it does not somewhat surprise me, but if you feel freer and more at ease this way, I will not permit myself to be hurt by so strange a change of face.

Goodbye, my friend. May you soon be cured of all your ailments, as I hope that now you may be (I have my own reasons for thinking this may be so). If you are, I will offer thanks to God for this bizarre ending of a friendship which has, for nine years, absorbed both of us. Send me news of yourself when you wish, from time to time. But do not think that a letter will be a prelude to further friendship. It is useless to believe that things could ever again be the same between us.

George Sand was striking no pose, but literally meant what she said. She gave up Chopin without any sense of romantic regret, and her only concern for him was centered on his health. She bore him no ill will, even though it hurt her to know that he had so willingly accepted the lies Solange had told him. She has been called callous because of the seeming ease of her parting with Frédéric, but her critics fail to realize she was drained of all feeling. Her daughter's perfidy, combined with her lover's credulity, had exhausted her both emotionally and physically.

All through the late summer and autumn of 1847, she did no work. She ate ravenously, slept long hours, and spent most of her days out-of-doors, walking, riding, and working in her garden. But her voluminous correspondence with many friends indicates that she neither grieved because her affair with Chopin had ended nor sought revenge against him. Her letters were calm, eminently fair, and she obviously pitied the man who had been her principal concern for almost a decade. As nearly as can be judged, she was compassionate, but had set herself free, too.

In the autumn George sent Chopin's grand piano to his quarters in Paris. She had been informed, indirectly, that he wanted to give it to her in order to save her the trouble of shipping it to him, but she made it equally clear, through friends, that she would not accept gifts from those who were 'not close' to her.

A number of people who had been friends of the couple were appalled by the news that they had separated, but no one quite knew how to heal the rift. It had been too long in the making, and had developed too gradually.

George and Frédéric met just once more in their lives, and that occasion was accidental, even though a significant exchange took place. Chopin wrote at length about the incident in a letter he sent to Solange on March 5, 1848. The preceding day, he said, he and a friend paid a visit to Mme Marliani, and were just leaving her apartment when George arrived, escorted by Eugène Lambert.

The former lovers politely shook hands, and Chopin inquired whether George had heard from her daughter within the preceding two days. When she told him she had not, he said, 'Then permit me to inform you that you are a grandmother. Solange has had a baby girl, and I am delighted that I have the honor to be the first to inform you of the fact.'

They chatted for a few moments, principally about Solange's health, which was good, and then each went his separate way. Chopin's account is factual, dry, and displays no emotion.

George tells her own version of the meeting in her *History of My Life*, and the professional author gives the meeting a new dimension:

> I had thought that a few months spent apart from Chopin would heal the wound, make possible a tranquil friendship, and pour balm on memory. I saw him for a moment in March, 1848. I took his hand. It was as cold as ice, and trembling. I should have liked to talk with him, but he fled. It was my turn to say that he no longer loved me, but I spared him that pain, and left everything in the lap of the gods — and the future. I never saw him again. There were black-hearted people between him and me — good-hearted, too, but they did not know how to help. There were also a number of trivial people who preferred not to become involved in such delicate matters.

So the most famous of George Sand's many affairs ended on an anticlimactic note almost totally lacking in drama. It was just as well that the atmosphere was quiet and restrained; she needed a breathing spell, an opportunity to compose herself and direct her life into new channels.

As it happened, the break with Chopin occurred at a time when French political affairs were working toward a new, major crisis. George had already dabbled in politics from time to time, and liked to think of herself as an expert. Now, with France racing toward a major upheaval, she threw herself into the fight with all of her enormous energy and enthusiasm.

The French Revolution of 1848, one of many that broke out in Europe, was partly an outgrowth of the Industrial Revolution. The proprietors of the new factories that were springing up in major cities made huge profits, the new managerial, middle class earned large incomes, and the masses who operated the machines were paid starvation wages. Inflation was rampant, and peasants were as unhappy as city workers because their produce failed to earn them a living wage. In France the situation was complicated by King Louis-Philippe, who was proving himself a true Bourbon by eradicating the personal liberties his countrymen had held dear since the great Revolution of 1789. It was apparent to anyone with even a rudimentary knowledge of politics that the nation was on the verge of an explosion.

One of the wonders of French politics, according to the French, is that such an individualistic people should be able to band together to form parties. This individualism has been the despair of foreigners, who have sworn that, when there are as many as three Frenchmen gathered in a room, three separate parties develop.

George Sand was not only more advanced in her thinking than most of her compatriots, but at the same time her political opinions were indistinct, sometimes contradictory, so it is in no way remarkable that posterity has found it difficult to determine precisely where she stood on the eve of the Revolution of 1848.

She was able to say, without realizing she was contradicting herself, that she believed in democracy, but had no faith whatever in parliaments or parliamentary government. In some of the discussions that took place at Nohant on warm summer evenings she managed to infuriate old friends by simultaneously defending the opposing causes of the

Republicans and of the Bonapartist monarchists. She also thought of herself as a Socialist, and was firm in her insistence that she was a Christian, even though the Socialists of her day paid lip service to a vague form of atheism. She hated the oppressive Bourbons, and although she claimed that all kings were dictators, she willingly admitted that she might support a descendant of Napoleon if one were called to the throne.

She was also something of a mystic. She held, with Jean-Jacques Rousseau, that man was essentially good, and she believed the people could govern themselves if they received adequate instruction not only in the art of government but in the higher art of self-government, which in her opinion meant religion.

In only one sphere was her thinking very precise. She was a dedicated feminist, and since early womanhood had demanded equal legal and sexual rights for women. The members of her sex were exploited by men, and the customs, mores, and institutions developed over many centuries made women the slaves of love. Worst of all, woman could not escape from serfdom because man-made laws favored the male at the expense of the female.

In her *History of My Life*, as well as elsewhere in her voluminous works, George Sand lashed out repeatedly against the injustices of society toward women. A man who committed adultery was condoned, and society not only smiled indulgently, but actually congratulated him. A woman who committed adultery, however, was considered an outcast, and more often than not was subjected to severe punishment.

Women were ill-used, she declared, forced to live as imbeciles and subjected to harsh criticism because of their stupidity. When they were ignorant, they were despised. But when a woman tried to 'climb above her station' and became learned, male society mocked and scorned her.

Yet another strain was repeated again and again in her writing. Women understood the true meaning of love, which included sacrifice, but that was something no man could understand. In love a man wanted a woman to behave like a courtesan, and thereby reduced her to the courtesan's role, which made it possible for him to reject her at will. If she jilted him, she became an outcast. In marriage a woman was not treated as her husband's companion and equal, but as his servant. And she had no legal means of obtaining the equality that was her due.

The law had to be changed, she declared, and the double standard had to be abolished. It was woman's right to control her own finances, to obtain a divorce if she wanted one, to remarry if that was her desire. There could be no compromise, no halfway measures.

Strangely, George Sand neither wanted the right to vote for herself nor sought the franchise for others of her sex. Neither on the eve of the Revolution of 1848 nor later in her life, when her followers began to clamor for the franchise, would she give either active or passive support to the movement. It was premature, she said, for woman to be given the vote. Men had not been taught to use the franchise intelligently, and their education should come first. Meantime laws should be changed, and by the time woman was admitted to the polling place, she would have won the equality she sought in other spheres. Apparently it did not occur to this champion of women's rights, the most enlightened and advanced member of her sex in the entire nineteenth century, that only through the ballot box would women obtain the rights she sought for them.

George Sand cannot be faulted for her one blind spot, however. All of her other ideas, which since her time have become commonplace throughout the civilized world, were the product of her own thinking. She had no precedent to guide her; her demands rose out of her own intellect and her own yearnings. Had she achieved no distinction in the writing of literature, her original concepts on behalf of equality for women would have won her a permanent, secure place in history. It is small wonder that few of her contemporaries understood her, and that still fewer appreciated her efforts.

Most of her writing in the 1840s was concerned with social themes and the search for social justice. *Le Meunier d'Angibault* tells the story of a simple miller whose attitudes and behavior were too pure to be real, and a wealthy woman who lost her fortune and rejoiced over her new-found 'freedom'. In *Le Piccinino* she painted an exceptionally attractive portrait of little Louis Blanc, the leader of the activist wing of the Socialists, who was destined to become a poet of some standing, too, and would end his life as one of Victor Hugo's closest friends.

It was during this same period that she began writing yet another type of novel, one which assured her a permanent place as a literary figure. These were her Pastorals, and contrary to the view, held by many of her contemporaries, she did not just 'happen' to write them. They were the outgrowth of a deliberate, conscious effort, and were sparked by her reading of Virgil, a chore she undertook in an attempt to improve her knowledge of Latin.

The Pastorals reflected the warmth and simplicity of her love for the French countryside, and her descriptions of woods and valleys, hills and rivers, fields and lakes have sometimes been called prose poems. Her stories were simple, direct, and strong; in these books she dealt with the French provincials whom she knew and understood better than any other people. The purity and tone of the Pastorals are remarkable, and she achieved the difficult technical feat of setting down the rural dialects of her characters, yet simplifying the speech so the more sophisticated Parisian reader could understand them.

La Mare au Diable, the first of these novels, was an immediate success, and George made certain she would lose none of her previous readership by her rural setting. The tale was that of a wealthy farmer who married a poor girl, learned to appreciate her, and found happiness with her. *François le Champi*, which soon followed, was equally successful, and had an even less complicated story line, telling of a bastard child, abandoned in a forest, who won the affections of the wealthy woman who found and cared for him. The third Pastoral, *Jeanne*, is still regarded as something of a masterpiece, particularly in its descriptive passages. Published in 1844, it won the quick approval-of Balzac, Sue, Théophile Gautier, and Sainte-Beuve. Victor Hugo was persuaded to read it the following year, and remarked with some surprise, 'no wonder Mme Sand's work is so popular. There's no better writer in France today.'

Since the Pastorals were small books, they sold for less than more extensive works, and George earned less in royalty payments than she did from her larger novels. The reorganization of her life after her break with Chopin caused her to delve into every aspect of her existence, and she was somewhat startled to discover that, despite the income she obtained from her estates, she was on the verge of going into debt. Needing money, in 1847 she began the largest project she ever-undertook, her *History of My Life*, which would run ten volumes before completion.

'Never have I known such agonizing labor,' she wrote Sainte-Beuve. 'It is far more difficult to write about one's own feelings than to describe the characters who spring from one's imagination.'

In later years she would recall that 1847 marked a low point in her life, but there was one major compensation. In the autumn Augustine fell in love with a young man who reciprocated her feelings. Karol de Bertholdi was a Polish exile who taught school, and he came to Nohant under the auspices of Victor Borie, who was his friend. George used her influence to obtain a position for the bridegroom as a provincial tax collector. The position paid a comfortable salary, and George also gave the bride a dowry of thirty thousand gold francs, a princely sum she could ill afford.

Victor Borie told George repeatedly in his letters that a revolution would break out at any time, but she insisted he was daydreaming. All of Berry was peaceful, and at the beginning of 1848 the good citizens of La Châtre seemed contented with their lot. No one could have been more surprised than George Sand when the people of Paris suddenly lost patience with a regime that granted the vote to only one citizen in thirty and refused any changes in the so-called constitutional monarchy. The reform elements planned to hold demonstrations in conjunction with a banquet on February 22, 1848, and the preceding day King Louis-Philippe specifically forbade all such gatherings.

People of the working class districts built barricades of paving blocks, furniture, and the wood and stone of old buildings; the government retaliated by calling out the National Guard, but the citizen-soldiers refused to obey the call. Louis-Philippe finally realized the gravity of the situation and offered to negotiate, but it was too late. Radicals gathered in front of the house of the First Minister, Guizot. Someone fired on the guards, the soldiers returned the fire, and twenty citizens were killed.

The bodies of the unfortunates were paraded through the city on the night of February 23rd in a torchlight march, and the entire city responded. Riots broke out everywhere; on February 24th, Louis-Philippe and his family escaped in disguise to exile in England. A throne had been toppled in a scant seventy-two hours.

The monarchists had hoped to place the young son of Louis-Philippe on a righted throne, but the republican fervor was so strong that the Chamber of Deputies, in a show of wild emotion, established a new Republic of France. Pending the election of a National Assembly, a provisional government was established under a group of ten ministers. Lamartine, the poet, held the title of Provisional President or Chief Minister, and the Minister of Labor was Louis Blanc, the poet and historian.

When George Sand first learned of street fighting in Paris, she assumed that Maurice, who was in the city, would return at once to Nohant. Instead she received a letter from Delacroix telling her that her son was having the time of his life, spent all of his time in the streets, and seemed intoxicated by the fervor that was gripping people in every walk of life.

George left for Paris at once, ostensibly to persuade Maurice to come home, but actually to witness all the excitement herself. She had miscalculated in missing the start of the Revolution, but felt certain that she could catch up with events when she arrived.

To her astonishment the Revolution had already been won, and two of her colleagues were all-powerful members of the government. The moderate Lamartine, a close friend of Victor Hugo's, long had been an admirer of George's work, and she had reciprocated by admiring his poetry. They had spent evenings together at dinner parties and in cafés discussing both politics and literature, and although Lamartine was too conservative to approve of her personal way of life, he nevertheless trusted her.

Her relationship with the radical Louis Blanc, who was hated by Lamartine, was closer. He was the acknowledged leader of the Socialists, and George had corresponded with him for years, since her affair with the Socialist Michel de Bourges. No evidence exists to substantiate the story, still circulated, that George Sand and Louis Blanc had been lovers. They were members of the same profession, both considered themselves Socialists, and their mutual interests brought them together as friends. Both were too strong, too demanding, too argumentative to have had an affair.

Lamartine had made his headquarters in the Louvre, and even though the anterooms of his office were crowded with visitors, he received George Sand without delay when she called on him and spent more than an hour there while crowds in the outer office grew larger. Louis Blanc was even more cordial, and came to the head of the grand staircase at the Luxembourg Palace, where he made his office, when she went to see him. Hundreds saw him greet her by kissing her on both cheeks before leading her into his private office.

It soon dawned on people at large, as well as those in literary and theatrical circles, that George Sand had overnight become a power in the land. In a sense she became the indirect ruler of Berry because the Provisional Government followed her recommendations in the appointment of their representatives there. Friends whom she trusted became the official Commissioners of Châteauroux and La Châtre. Others who were no strangers to Nohant were given less important posts.

Her son was not forgotten; Maurice became Mayor of the village of Nohant.

All the members of the new regime knew she could write, and soon were asking for her help in composing the steady stream of directives, proclamations, circulars, and orders that poured from the offices of all ten Provisional Ministers. For George's convenience, Lamartine made an office and a small staff available to her in the Louvre, while Louis Blanc, not to be outdone, gave her a larger suite and a far larger staff at the Luxembourg Palace.

George displayed her customary energy and enthusiasm for her new, unpaid work. She appeared at the Louvre early every morning, and did not stop until time for a late lunch. Then she hurried to the Luxembourg Palace, where she continued to work long after dark. Lamartine himself is the authority for the statement that, within ten days of the Provisional Government's formation, George Sand was either writing or directing the preparation of at least half of the new regime's orders.

Early in March George returned to Nohant so she could be present at the ceremony in which Maurice would be installed as Mayor. She remained for two days, and those who sought to discredit her said she spent her time gossiping in the inns and cafés of Châteauroux and La Châtre. They were right, but did not understand her reasons. Paris was not the provinces, and she was carefully sounding out the reactions of the local middle class to the new regime.

What she learned was not encouraging. The bourgeoisie of Berry agreed with the middle class of Paris that the Provisional Government was far too radical. She already knew that the working classes of Paris, which solidly supported Louis Blanc, believed that most Ministers were too conservative and the reforms they proposed too timid.

She herself maintained her faith in the general mass whom she called The People, and in her correspondence with her friends in high places in Paris she stressed her conviction that 'The People will be just, wise, calm and good'. She disliked the feuding that had already broken out between factions, and in a letter to the cynical Balzac, who believed that the future would be chaotic, she declared that the middle class, being more substantial and better educated than the workers, would take the lead in the establishment of a permanent Republic that would satisfy the legitimate demands of all classes.

On her return to Paris, George immediately discovered that the dissemination of public information was in a mess. The machinery of government had broken down, and contradictory orders had been issued by the Ministers of Labor, Interior, and Public Instruction. Lamartine promptly proposed that the dissemination of all information by the Provisional Government be channeled through George Sand. His nine colleagues approved of the eminently sensible idea, and George became an official but unpaid member of the regime, with a large staff and an impressive suite of offices at the Louvre. It did not matter that Louis Blanc's nose was somewhat out of joint because she had to give up her other quarters at the Luxembourg Palace. As she explained to him in a patient note, she could not be in two places at the same time.

For all practical purposes George became an eleventh Provisional Government Minister, the head of a separate Ministry of Propaganda. There was one notable difference between her position and that of the other ten; she took part in their deliberations and offered her advice, but she did not vote. Many years later, reminiscing about the period, she remarked to Gustave Flaubert that she was so busy it did not occur to her that she was being denied the franchise.

It may be significant, too, that George's Ministry remained unofficial. In spite of her power she was never granted a title, and those who worked on her staff were not members of an independent Ministry, but were loaned to her by other departments of the Provisional Government. She was required to take no oath of office, and as a volunteer worker who drew no salary, she was free, at least in theory, to come and go as she pleased.

No member of the Provisional Government worked harder or enjoyed the experience more. A letter she sent to Maurice on March 24, 1848, summarizes her feelings:

> Here I am, doing a statesman's work. I have drawn up two Government circulars today, one for the Ministry of Public Instruction, the other for the Ministry of the Interior. It amuses me to think they will be dispatched addressed to 'All Mayors', and that you will be receiving through official channels your mother's instructions!
>
> Ho-ho, Mr Mayor, you had best walk with care! I suggest you begin by reading out, each Sunday, one of the Bulletins of the Republic (you might recognize the style of the author) to your assembled National Guard.
>
> Never have I been so occupied! Most days I do not know whether I am standing upon my head or my heels. There is someone "at me", pestering me all of the time. But this life suits me. It was made for me, and I for it.

In April a warm spring sun dispersed the fog and rain of winter, and Paris enjoyed the weather for which tourists had been praising her for centuries. Everyone in the city spent as much time as possible out-of-doors, and nature lover George Sand looked out of her Louvre windows at the green grass and budding trees in the gardens below. Not even a Minister of Propaganda, she decided, should be denied the joys of fresh air, sunshine, and grass. So, after returning each night to her apartment, she prepared a roasted chicken, hard-boiled eggs, and other dishes suitable for a picnic. At noon she went out into the gardens to eat, and after a day or two Lamartine joined her there. Thereafter any casual bystander could see the First Minister and the Minister of Propaganda eating chicken and bread, hard-boiled eggs and cheese, and drinking strictly limited quantities of rough wine as they enjoyed a noon respite from their labors.

According to a story that may be apocryphal, the civil servants who kept their jobs no matter what regime was in power became curious. What did the First Minister and the Minister of Propaganda discuss with such intensity that they almost came to blows? Since both seemed unaware of their surroundings, a few of the more daring civil servants wandered close to them and eavesdropped. One day they argued about the poetry of Seneca. On another occasion Lamartine insisted that the work of Robert Browning was far superior to that of his wife, while George argued he was denigrating the poetry of Elizabeth Barrett Browning simply because she was a woman.

The two artist-statesmen may have enjoyed their lunch hour discussions of literature, but the political situation was growing increasingly bleak. The middle class, the monarchists who had supported the Bourbons, and the more conservative of the proletarians were alarmed by the radicalism of Louis Blanc's faction in the Provisional Government. Yet the bulk of the working class, which called itself Socialist, was disgusted by the cautious, halfway measures taken by Lamartine and those who tried to walk the middle of the road. Out of a total population of about 1,500,000 at this time, more than one-third of a million men were unemployed. Pessimists predicted there would be further bloodshed.

The elections for the new Constituent Assembly were scheduled to be held late in April, and as the date approached, the situation in the capital became increasingly tense. George, who had committed herself to the sacred cause of The People, without quite knowing what she meant, became disturbed when she learned that monarchist elements remained strong in Berry and other provinces, and might win a majority in the new Assembly.

By standing together, the middle class and the workers could have avoided both conservative and radical extremes, electing an Assembly that would have given France the constitutional reforms actually desired by a majority of the people. But the French genius for individualism asserted itself with a vengeance, and factions formed within factions.

On April 23rd, a scant twenty-four hours before the election, Propaganda Minister George Sand threw herself into the fray with unprecedented vehemence, and the publication of Bulletin of the Republic Number 16, which she wrote, created a major scandal. In it she declared:

> If these elections do not assure the triumph of social truth, if they express only the interests of a caste, and if the trusting loyalty of The People is by violence deceived, then, beyond all doubt, instead of being, as they ought to be, the salvation of the Republic, they will sound its death-knell. Should that happen, there can be but one road to safety for those who have already built the barricades, and that will be for them to manifest a second time their will that the decisions of a false National representation shall be adjourned. Does France wish to force Paris into having recourse to this extreme, this deplorable remedy?

She went on to express the hope that this would not happen, but men of every political persuasion concluded that she was nevertheless inviting the proletarians of Paris to return to their barricades and resume rioting that had led to the downfall of the Bourbon monarchy.

Louis Blanc and the other radical Ministers denied they had authorized this new call to arms. The moderates joined the conservatives in demanding that the names, of the perpetrators of this outrageous infamy be published. George Sand unhesitatingly admitted her authorship of the notorious document, protesting loudly but in vain that she had not intended to incite the working class to commit fresh violence.

No one believed her, and Lamartine confided to several intimates that her lack of judgement shocked him. Inevitably, disorders took place on the day of the election, and inevitably George Sand was blamed for them.

The moderates won the election by an overwhelming majority, and when the new Constituent Assembly met on May 4th, there were demands from every quarter that George Sand be dismissed. But with more important matters to be settled, and for the better part of a week, while attempts were made to form a new Cabinet, George retained her post and continued to meet daily with the outgoing Ministers.

On May 10th a new Cabinet was formed, the Lamartine forces were victorious, and the radicals, including Louis Blanc, were dismissed from office. Inasmuch as George Sand had not held an official position in the Provisional Government, it was not deemed necessary to honor her with a formal dismissal.

The ultimate irony of the situation was that George's principles had actually prevailed. The good sense of The People had asserted itself, and France was committed to a future of progress toward greater liberalism, although at a pace that would not alarm the conservatives.

On May 15th the storm broke. The working classes swept into the streets, intending to force the new Government out of office, and a mob poured into the Chamber of Deputies, intending to force the dissolution of the new Assembly. Lamartine and his associates held firm. They called out the National Guard, which remained loyal to them, and order was temporarily restored.

In any event, a number of arrests were made, and the newspapers of May 16th blamed George Sand's infamous Bulletin for the disorders. She retorted that a document written and published more than three weeks earlier could not have incited the working men of Paris to riot, and her logic may have been unassailable, but the tide of public opinion had turned strongly against her. Before leaving her apartment that morning she was informed that her Ministry no longer existed and that her own offices were now being occupied by employees of the new Government. The political career of George Sand had come to an abrupt end.

Maurice, who had spent the night with friends, returned to his mother's apartment to tell her he had heard a rumor that a number of radical leaders were being arrested and imprisoned to await trial, and that her name was on the list. He went out to check on the story, and soon returned to report that the rumor was true. A number of Socialist leaders already had been hauled away to prison cells.

George was still free to return to Nohant if she wished, and no longer had any reason to remain in Paris, but nothing would persuade her to depart. Suppose the National Guard or the police came for her, and failed to find her. The whole country would say she had fled to Nohant in order to escape from the authorities.

She remained in Paris for forty-eight hours, deliberately going to restaurants, sitting for an hour in a café near the Chamber of Deputies that the members of the Assembly favored, and otherwise allowing herself to be seen in public. But her presence in the city was ignored. No one came to arrest her, and no one warned her she would be wise to flee while she could still go.

Whether any officials of the new Government seriously contemplated her imprisonment is unknown. Lamartine and his associates were too wise to make a martyr of a woman who would create a new storm if taken to jail. It was far better, they reasoned, to pretend she did not exist.

George understood their motives, and when she finally went to Nohant on May 18th, she felt badly humiliated. Not only was she being falsely blamed for a situation that was not of her making, but now she was ignored by former friends. Her vanity could not tolerate the snub. For months she had worked furiously for fifteen to eighteen hours per day, at her own expense, and in return France was abusing her. People who should have known better were accusing her of fomenting riot, and many who had regarded her as a close associate no longer respected her. If that was the way they felt, she could return the compliment.

Politics was a filthy, illogical game. Men paid lip service to principles and causes, but when they achieved power, they no longer cared about their constituents. George made up her mind to leave the political arena permanently, which is precisely what she did. Apparently it did not occur to her, when she went back to Nohant, that by holding her place as

Minister of Propaganda she had notably advanced the cause of women's rights to which she was so devoted.

XI

George Sand's reaction to her political misadventure was that of a scorned woman. She had been jilted, and therefore had no intention of permitting a former lover to hurt her again. But she soon discovered it was difficult to escape from the world, regardless of her own wishes. There were many in Châteauroux and La Châtre who blamed her for the upheavals in Paris, and there was talk in both towns of burning her estate to the ground.

George reacted as expected to the challenge, and wrote a pamphlet daring her foes to attack. If necessary, she said, she and the members of her household would defend themselves to the last. But she was dissuaded from publishing it by André Aulard, the new Mayor of Nohant, who was a lifelong friend. When people were aroused, he said, they were inclined to do foolish and even dangerous things. In fact, he declared, she would be wise to leave Nohant for a time until passions cooled.

Maurice returned from Paris and gave his mother the same advice. Friends in Paris, including Delacroix, Balzac, Sainte-Beuve, and Marie Dorval wrote to her, urged her to go away for a time. She refused, insisting that Nohant was her home and that no one would drive her from it.

Then, in late June, as George Sand had predicted in her famous Bulletin, class war suddenly ravaged Paris and the streets ran with blood. Scores were killed and wounded in the riots, and after order was restored, hundreds of radicals were arrested and imprisoned or sent out of the country. Among those deported was Louis Blanc, who remained in England in exile supporting himself there by writing history until, as an old man, he finally returned to France in 1871.

The conservative citizens of Berry were incensed by the outrages in Paris, and the danger to George Sand became very real. Only because Maurice was in even greater jeopardy did she finally consent to take a 'holiday'. Locking her most valuable possessions in cellar vaults, she closed her manor house and slipped away to Tours, where she rented a small hotel suite under her real name, Aurore Dudevant.

It was agonizing to read in the Paris newspapers that she was a coward, but she knew that if she replied, Maurice would return immediately to Nohant from his own country refuge. Some of the more liberal factions of the press sought articles from her to counter the continuing assaults on her principles, her actions, and her person, but she refused every offer, telling the few friends who knew where to locate her that she felt too ill. She needed a respite to regain her objectivity.

In other ways, too, the summer of 1848 was the worst period George had ever known. Louis Blanc and several other friends wrote to her from London to tell her that Chopin was there, and was informing everyone who would listen to him that she was responsible for the Paris disturbances, that she was mired in mud and dragging down all who associated with her.

After his return to Paris late in the summer, Chopin contributed further to George's distress. Augustine's father, Brault, had just tried to blackmail George by printing a vicious pamphlet in which he accused his distant relative of having taken Augustine to Nohant for the purpose of making her Maurice's mistress, and then having married her off to the first man who appeared on the scene after Maurice grew tired of her. George's attorneys halted the dissemination of the pamphlet, but a number of copies had already been distributed, and someone called one to Chopin's attention.

He deplored the act of the girl's father in publicizing the story, he said, but every word happened to be true. Further emphasizing his own attitude, he sent the copy to Solange in a large bouquet of flowers, and she, of course, took delight in passing along every detail of the incident to her mother.

George displayed true nobility in her reply. Ignoring her daughter's role in the matter, she said of Chopin, 'I cannot bring myself to pay him back in his own coin for all the hatred and rage he has shown me. I think of him frequently, always as a child who has become unbalanced, bitter.'

She did not waver in her political views, either, in spite of the hatred directed toward her. In a letter to Joseph Mazzini, the Italian patriot whom she had known in Paris, she declared, 'Only if all work together — reactionary bourgeoisie, democratic bourgeoisie, and Socialists — will The People achieve self-government.'

Other events added to her misery. Hippolyte, her half-brother, was seriously ill, and was not expected to live. Marie Dorval's son-in-law, an actor, was unable to find work, and Marie was forced to go on tour again in order to support her daughter and three small grandchildren, two of whom were sickly. Her own health was impaired, so George intervened and quietly helped to support the family.

During the months of her stay at Tours George saw no one except Maurice, who visited her regularly. A number of her friends wanted to come to her, but she held them off, saying she was not fit company for anyone. She needed solitude, she told them, and above all she wanted rest.

But after spending two or three weeks doing virtually nothing her restless nature reasserted itself, and she turned back to her own work. She wrote several portions of her *History of My Life*, making greater progress on it than she had ever before shown. Letters from several Paris publishers indicated there was a growing market for her Pastoral novels, and she showed her true mettle as a professional writer. Ignoring the collapse of her world, she wrote one of the most charming of her Pastorals, *La Petite Fadette*. When published in 1849, the novel not only won back whatever readership her political activities might have cost her, but was popular with thousands of new readers as well.

Finally, in the autumn of 1848, a sober and restrained George Sand returned to Nohant. As Mayor Aulard had predicted, her neighbors had grown calmer, and when she first appeared in La Châtre, a number of citizens approached and apologized to her for their threats of the previous summer. Quietly, without calling attention to herself, George resumed normal life under her own roof and again took her place in the local community.

On Christmas Day, after drinking an entire bottle of brandy at a sitting, Hippolyte died, unmourned by his widow and children. George wrote a short memorial to him, then tried to put him out of her mind. He had been a stranger to her for years, their lives had led them in opposite directions, and it was difficult for her to remember the boy with whom she had climbed trees, hiked, and fished.

The year 1849 promised to be a far better year, and early in January Augustine Bertholdi gave birth to a healthy son. His parents named him Georges, and a letter dispatched by his father on the day of his birth asked George to act as his godmother, a responsibility she happily accepted.

The good news was balanced by fresh tragedy. In the spring Marie Dorval died in Paris after wearing out what was left of her fragile health on tour in the provinces. The last of her old friends and lovers to see her was Alexandre Dumas the Elder, who held back his tears until he left the sickroom. Marie had also asked to see Jules Sandeau, but it was typical of him to be delayed, and he arrived an hour or two after she died.

George Sand took upon herself the burden of providing for the impoverished family. Through friends in the theater she found employment for Marie's son-in-law, who survived for many years playing small roles. George also supervised and paid for the education of Marie's two surviving grandchildren, Marie and Jacques Luguet. For many years thereafter, they came to Nohant every year to spend their summer holidays with her.

On October 17, 1849, Frédéric Chopin died in Paris. Among the last to see him was Solange, who left no account of her visit. Many who gathered in his apartment were hysterical, and so many wrote conflicting accounts of his last hours that it is impossible to determine with any accuracy whether he mentioned George at the last or whether he spoke of others. The news reached George the following day. She placed a lock of his hair in an envelope, sealed it, and wrote on the outside, 'Poor Chopin. October 17, 1819.' It was her only comment.

The death of Chopin and the disillusionment with politics caused by her participation in the Revolution of 1848 marked a turning point in George Sand's life, and her next few years were relatively uncomplicated and tranquil. She again became a grandmother on May 10, 1849, when Solange gave birth to a daughter, Jeanne, at Casimir's estate in Gascony. George and Solange were on speaking terms again and corresponded irregularly, but the girl had taken advantage of their break to mend relations with the man she believed to be her father, and who thought of her as his daughter. When Solange and her husband needed financial help, however, they automatically turned to George.

Clésinger, who was winning distinction as a sculptor in Parisian artistic circles, was unable to show the acumen in financial affairs that he displayed in the management of his own career. He and Solange squandered her dowry, and as his income was uncertain, George-promised them three thousand gold francs a year. They not only accepted, but immediately plunged into the social life of Paris. The mistress of her own home, Solange gave lavish dinner parties at which authors, artists, and actors were frequent guests. She bought herself a coach and a team of horses, hired an English coachman, and purchased new furniture far beyond her means.

George deplored her daughter's extravagance, and felt certain she was putting herself and her husband further into debt, but the sound advice she gave in her letters was ignored. She did not know that Solange's marriage was already falling apart, that Clésinger's heavy drinking was making him far more erratic than usual, and that Solange was finding a convenient way to augment her income. Behaving with a discretion no one would have believed her capable of achieving, the girl was . secretly accepting very considerable financial assistance from gentlemen of means, to whom, in return, she granted the favors customary in such transactions. No one outside a small, exclusive group of blue-bloods and aristocrats was aware of her new profession, and she displayed remarkable dexterity in juggling her two lives. Her conduct in public was impeccable, and although she was rapidly acquiring a reputation as the most beautiful young woman in Paris, no one in her social circle dreamed that she had privately launched herself on a new vocation.

One of the very few who learned of her trade was Victor Hugo, who probably slept with more women in his lifetime than any other nineteenth-century man of public affairs. How he discovered that Solange had become a courtesan is unknown, but out of respect for her mother he refrained from utilizing the services she offered, a rare act of self-discipline on his part. Not until much later, when Solange acquired a reputation that made her the most notorious young woman in all of Europe, did he reveal in his correspondence with George that he had long been aware of her life as the most expensive prostitute of her time.

Maurice, meanwhile, was building a solid career as an artist and political cartoonist, earning enough to become financially independent of his mother. But he continued to lean on her emotionally, making his Paris home in her apartment and spending a portion of his time at Nohant. He fell in and out of love with several young ladies, always shrinking from marriage. George hoped he would marry, but urged him to find the right wife, and in her steady correspondence with him whenever they were apart urged him not to take the important step until he was certain he loved the girl. Love, she told him, was the all-important element in marriage.

Meanwhile, some of Maurice's friends began to play important roles in her own life. Emile Aucanté, a brilliant young lawyer who frequently visited Nohant, gradually became her most important professional advisor, and in time acted as her representative in dealings with publishers. Aucanté first helped her in the complicated negotiations in selling the Paris properties George had inherited, doing so well that she turned to him repeatedly for help. Over a period of many years he became closer to George than he was to Maurice, and the intimacy of the association led a number of George Sand's early biographers to assume they also became lovers. No evidence or substance has ever been found to verify this.

Victor Borie, who was rapidly becoming one of the more influential young editors in Paris, also developed a friendship with Maurice. But George had 'discovered' him first, and whenever he came to Nohant for a visit, she treated him more as her own guest than as her son's. Eugène Lambert, whose portraits of cats were winning him a reputation as great as he was achieving with his landscapes, was another who came to Nohant for several weeks at a time.

Another of Maurice's friends was Alexandre Manceau, an artist and engraver whose etchings would be recognized as some of the best of the period. He was thirteen years younger than George, suffered from a number of chronic ailments, and was considered exceptionally handsome. He became George's favorite on his first visit to Nohant, and by early 1850 occupied a permanent place in her entourage as her secretary, assistant, and general confidant. There can be little question that George sometimes slept with him, and their relationship made Maurice uneasy. He protested, late in 1850, when George planned to stay at Manceau's apartment during a visit to Paris, and she went to her own home instead only because her son insisted.

Manceau was so much the type of man toward whom she turned that her affair with him, seen in perspective, was probably inevitable. At least she had learned a lesson from her romances with Sandeau, Musset, and Chopin, and did not fall in love with Alexandre. Her regard for Maurice, and fear that she might lose his respect, no doubt caused her to exercise unusual self-restraint.

A partial return to the political arena tempted George when Prince Charles Louis Napoleon Bonaparte was elected President of the Republic on December 10, 1848. She had met him ten years earlier, in Paris, prior to the time he had been sent into exile by Louis-Philippe, and during all these years she had maintained an infrequent but steady correspondence with him.

George wrote a number of articles for various Paris newspapers in which she lauded the new President, and she continued to praise him even after he staged a coup late in 1851, making himself Emperor under the name of Napoleon III. Those who have criticized George for her inconsistency, accusing her of shedding her liberalism, have missed the point of the position she took. Not only had she been a lifelong admirer of the first, great Bonaparte, but Napoleon III was her personal friend. Although she came to deplore many of his policies, her personal relationship with him remained unaltered for many years. She was able to maintain friendships with a number of people whose ideas and political principles she deplored, and she saw no reason to alter her feelings because Napoleon III was a dictator who curbed the liberties of all Frenchmen.

George was drawn even closer to the younger Napoleon through no fault of her own. One of the strongest influences on the President of the Republic was exerted by Comte Alfred d'Orsay, a wealthy banker and industrialist. Around 1850 the latter began an affair with Solange that soon became public knowledge, and within a short time he was recognized as her protector by everyone in France and elsewhere who kept in touch with such matters. George's relationship with her daughter had improved somewhat, and they now saw each other on infrequent occasions; if George disapproved of the affair, she kept her opinions to herself.

By the autumn of 1851, in any event, she was openly accepting the affair. Solange, who had left her husband on and off over a period of several years, returned to him once again, without breaking oil with d'Orsay. It was in 1851 that George took her first long step into the theater, writing a play, *Le Manage de Victorine*, that was given the mid-nineteenth century equivalent of a little theater production in November of that year. Sitting with her during the opening night performance were Solange, Clésinger — and the Comte d'Orsay.

It was through d'Orsay that George met the new ruler's cousin, Prince Napoleon-Jérôme, also a nephew of the first Bonaparte, whose views were similar to her own. Jérôme, with whom she shared a liking for good cigars and old cognac, became her lifelong friend. Thanks to him she eventually became friendly with the Empress Eugénie, who admired her work. Through both she was able to exert a mild, indirect influence at the new royal court.

In any event, she was strong enough to intervene with the new Emperor, usually successfully, on behalf of friends who were arrested and threatened with imprisonment or deportation. Among those whom she saved from such a fate was Victor Borie, who was granted an Imperial pardon, and she was equally helpful to a number of her old Berry friends who had also been hauled off to jail because their views were too liberal for the new regime.

She had learned a number of lessons from the Revolution of 1848, however, and did not forget them. A thin thread of sorrow deploring the reactionary activities of the new regime may be found in her voluminous correspondence, but she unburdened herself only to old friends she knew she could trust. The collapse of her own political dreams had taught her harsh reality. She knew she was incapable of opposing Napoleon III openly, so she carefully refrained from making him her enemy.

George Sand lacked the incredible strength of Victor Hugo, who went into exile and remained there until the fall of Napoleon III almost two decades later, though the Emperor himself personally invited the exile to return. Her admiration for Hugo's stand was great, and for the first time in all the years she had known him, George opened a correspondence with him. In one of the more memorable of her letters to him, written on March 23, 1854, she told him, 'I envy the courage that has made it possible for you to have made yourself the symbol of liberty. Alas, I must remain in France, respectfully raising my hat when royalty passes, so that I might gather up a few crumbs of freedom to feed those of our friends who dare to say too much and lose favor with the regime. You accomplish more by your very absence from France for a single day than I can achieve in a year of carefully hoarding and using what little influence I may possess with those who are near the throne.'

An activity that George regarded as an escape from reality and that, in the long run, proved enormously beneficial to her career, gave her enough distractions to make the new tyranny of Napoleon III bearable. Early in 1851 she had a professional puppet theater built on the stage at Nohant. Maurice carved the puppets and George not only made the costumes, as she had been doing for several years, but began to write plays to be performed there.

These efforts were labors of love; she lavished far greater care on them than she did on the books she was writing for profit. The audience of relatives and friends at Nohant were valuable, too, their reactions telling her what was effective and what failed, and she constantly rewrote her plays for puppets. One, entitled *Nello, ou le Joueur de Violon*, was subjected to eight complete rewrite jobs.

The work George did for her puppet theater — which she regarded as sheer pleasure — paved the way for her second career as a playwright. Her plays were to earn more money than her novels, though contributing less to her renown. *Nello*, to take the obvious example, became a play for the commercial Paris theater, and was presented at the Odéon Theater in September, 1855, under the title of *Maître Favilla*.

The young men of the Nohant household, most of them friends of Maurice who had become George's satellites, played the leading roles in dramas that would find their way onto the Paris stage. Almost by accident, these plays were tried out 'on the road' at Nohant before being presented with real actors before a ticket-buying public in the world's most active theatrical center.

By the 1850s George Sand had entered her change-of-life period, which had a calming effect on her volcanic character, and her behavior no longer startled and delighted the gossips of Paris. She wrote regularly, steadily, her pace rarely varying. She spent most of her time at Nohant, going into Paris only on the infrequent occasions when she had to confer in person with publishers or producers. She preferred, when possible, to summon even these men to Nohant rather than travel into the city.

Her daily routine became habitual. She arose at about 9.00 a.m., and after eating a light breakfast in her bedroom or private sitting room, went out alone for a long walk. She returned at noon, spent an hour or two dictating letters to Manceau, and then, for the first time that day, saw her guests at lunch. In the afternoon she went for another walk or rode through the fields or drove into La Châtre on errands. More often than not she was alone, although a favored guest might be asked to accompany her.

She always returned home in time for tea, the English custom she now kept until the end of her life, and then retired to her bed for an hour's nap. Dinner was served at 8.00 p.m., and was the most social time of day, the hour George reigned supreme. Later there might be a performance of a play in the puppet theater, or someone might read aloud from a new book. There might also be a burst of creative activity: Maurice, Lambert, and other artists would make sketches, George would work on puppets' costumes, and any composers who were guests would be invited to sit at the piano.

George herself usually played a passive listener's role during the evening's activities. She noted carefully everything that was said, and Manceau is the authority for the statement that conversations in the parlor at Nohaht were sometimes repeated almost verbatim as dialogue in a new George Sand book.

Between 11.00 p.m. and midnight George retired to her study for her most serious activity of the day, her work. Manceau saw to it that sharpened quills, a jar of ink, and ample supplies of paper awaited her. The door closed behind her, and under no circumstances was any member of the household permitted to interrupt her. Even the most pressing of emergencies were not called to her attention until the following day.

George wrote steadily, smoothly, paying no attention to the clock on the mantel, and worked until she filled her day's quota. If the writing was swift, she might finish her fifteen to twenty pages in three or four hours, but if she labored, she might spend twice that time to finish. She sometimes suffered from headaches that attacked her when she awakened in the morning and grew worse throughout the day, but she refused to let them interfere with her daily output. On occasion, when she was suffering intensely, she dictated her work to Manceau, and apparently could make the transition from written to verbal expression of her thoughts without difficulty. According to her own estimate, she dictated approximately four to six complete books to her secretary-confidant-friend-lover over a period of years.

Only on rare occasions could she be persuaded to take an active part in the after-dinner talk and games. Manceau's *Diary*, which he kept meticulously during his tenure at Nohant and elsewhere, indicates that one of the most notable of these events occurred when George received, from Victor Hugo, a copy of his new book of poems, *Les Contemplations*. No one else, her guests insisted, was capable of reading such work aloud to the company, and she consented when she realized they were demonstrating genuine shyness, a feeling she well understood. The reading took many nights because George often interrupted herself to discuss the poet's handling of his subject, his mood, and his technique. On more than one evening, Manceau wrote, she revealed that she wished she could write poetry. She had tried many times, she said, but had been so dissatisfied she had destroyed her efforts. Only a few fragments of her poetry have survived, none sufficiently long or detailed to enable posterity to determine whether she should have persevered.

Some of George Sand's ideas regarding the operations of her household were unusual, and for their day were extraordinary. She refused to converse with servants in the third person, believing that form of speech archaic and unnatural. She employed nine full-time persons, and it was said she paid the highest wages in the entire province of Berry. There was no difference, she insisted, between a so-called master and a so-called servant; all were equals, and were entitled to treat each other accordingly. Because the laborer was worthy of his hire, he would do his best work if well paid, and she gladly offered high wages in return for expert service. In return she demanded both efficiency and loyalty. It was an unwritten rule that nothing regarding activities at Nohant should be repeated to outsiders, and her staff supported her to the full. Only twice, over the period of many years, was it necessary for her to discharge a servant who spoke out of turn.

Her own special province was the flower and vegetable garden, which George tended herself. A full-time gardener was in her employ, but even he was not permitted to touch either the flower or vegetable plots unless she happened to be absent in Paris.

Old friends, who came to Nohant, such as Sainte-Beuve, scarcely recognized the calm, considerate woman who never raised her voice or indulged in displays of her previously volatile temperament. After a turbulent half-century on earth, George had finally matured.

But her daughter now supplied more than a compensatory quota of the quicksilver missing from her own nature. Solange was hard-bitten, cynical, and greedy, and having been aware of her mother's various liaisons since earliest childhood, was determined to achieve an even more spectacular record. Perhaps she lacked George's talent, but no one would ever be able to say that Solange was less notorious or shocking than her mother.

The irony of the situation was that George could not understand why Solange went out of her way to behave immorally. It never occurred to George Sand that she herself had set her daughter an example. She believed her own conduct had been impelled by love and high principles, and she was unable to understand that, regardless of how she herself felt about her past, society at large regarded her in a far different light.

Her old friend, Honoré de Balzac, who knew her better than most, discussed her bewilderment a few months prior to his death in 1850. Writing from Russia, where he had gone to woo and marry his beloved Mme Evalina Hanska, he declared:

> Poor George! I grieve for her whenever I read the sly gossip in the Paris newspapers about her daughter. She herself likes to believe she has led an exemplary life, and that Solange has betrayed her. She cannot see, I am sure, that her own lack of discipline is responsible for the conduct of the depraved young Mme Clésinger. I am tempted to quote to George from the Old Testament that most powerful passage about the sins of the fathers being visited upon the children, but, alas! she would not understand why I singled her out for the receipt of such information. I myself condemn nothing George has ever done; her life has been her own to lead. How I wish, though, for the sake of her own tranquility in her old age, that she would recognize the importance of the role she played in shaping the character of her daughter. How better to learn now, to berate herself and be done with it, than to wait until her mind and heart grow too feeble to withstand the rigors of truth.

Had Solange been married to a firm man of principle she might have developed into a woman of stature, but Clésinger was the worst of all possible husbands for her. He was an undisciplined, self-indulgent drunkard, a man incapable of saving money or investing wisely, and he squandered his talents. Certainly he brought out all of the worst qualities in his wife.

'Clésinger,' George said, 'may be the more insane of the pair, but no one could ever call him the more malicious.'

Solange's hostility toward her mother sometimes went to almost unbelievable extremes. In 1850, when Clésinger went into bankruptcy and George extended herself to straighten out his financial situation, Solange told all of her mother's old friends in Paris that her own life was being made miserable because the bailiffs who hounded her for money had been put on her scent by George.

When a real crisis occurred in the girl's life, however, she came straight home to her mother. In late January, 1852, Solange left Clésinger for the last time, and accompanied by her little daughter, Jeanne, who was known in the family as Nini, she made an unexpected appearance at Nohant. She no sooner settled down than she began to quarrel violently with her mother, and after a stay of less than a month she departed for Gascony, where she intended to visit her father.

One beneficial result of the visit was that Solange could not be bothered with her daughter, and left Nini behind. No woman was ever a more doting grandmother or more mindful of her obligations than George. She not only remembered vividly how much she owed her own grandmother, but she realized how much Nini depended on her, and she gave the child all the affection and attention of which she was capable. She had treated the children and grandchildren of others with generosity, and now that her own flesh and blood were involved, there was no limit to what she would do for Nini.

She did not extend the same generous love to Solange, who found life at the Dudevant castle in Gascony far too dull for her tastes, and seeking more drama, retired to a convent near Paris. There, as a paying guest who was being given refuge, she wrote a long, rambling letter to her mother, in the course of which she blamed George for all of her mishaps. Refusing to accept the entire burden, George replied in an extraordinary letter. Written on April 25, 1852, it reveals much of George Sand's own depths of character:

> I spent many of the best years of my own youth living in what you call 'isolation', and working hard between four dirty walls; allow me to inform you that although I regret much, I do not regret them. The sort of isolation of which you complain is another matter. It is the direct result of your own deliberate choice. It may be that your husband does not deserve to be so bitterly disliked or so impulsively set aside. If this separation was necessary, I cannot help thinking it might have been achieved with greater dignity, more patience, more prudence. But you wanted it this way, and you have your wish.
>
> In my view it is not attractive of you to complain of the immediate consequences of a resolution which you took entirely of your own accord, and in spite of the parents, the friends and the child, of whose absence you are now so painfully conscious. The thought of your child should have persuaded you to be patient for a longer time. As to parents — and you refer to me, of course — I constantly urged you to wait until a more opportune time, when you would be provided with a sounder motive.
>
> I fail to see why the friends you made when you chose to make your home elsewhere than with me in the great world should be likely to prove themselves more loyal than my old friends, who were your friends, too. There is not one of my old acquaintances who would not readily have forgiven your extraordinary behavior to me and welcomed you as of old. There are not many of them, it is true, and such as there are neither important nor fashionable. But that is not my fault. I was not, as you were, born in the purple, and in making friends I followed the promptings of my own simple tastes. If it is true, as you say, that all of your misfortunes have stemmed from the fact that you are my daughter, I can do nothing to alter that unhappy fact.

The only thing that will console you is money — large sums of it. In luxury, laziness and the whirl of fashion you might succeed in forgetting the emptiness of your heart. But I could give you what you need only by working twice as hard as I do now, which means I would be dead in six months, since even my present program is beyond my strength. You would not be rich for long, so my sacrifice would be made in vain, since what I shall have to leave will by no means provide wealth for you or your brother. Besides, even if I could work twice as hard and yet remain alive for a few years, why should it be my duty to transform myself into a galley-slave or an old horse merely to supply you with luxuries and a life of pleasure.

What I can give you, you shall have. You can treat this house as your home, on condition that you do not upset everyone here by your insane behavior, or drive them to despair with your ill-natured ways. I will keep your daughter and attend to her rearing for as long as you wish. But what I will *not* do is pretend to sympathize with the difficulties and privations you will have to endure in Paris. The remark in your letter about 'women of judgement and warm affections who let themselves slip, like poor girls without minds of their own, into a life of pleasure and vice', makes me think that perhaps your husband did not always lie when he claimed you had uttered certain threats. He may be mad, but so are you — diabolically mad.

There are moments when you seem not to know what you are thinking or what you are saying. You were in that state when you put that odd remark into your letter to pre. If you often say such stupid things, I don't wonder that you sent Clésinger out of his mind.

So you find it difficult, do you, to be lonely and poor, and not to slip into a life of vice? It is all you can do, is it, to be cooped up within four empty wails, while women are laughing and horses are galloping outside? 'What a terrible fate!' as Maurice would say. The real tragedy is to have the sort of mind that thinks, as yours does, that you *must have a life either of happiness or vice.*

Very well, then. Just try a little vice! Just try being a prostitute! I do not think you would make much of a success of it. Why you could not begin to hunt out luxury at the cost of seif-love, it is not so easy as you seem to think to accept dishonor. A woman must be far more beautiful and intelligent than you are before she can hope to be pursued, or even sought out by men who are eager and anxious to pay for her favors — or else she must be a great deal more experienced in the art of making herself desirable, more skilled in *feigning* passion and wantonness and those allurements of the dubious, delicious kind of which, thank God, I do not even know the names! Men with money to spend want women who know how to earn it, and that kind of knowledge would make you feel so physically ill that the preliminary bargaining soon would be broken oft.

I have known young women who have conquered the passions of heart and body, and have been terrified out of their wits lest domestic unhappiness might lead them into giving way to the impulse of a moment. But I have never known a single one brought up as you have been, *in an atmosphere of personal dignity and moral freedom,* who has dreaded unhappiness and isolation because of such dangers as you mention. A woman of heart and judgement may, no matter how strong her character, feel frightened of being swept off her feet by love, but never by cupidity. If I were the Justice appointed to deal with your case, and had read the precious reflections to which you have just treated me, I should certainly *not* give you the custody of your child!

Solange made no direct reply to her mother's letter, and did not refer to it in any future correspondence. It must have been difficult to be George's daughter and be overwhelmed by her.

XII

'I was intended by God to be a grandmother,' a happy George Sand wrote to Maurice in the late spring of 1853. She and Mini had become inseparable, and spent all of the child's waking hours together. The little girl ate breakfast with George, accompanied her on her morning walks, and, while her grandmother was dictating letters, took part in the session by learning her alphabet, then learning to read. George reactivated the miniature garden that her own grandmother had made for her, and sometimes, as a special treat, Mini was allowed to stay up at night and watch the puppet shows, some of which were written especially for her. She also accompanied George on trips to Paris, and was taken to the theater there, principally because there was no one with whom she could be left. She fell asleep during adult plays, of course, and Manceau had to carry her to the waiting carriage at the end of the evening, as Prosper Mérimée had carried Solange.

Occasionally Solange came to Nohant for a visit, but could not adjust to the quiet life and routines of country dwelling, and rarely remained for more than a few days. Her behavior was far better than it had been for a long time, however, and she drew somewhat closer to her mother, an improvement that George attributed to the influence of Nini. The little girl appears to have been the major factor in bridging the wide chasm that separated her mother and grandmother.

The idyll of Nini's life at Nohant ended abruptly and melodramatically in May, 1854. Clésinger had learned that his wife was having an affair with Conte Carlo Alfieri, a prominent Italian nobleman and one of the leading figures in the parliament of the Piedmont. He obtained enough evidence to prove the affair was taking place, and then went to court to obtain a legal separation. No sooner were the preliminary papers in his hands than he descended on Berry, accompanied by a brace of lawyers. He demanded the custody of his daughter, and George hastily summoned her own attorneys from La Châtre, but they were powerless in the situation, and the little girl was forced to depart with her father, weeping bitterly.

George was heartbroken, but all of her attorneys informed her there was nothing she could do.

A miracle of sorts took place when Solange suddenly decided to become a Catholic. She took instruction, then went off to a spiritual retreat, from which she wrote to her mother, 'I shall plagiarize Henry IV and say, "My daughter is well worth a Mass."'

The wheels of justice turned almost as slowly in the mid-nineteenth century as they do more than one hundred years later, and the case of Clésinger vs Clésinger was not heard until December, 1854. The court found both husband and wife guilty of so many transgressions that it refused to rule in favor of either, and, at least temporarily, would not grant a formal legal separation. But the disposal of the person of the couple's daughter, Jeanne, was of primary, immediate importance, and the court decided that neither parent was a fit custodian. Nini was awarded to her grandmother, the court having investigated the child's own desires and having learned in detail who had been taking care of her.

The decision was made one week before Christmas, but George was unable to obtain custody of her granddaughter at once because of a technicality. The court had adjourned until the end of the Christmas holidays, and Clésinger appealed the case to a higher court, which automatically halted the execution of the court order until an appropriate form could be signed. He had to put Nini in a boarding school, however, since he himself had been denied custody.

One day early in January, 1855, Clésinger appeared at the school and took Nini out to dinner with him. The weather was bitterly cold, the father failed to notice that his daughter was dressed in summer clothing (according to George Sand's account), and Nini came down with a bad cold. Complications developed, the child became gravely ill, and Solange arrived at the school just in time to take her daughter in her arms before she died.

The news stunned George when a hastily written note from Solange reached her on January 14th. She retired to her bedroom, where she refused all food and would admit no one for forty-eight hours. At no time thereafter would she describe or discuss her suffering with anyone, and she emerged only when Solange arrived on the 16th, bringing Nini with her in a coffin. The funeral was held in the chapel at Nohant that same day, with friends of George, Solange, and Maurice in attendance, as well as many from La Châtre and the village of Nohant. Jeanne's father was conspicuous by his absence as the little girl was laid to rest in a grave near those of her distinguished maternal ancestors.

By the next day George decided to interrupt her other work in order to write a book about the short life of the child, to be called, *Après la mort de Jeanne Clésinger.* Her motives were not morbid, and the book, when it was written, proved to be joyful and light-hearted, expressing all that a sensitive and perspicacious woman had found charming and fanciful in the short life of an imaginative, bright little girl.

Maurice was worried about his mother's mental and physical condition, however, and so were Manceau and Aucanté. All three finally persuaded her to make a trip to Italy to distract her, and she finally consented, provided the trio accompanied her.

They left late in February, by which time George was determined to look toward the future. She refused to grieve, at least in public, and by the time the party reached Genoa, by sea from Marseilles, she was regaining the weight she had lost. The party travelled first to Florence, where a brief halt was made, and then went on to Rome.

George's reactions to the Eternal City indicate her state of mind, which could not have made life easy for her son, her attorney, or her secretary. Rome, she declared in her letters, was a city of 'humbug'. She found no grandeur or sublimity in the spectacle, and called the sights 'trivial'. Rome, she said, was 'a disgusting medley of ugliness and filth'. There were beggars everywhere, and the entire population was devoted to the principle of trying to cheat tourists.

Having rid herself of a few frustrations, George returned to Nohant, after a six-week absence, in a somewhat better frame of mind. A number of relatively minor vexations further occupied her mind. Augustine de Bertholdi and her husband, while not ungrateful for all George had done for them, again needed her influence on their behalf. Bertholdi wanted to be transferred to a post near Paris, if not to the capital itself. And Augustine hoped George would introduce her to Prince Jérôme Bonaparte, who, the young woman had been given to understand, often made enterprising couples his protégés, particularly when the wife was young and attractive. George's pen burned indignantly when she replied that she would not present Augustine to her friend, Prince Jérôme, under any circumstances.

Another disappointment was Solange's refusal to pay another visit to Nohant that year. Her excuse was flimsy: the place would not be the same to her without her stable of riding horses and the many dogs she had kept there. But George was forced to accept her decision and allow her to put her own life together again in her own way.

If Solange absented herself from Nohant, however, virtually everyone else George Sand loved and knew came to see her in the spring, summer, and autumn of 1855. Relatives and friends alike knew the void in her life that had to be filled, and each became a seif-elected delegate to fill it. She had so many visitors that their presence interfered with her work, and she longed for a simple, rustic retreat to which she could withdraw and work in solitude.

She found such a place almost by accident One day early in the autumn of 1855, when Nohant was bursting with guests, she went off on horseback, accompanied only by Manceau, to get away from everyone. In the course of their ride they came to the little valley of the Creuse, situated in the hills of Berry. Exploring the area, they came to a tiny village called Gargilesse, which stood on the banks of a small river of the same name. Beyond the village the vegetation was so thick it almost seemed tropical, the weather was far warmer than anywhere else in Berry, as the valley was protected by high hills from the winds, no matter what their direction, and there was no sound but that of the river churning as it flowed over a rocky bed. This, George decided, was where she wanted her rural retreat.

Manceau made it his business to find the right place, and after a search of only a few days located a cottage of only five rooms which seemed perfect. He bought it, had it painted and refurbished, and then presented it to George as a gift.

She promptly fell in love with the place, and thereafter used it frequently over a period of years. Whenever she felt under pressure at Nohant, she rode to her cottage, a journey of only an hour or so, and felt completely cut off from the entire world. She could work there during the day as well as at night, and her isolation was so complete that most people had no idea where to find her. She simply disappeared from sight.

When she went to Gargilesse, George could indulge her passion for cooking, and prepared all meals herself. 'I enjoy stirring food in a saucepan,' she told Manceau, 'when I know that I am not forced to cook every day of my life. That is the sort of woman's drudgery to which most members of my sex are condemned, but I am afraid my temperament would not allow such docility.'

Sometimes she went to Gargilesse alone, and on other occasions Manceau accompanied her for her visits of one to three days. Only he could be self-effacing enough to disappear from sight and remain uncommunicative until George finished working on her current manuscript and wanted his company. Of all her other relatives and friends, only Maurice was privileged to see Gargilesse. No one else was invited there.

In 1857 George Sand's past cast its shadows on her present. Jules Sandeau, to the astonishment of everyone who had known' him since his youth, was nominated for membership in the most prestigious body in France, the French Academy. His attempt to win the seat failed, but another effort was made two years later, and succeeded.

Also in 1857, Alfred de Musset dropped dead, his body worn out by his years of dissipation. Some of his friends said he had never recovered from his affair with George Sand, and old, half-forgotten gossip about their affair was revived in the salons and cafés of Paris.

In the following year George made her peace with her old publisher, Buloz, and it may be he who suggested that she write a novel about her relationship with Musset. Whether the original idea was his or her own does not really matter; George believed she had achieved enough objectivity to write the book, and went to work with a vengeance.

The result was one of her best known, most controversial, and least merited novels, *Elle et Lui*. She presented herself as virtually perfect, a woman of nobility and compassion who gave herself to a younger man because of her hope that he would overcome his obvious faults and live up to his high vocational promise. Buloz was appalled by her portrait, and urged her to show her heroine in three-dimensional terms. George made a half-hearted attempt, and to some slight extent managed to make her heroine less of a saint, but no one, not even a total stranger, could have believed in the sanctity of her character.

The book created an expected sensation, and in 1858, when it was published, several printings quickly sold out. Everyone who had been close to Musset was horrified and angry, and Paul de Musset tried to salvage his brother's good name by writing a reply under the title, *Lui et Elle*. His account was a parody of what George had written, and some of his scenes, which were identical to hers, presented a totally different point of view. In the opinion of Alfred's brother, it had been the young man who had been the sensitive genius, but had been ruined by a woman who was rapacious, domineering, and greedy. All of literate France read the Paul de Musset book, and snickered.

The final touch was provided by someone the upset George had never met, one Louise Colet, a handsome woman who had never shown any talent in her chosen profession, that of an author, but had achieved renown of a sort because of her sensational love affairs and her violent temper, which she often unleashed in public. Trying to cash in on both sales and publicity, Mme Colet wrote a very short book, scarcely longer than a pamphlet, which she called *Lui*. Her work was crude and vulgar, with no discernible talent, but she attracted a reading public because she presented a portrait of a monster who bore a strong surface resemblance to George Sand.

Had the libel laws of France been more stringent, George could have won a lawsuit against Mme Colet, and might even have been able to collect damages from Paul de Musset. She had no basis for legal action, so she had to find some other way. She had kept all of Alfred de Musset's letters, along with copies of her own, and conceived the idea of publishing them. Then the world would see that the affair had not been one-sided, that Musset had reciprocated her love, and that she was not the man-devouring ogre who, in two different books, had been presented to the world in such horrifying detail.

A sixth sense impelled George to seek the advice of Sainte-Beuve, before she gave in to her own desire and the pleas of Buloz, who knew that a volume of the Sand-Musset correspondence would be the biggest-selling book of the year. Never had she presented her arguments with such care, and she bombarded the cautious Saint-Beuve with letter after letter.

In his own youth Sainte-Beuve often had been short-sighted, and sometimes had been guilty of giving bad advice to authors. But he had spent a lifetime cultivating grapes in the literary vineyards now. His own scandalous behavior over the years had given him a deeper insight into human nature. The desire to publish the Musset correspondence, he told George, was a natural, normal human impulse, and he was convinced that posterity deserved such a publication. But George's timing was wrong. If she brought the book out now, it would merely feed the flames of gossip, which would destroy her dignity. Her stature as an author made it imperative that she keep silent and allow the Paul Mussets, Mme Colets, and others on the periphery of the literary world to say what they would about her. If she could exercise enough patience, her own time would come, and she would be able to set the record straight.

The advice was sound, as George well knew, and with great reluctance she accepted it. Buloz received a letter telling him she had decided to postpone, indefinitely, any publication of her correspondence with Alfred de Musset.

Sainte-Beuve knew what a financial sacrifice George was making, and what strength of character was required for a professional writer to reject the vast sums that the publication of such correspondence would have earned her. Also, he falsely believed she was suffering from serious financial reverses, an idea that might have been passed on to him, maliciously or otherwise, by Solange.

In any event, at the next meeting of the Académie Française, august member Sainte-Beuve proposed that the organization give its most coveted award, the Gobert Prize, to the greatest woman author in the history of France. In addition to the honor, the prize consisted of a substantial twenty thousand gold francs.

Alfred de Vigny, also an Academy member, had not been fond of George Sand for many years, not even on speaking terms with her for two decades. Her relationship with Marie Dorval had ruined his affair with his mistress, and he made no secret of his contempt for 'the Lady of Nohant', as he called her. But de Vigny proved he was big enough not to let his literary judgements be warped or influenced by personal considerations, and enthusiastically seconded Sainte-Beuve's motion.

The matter was debated at length in the press, and a third Academy member who had no reason to favor George's cause emerged as her public champion. She, along with Victor Hugo and Honoré de Balzac, Prosper Mérimée declared, was one of the literary giants of the age. George herself maintained a dignified silence, at least in public, but wrote privately to a few friends that she knew the members were too backward-looking to grant her the award.

Her prophecy proved correct, and Sainte-Beuve's motion was rejected by a vote of 18 to 6. He and de Vigny decided to make a second attempt, and assiduously canvassed their fellow members, among them Jules Sandeau, who had not been present when the first vote had been taken. But Jules, unlike de Vigny, could not separate his appreciation of literature from his own past, and was absent when a second vote confirmed the first by the same score.

That would have been the end of the matter had the Empress Eugénie not intervened. This Spanish noblewoman, a patroness of the arts and by all odds the best dressed woman in all Europe, publicly suggested that precedent be smashed and that George Sand be elected a member of the Academy.

The members themselves remained silent, but a great controversy arose in the penny press, which exploited the subject to the full. Fresh fuel was added to the flames by the publication of an anonymous pamphlet which told, in semi-fiction form, about the election of a woman to Academy membership. It was called *Les Femmes à l'Académie*, and was so powerful, so skilfully written, that it could have been done by no one other than a professional writer. There is some evidence to suggest it was done by Mérimée, and that Sainte-Beuve edited it in order to remove any strong traces of his colleague's style.

A great many people were certain that George herself had written the pamphlet and published it herself in order to further her membership. Nothing could have been more remote from the truth. She knew that the prejudices against women were far too strong to permit her election, as the Academy's stand on the award to her of the Gobert Prize had so convincingly proved. But the story persisted, all the same, so she wrote and published a reply, *Pourquoi les Femmes à l'Académie*? She prepared it with great care, and was careful not to malign the talents of the members, whom she repeatedly called men of great stature. Nevertheless, she declared, she had no desire to become associated with a body that fixed its gaze on the past rather than the future, that knew nothing and cared less about the world in which modern French men and *women* lived.

That ended the subject of her admission to the august company of the Academy.

By 1860 George was in despair about a matter far closer to her heart. Maurice, who celebrated his thirty-seventh birthday in that year, was still a bachelor, and although he had been betrothed to several young ladies, each for a short period of time, it appeared that he might remain a lifelong bachelor. George was ready to abandon her hope that there would be grandchildren with whom she could play at Nohant, and that the lineage of Maurice de Saxe would endure. She herself was fifty-six, and for the first time in her life seemed conscious of her rapidly advancing age.

Then Maurice found a bride in 1861. Lina Calamatta, many years his junior, was the daughter of Luigi Calamatta, one of the best engravers in Paris. The family was Italian, but Lina, although born in Italy, had received most of her education in France, and spoke, read, and wrote French as though it were her native tongue. She was exceptionally pretty, a young woman of charm and intelligence, as well as the possessor of a lively wit. Maurice had known her since she was a child, but seemed to fall in love with her overnight, and she returned his devotion.

George and her daughter-in-law established a rapport from the time of their first meeting. George was struck by her friendly, direct manner, and particularly appreciated the girl's approach to her. Lina was not awed, refused to become a sycophant, and insisted on making her own views known, but at the same time she was lovingly deferential to the older woman. They managed to live together under the same roof at Nohant without clashing, and George, who soon came to regard Lina as a daughter rather than a daughter-in-law, actually began to turn over management of the establishment to the younger woman as soon as Lina could absorb the details of what was required.

George's wishes for a grandchild were fulfilled in 1863 on Bastille Day, July 14th, when the first of Maurice's children, Marc-Antoine Dudevant-Sand, was born. George was so delighted that she personally fired each of the miniature cannon that had been set up on the lawn for the celebration of the holiday.

It may be significant that the first friend to whom George wrote the good news was Alexandre Dumas the Younger, who had become increasingly close to her over the period of almost a decade. His fame as an author already as great as that of his illustrious father, young Dumas was almost universally regarded as the most outstanding French writer of his generation. As George informed his father, she liked and admired him because he had a social conscience, because he never spoke disparagingly of any colleague, and because he always showed compassion for the weak, the poor, and the crippled in spirit.

Over a period of many years the pair frequently worked together. Dumas, who considered himself a playwright, adapted George's novel, *François le Champi*, into a play, which he called *Le Fils naturel*. Another of her novels, *Claudie*, written on the subject of an unmarried mother who was betrayed, became the subject of two Dumas plays, *Les Idées de Madame Aubray* and *Denise*. At the urging of Dumas, George transformed her own play, *Le Manage de Victorine*, into a novel, *Le Marquis de Villemer*. Then, at the insistence of young Dumas, she made it into a play again under this same title, and he helped her with her plotting construction, which was second nature to him, but which she always found difficult. It became one of the greatest theatrical successes of its time, and was played in repertory by every Paris company of substance for many years.

In spite of her advancing age, George lost none of her facility, and the younger Dumas, among others, marveled at her ability to write a book of substance in a short time. It was miraculous, he said, when he learned, in 1862, that in a scant six weeks she turned out the manuscript of *Mademoiselle La Quintinie*, which was, in essence, a study in fiction form of the practice of Confession in the French Catholic Church.

Another who joined George's circle of literary friends in the 1850s was Gustave Flaubert, whom she chided for being a perennial bachelor. He was, she said, the only writer on earth who could be unabashedly, sentimentally romantic and cruelly realistic at the same time. She and Flaubert struck up a correspondence that grew through the years, and posterity is indebted to these letters for the views of the elderly George Sand on matters pertaining to life and love, humanity and literature, politics and death.

By 1863, however, Nohant was no longer a Garden of Eden. Manceau, who was a man of considerable talent as an engraver, poet, and even playwright, managed George's vocational, personal, and domestic affairs with selfless brilliance. He had no interest in fame or money for his own sake, and actually spent the income from a play he wrote, which was successfully produced at the Odéon Theater in Paris, on George's household.

His efficiency and intimate knowledge of George's business irritated Maurice, whose jealousy of a man only a few years his senior became increasingly worse. George remembered what jealousy of Augustine de Bertholdi had done to Solange, who was now spending her life living first with one millionaire, then another. She also believed it was not wise for a mother to remain under the same roof with her married children.

So, immediately after Christmas, 1863, she startled Lina and Maurice by telling them she and Manceau were going to Paris, where they had taken an apartment at 97 Rue des Feuillantines. In order to show that she bore no bitterness against her beloved son and daughter-in-law, George made them a handsome gift. Delacroix had recently died; and George, who owned twenty of his pictures, sold eighteen of them, keeping only the first and the last he had given her, 'La Confession du Giaour' and 'Le Centaur'. She had been paid eighty-five thousand francs for the rest, and set up the sum in a trust account that paid the annual interest of three to four thousand francs to Maurice and Lina.

Her generosity stunned the pair, and the shame-faced Maurice begged her to reconsider her plans. If she chose to permit Manceau to dwell at Nohant as her guest, where her son also lived with his family and where there were other guests coming and going, that was her business, and placed her beyond criticism. But it was a far different matter for her to set up housekeeping in a Paris flat — at the age of fifty-nine — with a man many years her junior.

The unperturbed George told them the rest of her news. *Villemer* was earning her enormous royalties, and she had invested some of the money in a house at Palaiseau, near Versailles in the Paris suburbs. She and Manceau would be spending their weekends in the country, and would go to Palaiseau whenever city life palled on them. As firm now, when she was nearing her sixties, as she had been in her twenties, George was indifferent to the world's opinion of her way of life.

Maurice and Lina desisted, in part because they knew it was useless to argue with her, and partly because they hoped she would change her mind after spending a short time in the city. So they said nothing more until George paid them a brief visit at Nohant in April, and at that time they made the mistake of preaching abstinence to her. An entry in George's *Diary* on April 25, 1864, not only indicates her state of mind, but proves that, in some ways, she had not changed:

> Abstinence! Abstinence from what, you young idiots! It would be well if *you* observed a lifelong abstinence from evil! Has God made what is good so that we must deprive ourselves of it? I would suggest that you abstain from enjoying the warmth of the sun, or from regarding lilacs in flower. I, for my part,

work, without abstaining from a regret that I do not work more. But I am sometimes bored by my countless hours at my desk, and when that ailment strikes, I have little heart for work, although it is my mainstay, my nourishment, my all.

When the departing couple settled in Paris, Manceau engaged a cook and a housemaid who would work both in the city flat and the country house, and a gardener, who would be stationed full-time at Palaiseau. They intended to lead a simple life, George said, and had no need for the full staff of servants they had enjoyed at Nohant.

Maurice and Lina were undecided what to do about the huge manor house, which they felt was too great a financial burden for them to manage alone. Pending a final decision, they closed the place and went off to Gascony for a visit with Casimir and his common-law wife. Casimir had already met Lina, and had been charmed by her, which had confirmed George's opinion that no one could resist her.

In mid-July a fresh tragedy struck swiftly. George received word via a new means of communication, the telegram, that Marc-Antoine was seriously ill, and asking her to come at once if she wanted to see him again. There were new means of travel now in a rapidly changing world, so George and Manceau went to Bordeaux by overnight express train, and the next morning transferred to a local train that took them close to their destination.

By the time they reached the gloomy Dudevant castle, it was too late. Marc-Antoine Dudevant-Sand had breathed his last.

George remained in Gascony for twenty-four hours, and this sad visit was the last time she ever saw her husband. She and Casimir were polite to each other, but had little to say, either in private or in the presence of others. At the dinner table George ate virtually nothing, but chain-smoked exceptionally long cigarettes, always taking care to follow her inviolable custom of dropping the butts into a bowl half-filled with water. Before she departed she urged Lina and Maurice to return to Nohant, saying she would give them an additional three thousand francs per year to help them. Above all, she said, they should have other children. If they allowed themselves to become too discouraged, their own lives would be ruined.

Maurice and Lina followed George's advice to the letter, and immediately reopened Nohant. Their respect for her was so great that, it would appear, it did not occur to them to act in any other way. Within a short time they were writing to her to the effect that they hoped to have more children as soon as they recovered from the shock of Marc-Antoine's death.

George, still accompanied by Manceau, went straight back to Paris, where she made a determined effort to pick up the threads of the new life she was making for herself there. On the surface, at least, nothing was changed. She went to the theater several nights each week, she dined with friends in restaurants, and she attended the literary salons of various colleagues.

By the end of the summer a new worry was added to her burden. Manceau's health was deteriorating rapidly, and it was apparent that he was suffering from consumption, the same disease that had killed Chopin. He coughed incessantly, sometimes ran a fever, and on his worst days frequently spat blood. By early 1865 George was forced to curtail her social life in order to take care of him, and in the spring, when the weather improved, they moved out to the house at Palaiseau and stayed there.

It was extraordinary how history was repeating itself. George had looked after Musset for a short time when he had been ill in Venice, and later had nursed Chopin for months in Majorca and Marseilles, subsequently supervising his daily regimen for years. Now she had to do the same for the man who was the last of her lovers. The principal difference is that she was not now and at no time had been in love with Manceau. She was devoted to him and felt fiercely loyal to him, but he had always been so undemanding, so willing to sacrifice even his personality for her sake, that they had never struck romantic sparks.

It might be an exaggeration to say their relationship was tepid. Manceau was so in awe of George that their affair could be nothing other than dull. Manceau always referred to George as 'Madame', even in the *Diary* he kept for personal satisfaction and for the sake of posterity. He never failed to show her the respect he believed her due as one of the great authors of the age, even when she neglected him or, because of her preoccupation with herself, showed him little consideration.

During Manceau's final days, George more than compensated for any unintended slights over the years. For more than five months she did not stray beyond the sound of his voice. Both of them knew he was dying, but George would not accept the inevitable, and in her *Diary*, as well as her letters to Maurice, she stressed one theme: she would give Manceau the strength to recover.

In spite of her best efforts, however, Manceau died as George held him in her arms on the morning of August 21, 1865. Now that the fight was ended, she accepted his passing with tranquility.

Even in death Manceau was still loyal. He left several small properties to Maurice, and made George his literary executor, giving her the right to do as she pleased with his play, his poems, and his *Diary*.

For two weeks George insisted on remaining alone at the little house in Palaiseau, and only then finally consented to rejoin Maurice and Lina at Nohant. She saw no one during that fortnight, cooked her own meals, spent most of her days in the little garden where Manceau had enjoyed his last sunshine.

This was a final testing time, the ultimate step as George herself moved toward old age, and she seemed well aware of what was taking place within her. As indicated in her correspondence with Flaubert and others, her thinking ranged from theology to politics to the advancement of the rights of women she had so long advocated. Of these, she herself considered the most important to be her return to a positive approach to religion. She was not prepared to embrace the Catholicism she had abandoned three decades earlier. Yet the death of Manceau caused her to ponder at length on the mortality of man, and she summarized her conclusions in a letter to an old friend in La Châtre:

Let us… believe in God. Feeling prompts this. Faith is an excitement, an enthusiasm; it is a conclusion of intellectual magnificence to which we must cling as one would to a treasure, and not squander our way through life in the small coin of empty words, or inexact, priggish argument.

Let time and knowledge work their changes. Centuries must pass before men can hope to understand the ways of Goa in His universe. As yet man knows nothing of the ultimate. He cannot prove that God does not exist; he cannot prove that He does…

Let us, whatever happens, still have faith and say, "I believe", which is a very different thing from saying, "I assert". Let us say, "I hope", which is a very different thing from saying, "I know". Let us shake hands on this notion, this determination, this dream-which is the dream of all good men…

George's friendship with Prince Jérôme Bonaparte and the Empress Eugénie, and the fact that the Emperor always replied to any communication she sent him, did not deter her from becoming increasingly critical of a regime that was vigilant in its denial of the personal liberties Frenchmen held dear. Her mysticism had vanished during decades of observing politicians at work, and she had lost her illusions, yet she managed to cling to the hope that France some day would establish a stable form of self-government.

Visible expansion in the field of women's rights offered George a great deal of encouragement. Thanks to her own example, scores of women were working on newspapers, writing books, poems, and plays, and making their own influence felt through publishing. Most of the old professions — law, medicine, and architecture — still banned women from practice, but she predicted that day would end within her own lifetime or soon thereafter, and said that her granddaughters would be admitted to the University of Paris or any other institution of higher learning in the country they cared to attend.

Industries were expanding rapidly, and women as well as men were given jobs on assembly lines. George rejoiced because the age-old custom of confining woman to her home was ending, but she was less than certain that the assembly line solved any problems. Women were being paid even smaller wages than men for such work, and there was little improvement in the living conditions of the poor. It was essential that woman fight for her rights, but she found it hard to believe that the acceptance of starvation wages was one of them.

Feminist leaders in Great Britain and the United States were beginning to agitate for the ballot, and a number of women in

France were starting to do the same. But George still refused to follow the lead of the Anglo-Saxons, clinging to her view that man should be taught how to use his franchise intelligently, and that it would be wise for woman to wait. Her attitude on this subject remained unaltered, and she clung to it for the rest of her life.

George more or less summarized all these views in the novel *Monsieur Sylvestre*, which she wrote in 1865 and which was published in the following year. The cynics who believed the cause of justice was lost were mistaken, she declared, and so were those who insisted that changes in legislation would produce Utopia. It was necessary for man to utilize his institutions, she said — the churches, government, industry, the arts — so that each individual would learn for himself how to live happily within the community of men, at peace with himself as well as with his neighbors.

Looking back on her own life at the age of sixty-one, George was convinced that she herself was happy. She had lived as she wished, and, through suffering, had been taught not to repeat her mistakes. Her health was still good, although she complained of headaches and occasional stomach disorders. And she had become the most famous woman of her time; most of her books were being published in Italian, German, Dutch, Swedish, and Spanish, and occasionally one appeared in English, too.

She had only one major, unfulfilled desire: she wanted a grandchild.

XIII

After the death of Manceau, George Sand reordered her life by taking a somewhat smaller apartment in the same Paris building and hiring a couple to look after the house at Palaiseau. She continued to use both residences, but spent much of her time either at Nohant or her rural retreat in Berry. Her need to own so many homes, which became more pronounced as she grew older, was one of her idiosyncrasies. In modern times that trait has been called a lack of inner security, and may have stemmed from a feeling that she had failed to establish genuine roots anywhere.

George herself attributed the desire to own a number of homes to a sense of restlessness that sometimes possessed her. There were times when there was nothing she enjoyed more than being surrounded by her family and friends at Nohant, but she would awaken one morning feeling that the whole world was closing in around her, and had to escape to the solitude of Gargilesse. There were few things she relished more than attending the theater, then going on to a restaurant to argue the merits of the play with colleagues. When this existence palled on her, as it always did, she could go to Palaiseau, and Paris ceased to exist for her. She spent the rest of her life traveling from one of her four homes to another, never remaining in any one for more than brief periods. No one interfered, and her children knew better than to criticize what they considered erratic behavior. She had always done what she wanted, and it was far too late to cure her of the habit.

Perhaps the most important event of her later years was the birth, late in 1866, of Maurice's and Lina's second child, a girl. She was called Aurore, after her grandmother, and was the fourth in the family to bear the name. George immediately called her Lolo, and soon the entire family adopted the nickname, by which the second Aurore Dudevant-Sand was known thereafter.

Lolo filled a vacuum in George's life, but a woman long accustomed to intellectual companionship had other needs, and these were filled by Gustave Flaubert. He and George had enjoyed an amiable relationship for several years, and their friendship was cemented when he defied her ban on company and insisted on visiting her at Palaiseau after Manceau's death. Thereafter George paid him a visit at his home, Croisset, and the pair became 'intellectually inseparable', as Ivan Turgeniev, their mutual friend the Russian novelist, observed after seeing them together at Nohant.

The claim made by some of George's malicious contemporaries that she found it necessary to take a lover even in her old age, and that she settled on Flaubert simply because no one else was available, is sheer nonsense that does discredit to both. Their voluminous correspondence, which fills many volumes when published in full, reveals that at no time were they more than friends. They understood each other, their thinking was remarkably similar in many ways, and each filled a need in the other.

Gustave Flaubert was seventeen years younger than George Sand, but the failure of his body to produce certain chemicals in a balanced supply had made him ill since youth. He himself thought he suffered from epilepsy, and his hypochondria made him look far older than his actual years. He was endowed with a magnificent physique, but a loathing for physical exercise and a love of good food made him pudgy. When George first became friends with him, he was balding and myopic.

Born in Rouen, Flaubert was the son of a distinguished physician and a Norman noblewoman who could trace her ancestry to the ninth century. It was from her that Flaubert learned to despise the middle class and all it represented, a hatred that was almost a mania. Trained for the law, he turned instead to writing, and never knew any other profession.

A lifelong bachelor, Flaubert bought his house at Croisset, pear Rouen, overlooking the River Seine, after the death of his father and sister, and lived there for many years with his mother. He indulged in countless, brief affairs, but only one was significant: for a decade he enjoyed an intimate relationship with Louise Colet, the writer of dubious talents whose short book, *Lui*, had caused George Sand so much grief.

Flaubert's passion for revising his work until he made it perfect was legendary even in his own lifetime. Few authors, if any, have ever displayed such remarkable diligence in polishing their prose. Frequently he read his work aloud while playing appropriate mood music on a piano, and would tear apart an entire fabric if a sentence or even a phrase failed to meet his exacting standards. Often he completed no more than a single page in a week of unceasing work, and if that page satisfied him, he was content.

The publication of *Madame Bovary*, his masterpiece, in 1856, overnight established him as one of the great authors of the century. Émile Zola, Alphonse Daudet, and other writers of the younger generation hailed Flaubert as the most realistic of authors in the history of French literature, and not until long after his death in 1880 did it gradually dawn on critics and students that his work was far more than purely realistic, and could be interpreted as symbolism.

Why George Sand and Gustave Flaubert were drawn to each other is a question that has puzzled and delighted the amateur literary psychiatrists of the twentieth century. It well may be that George found in her friend a younger man who provided her with a substitute for an affair, and it is possible that Flaubert regarded her as a surrogate mother. But their correspondence, which speaks for itself, indicates that they were two exceptionally talented, lonely people, both needing the companionship of an equal in whom it was possible to confide.

That equality was the real core of their friendship. Differences in age and sex were unimportant, and neither was concerned about the scandals in which the other had been involved. Their relationship was similar, in a sense, to that which George had enjoyed with Balzac, although it was far deeper. She and Flaubert respected each other as artists and as people; the very absence of sexual tensions made it possible for them to draw close without feeling strained or self-conscious.

Flaubert was interested only in the written word, and forgot literature only when eating a magnificent dinner or drinking a superb wine. George, on the other hand, was fascinated by everything in the world and claimed that she wrote only because of the need to support herself in the manner she enjoyed. Yet this seemingly ill-matched pair found a common meeting ground, and could spend entire days arguing the merits of someone else's novel or play. George was awed by her friends perfectionist standards, while Flaubert could only shake his head in wonder over her ability to write fifteen or twenty pages in one night of work.

Flaubert was not George's only new literary friend in her later years. Another was Turgeniev, a frequent visitor to Nohant, who found that the censors of Napoleon III created far fewer problems for an author and were infinitely less hazardous to his personal health than the secret police of the Tsar. A third friend was an exceptionally attractive young woman, Juliette Lamber, who made her appearance on the literary scene in 1861, when trying to find a diversion from an unhappy marriage.

One of the more curious relationships formed by George Sand in the late 1860s, when she was achieving ever-greater respectability, was her friendship with the notorious American actress, Adah Isaacs Menken. Long devoted to authors and herself a poet of questionable talent, the controversial Adah Menken, who achieved stardom in a play called *Mazeppa*, in which she was carried on a runway built in the auditorium of a theater, strapped to the back of a horse and wearing flesh-colored tights. One of her four husbands had been the heavyweight boxing champion of the world, who had abandoned her because she had beaten him for drinking too much.

Among her many devoted friends were Walt Whitman and Dickens, Swinburne and Rossetti, and Bret Harte. Her exceptional intelligence and sensitivity to writers, as well as her great beauty and charm, more than compensated for her promiscuity and flair for embarrassing publicity.

She arrived in Paris in 1868 awaiting the birth of her child, before launching her French theatrical career. Within days of her arrival she achieved local fame by being photographed sitting on the lap of Alexandre Dumas the Elder, who was already infatuated with her.

In almost no time Adah Menken became acquainted with every French author of note, and the most solid of her friendships was that which the young woman, then in her early thirties, formed with the sixty-four-year-old George Sand. They dined together frequently, and after the birth of Adah's baby, George became the infant's godmother.

Parisians had seen George wearing her once-familiar trousers only infrequently of late, but she revived her habit of appearing in men's attire when she and Adah went out together. The flamboyant actress also wore trousers and regularly smoked cigars, a habit that she long enjoyed.

For more than a generation Parisians had suspected the worst of George Sand, and her association with Adah Menken raised eyebrows anew. Whether there was more to their friendship than met the eye is a question that has never been answered. But it appears possible that contemporaries of the two women may have been right.

Adah, who was usually circumspect in her language, frequently referred to her friend, in various letters to others in London and New York, as 'my darling George'. After *Mazeppa* opened in Paris and won her an enthusiastic following, a number of parties were given in her honor. Prior to one of them, in a note to Théophile Gautier, Adah may have revealed more than she intended when she wrote: 'I am looking forward to seeing all of you on the night after next, and only hope my darling George will be present. She so infuses me with the spirit of life that I cannot bear to spend an evening apart from her.'

Her friends knew of the relationship and considered it Lesbian, but it was ephemeral. Within a few months George had more substantial interests to occupy her, and Adah, soon to die a sudden and tragic death, transferred her enthusiasms elsewhere. The incident, if indeed there had been one, was ended. George took on the responsibility of supporting Adah's child for some time.

Juliette Lamber had become a protégé of Marie d'Agoult, who discovered that the girl was an admirer of George Sand and made her life miserable as a consequence. Jealousy, Juliette eventually revealed, made it impossible for the woman who wrote as Daniel Stern to discuss any other subject. When Juliette's husband died, she married the man she loved, Edmond Adam, a newspaperman, and the illness of Marie d'Agoult soon thereafter made it possible for her to strike up a friendship, in 1867, with George Sand.

The books Juliette wrote under the name of Madame Adam, most of them political commentaries and works of literary criticism, indicate her love for her husband was both deep and genuine. So it is unlikely, rumors of the period to the contrary, that she engaged in a Lesbian affair with George. Their correspondence gives no hint of any such relationship, and it must be remembered that a turning point occurred in George's life after the termination of her affair with Chopin. She and Manceau occasionally slept together, but after his death she put her active sex life behind her.

In her *Mes Sentiments et nos Idées avant 1870*, Juliette Adam quoted George at length, and posterity is indebted to her for a portrait in depth of the elderly George Sand. On one occasion, Juliette said, her friend and mentor told her what to reply if anyone ever accused George Sand of disloyalty:

> Tell them, 'George Sand may have lost her right to be judged as a woman, but she can still claim to be judged as a man, and in love she has been more loyal than any of you. She never deceived anyone, and has never engaged in two adventures of the heart at the same time. All that can be held against her is that, in the course of a lifetime during which the creative arts meant more to her than anything else, she sought the society

of artists, and preferred the moral standards of the male to those of the female.'

Let me admit without further ado, my dear Juliette, that when a woman ceases to be a woman, *she makes herself inferior.* It is well and proper that you, living as I once lived, surrounded by men and no doubt adored my many of them, should remember this: *any exceptional woman who can call a superior man her friend is to be envied.* As a lover, a man is the same for all women, and often is the better lover when the woman is crude and stupid.

I have known utter and complete love — not once, alas, but many times — *but, if I could begin my life again, I would elect to remain chaste.*

Late in 1867 George learned the best of all possible news, that Lina was expecting another baby, and soon thereafter, in the first months of 1868, she went off in high spirits to visit Juliette and Edmond Adam at their winter home on the Riviera. During her stay she heard that Solange was less than twenty miles away, spending several months at Cannes in the company of someone her mother described to Lina only as 'a foreign prince of great wealth'. By now it was impossible for George to pretend she was unaware of her daughter's chosen vocation, but no one could force her to accept a way of life that was repugnant to her, and she elected to avoid Cannes as she made trips to one town or another in the area.

When George returned to Nohant in the spring of 1868, she met her new granddaughter, Gabrielle Dudevant-Sand, who was destined to become the great beauty of the family. George's life was now complete.

In the summer of 1868 Nohant was filled with guests. Juliette and Edmond Adam were there, as were Flaubert and Turgeniev. Théophile Gautier came, too, having been persuaded at long last to spend at least a few days in the country home of his old friend, and in his correspondence he revealed his reactions to his astonishing hostess.

Every morning, he declared, George went bathing in the cold waters of the river and stood for a long time, immersed to the neck. She claimed, he repeated, that the water revived her, gave her new energies. The guests, following the custom George had instituted many years earlier, spent their days doing whatever they pleased, but they soon discovered one significant change in the schedule: lunch was served early, because everyone was expected to sit down at the dinner table promptly at 6.00 p.m. Now that George was growing older she became hungry early in the evening.

The evening's activities in the salon-puppet theater were the highlight of the day. At the very least there was conversation on literary, political, moral, and theological subjects, most of which were suggested by George, who subsequently took no part in the conversation as she sewed new dresses for her grandchildren. Some evenings either Flaubert or Turgeniev read from an as yet unpublished work and sought the comments of the assembled company. Their willingness to subject their efforts to this semi-public airing gave George the courage to follow their example, and for the first time since she had started inviting guests to Nohant almost forty years earlier, she read excerpts from her own forthcoming books.

The evenings everyone welcomed were those involving the puppet theater. On these nights, George, Flaubert, and Turgeniev pooled their talents to improvise plots, and Théophile Gautier wrote to his daughter in Paris that he was sorry he could not write rapidly enough to transcribe their conversations. Rarely, if ever, had three such literary giants worked together for the sake of providing a small company of people an evening's entertainment. Unfortunately for posterity, none of these plays survived, as none was reproduced on paper.

During the summer of 1868 George finally managed to rid herself of some of the frustrations Solange had caused her for so many years. She utilized the method that so many authors before had used, and told her daughter's story in a novel, *Mademoiselle Merquem*, in which she not only painted Solange in a harsh, unflattering light, but tried to tell the truth about her. Obviously, it still hurt to know that Solange, who was now forty, was still the most famous courtesan in Europe. But it did not occur to George, who still paid her a regular allowance, that she herself might be partly to blame for Solange's situation.

Apart from her concern over a wayward daughter, George, in her own words, was leading 'a life that becomes more tranquil with each passing day. Many of my contemporaries look backward toward the past, but it cannot be done. I have learned that one can live only in the present, either for its own sake or that of one's future.'

Occasionally a new worry cropped up. In 1869 Maurice told her that his father's letters indicated Casimir was becoming senile, and it crossed George's mind that her husband might leave his estate to his illegitimate child instead of Maurice and Solange. She mentioned her concern to both of her children, then began to urge them to stand up for their rights.

Casimir was evasive in his replies when his legitimate son and daughter tried to pin him down on the subject of the disposition of his estate, and the more he side-stepped, the more alarmed George became. Taking charge of the matter herself, presumably because she knew Casimir far better than did either Maurice or Solange, she filed suit against him on their behalf.

The case was complicated, but George persisted, and within a year and a half she drove Casimir into a corner. He was forced to sell his castle and move to a small house in a nearby village. The liquidation of his estate brought him a sum in excess of one hundred and sixty-five thousand francs, approximately twenty-five thousand of which he gave to his illegitimate daughter. He transferred the appreciable sum of one hundred and forty thousand francs to Maurice and Solange, dividing it between them. Then, having lost his last battle to George, Baron Casimir Dudevant expired at his new home on March 8, 1871. His legal widow did not mourn his passing.

But the death of her old friend and advisor, Sainte-Beuve, in October, 1869, was a severe blow that made her conscious of her own mortality. Flaubert escorted her to the funeral, and although she had long followed the principle of concealing her deeper emotions in public, she wept at the graveside ceremony.

On July 14, 1870, two weeks after George's sixty-eighth birthday, Napoleon III declared war against Prussia. George, who had become increasingly critical of the Emperor's foreign and domestic policies in recent years, was irritated by what she considered his stupidity, and privately predicted he would be shot down by his own troops if he dared to appear on the battlefield.

Gradually her anger turned to alarm. The censorship was so strict that the newspapers were permitted to print nothing of consequence regarding the progress of the war, but it was impossible to conceal the collapse of the Empire. By early September word trickled down to Nohant that Napoleon III had been captured by the Prussians, France's finest armies had either been destroyed or captured, and a strong Prussian corps was marching toward Paris.

A day or two later Maurice learned in La Châtre that a Republic had been proclaimed in the capital and that Victor Hugo immediately had ended his eighteen-year exile and had returned to Paris, entering the country from Belgium. George's feelings were summarized in a brief note she wrote to one of her old Berry friends, now in Paris: 'Long live the Republic! — no matter what may happen, and these days I fear the worst!'

She wanted to go to Paris, but Maurice flatly forbade her to leave Nohant. It was becoming clear that the Germans intended to lay siege to the city, and that Paris planned to resist. No matter how much George longed to join old friends at the scene of action, her son decreed, a city besieged by the finest soldiers Europe had known since the legions of Napoleon I was no place for a grandmother of sixty-eight, regardless of her determination to fight to the end.

The siege of Paris was undertaken on September 15, 1870, and lasted until the following January 28th, when the exhausted, battered city was forced to capitulate. But the travail of Paris was not yet ended. Officials of the Provisional Republic gathered in Bordeaux to form a permanent government that would be able to meet the exorbitant demands of the Prussians and sign a peace treaty. Meantime the working people of Paris revolted against the National Assembly. They were joined by thousands of disillusioned intellectuals and members of the middle class, and the 'Communards', as the Parisians called themselves, took charge of their own destinies after several days of bitter street fighting.

About half of the members of the Commune were Republicans, many of the older men were George's lifelong friends, and again she expressed a desire to go to Paris immediately. Again Maurice put his foot down, and took no chances. In order to make certain his mother did not sneak off at night, he not only ordered the servants not to allow her to use a horse, but himself kept the stables under lock and key. George was forced to follow the heartbreaking events of the following weeks from a distance.

When the Prussians threatened to return and take permanent possession of the enemy's capital, the National Assembly was forced to act, and sent an army to take Paris. An undeclared civil war raged in Paris from April 1 to May 28, 1871, and the most civilized city in the world became a place of death and destruction.

The victory won by the forces of the National Assembly late in May did not end the terror. Fifteen thousand Communards had been killed and at least three times that number had been wounded, but the forces of reaction wanted to make certain the rebels would not rise again. Special tribunals were established, and an estimated one hundred and twenty-five thousand persons were exiled, the 'more dangerous of the conspirators' being sent to French penal colonies in South America, the rest to the French island of New Caledonia in the Pacific.

A fuming George Sand identified herself with the Republican members of the Commune, and unable to take action of any kind either during the revolt or during the period of retribution that followed, she was horrified by the excesses committed by the rebels, then stunned again by the retribution exacted by the Right. The Republicans were to blame, she declared, for not keeping the more radical elements under control. The monarchists were equally to blame for their trials and harsh punishment of many who were innocent as well as those who were guilty.

The barricades, she wrote, should be removed from the streets of Paris without delay! Her comments, which appeared rather mysteriously in leaflet form and were widely distributed in Paris, aroused men of both factions against her. The people would triumph only by climbing over the barricades, the dedicated Communards retorted, while the supporters of the National Assembly declared that there would be chaos in the streets again if the barricades were removed.

The disgusted George, who found it inconceivable that her fellow Frenchmen could be so short-sighted, was inundated with letters from both sides attacking her for the stand she had taken. She answered all of them in the same way, saying, 'I am myself neither a Communard nor a monarchist. I continue to adhere to the teaching of the Gospel according to St John.'

Under the terms of the peace treaty imposed by the Prussians, France was forced to pay a crushing indemnity and cede her provinces of Alsace and Lorraine to the enemy. Beaten to her knees, she was unable to reject the harsh demands.

The Prussian terms were so overwhelming that George thought her countrymen might come to their senses and stand united. As a landowner in a rich agricultural province she knew the nation would recover swiftly if men of every political persuasion buried their differences. Food supplies for the nation were ample, as were raw materials for factories, and France, if united, could make herself prosperous and strong again. But the national genius for stubborn individualism once again asserted itself.

George, on a brief trip to Paris, dined with Victor Hugo for the first time since his return from exile. They agreed there were almost as many political parties as there were members of the National Assembly, and they shared the fear that the neomonarchists might doom the Republic by placing another Bourbon on the throne.

For the next year the issue remained in doubt, and even after the Republic became somewhat stronger, it was assailed by so many enemies that its long-range future was uncertain. George Sand weathered the storm in remarkably good humor. She was thoroughly disgusted with politics and politicians, she realized the future might be bleak, but she knew there was nothing she could do to alleviate the situation, so she tried to concentrate on her own concerns. Flaubert gloomily predicted that the country was on the verge of collapse and that he hoped the case of ague from which he was suffering would prove fatal. George's answer, in the spring of 1872, is indicative of her basic state of mind:

> This is no time to be sick, old troubadour, and certainly is no time to grumble. What we must do is cough, wipe our noses, get well and declare — aloud, very firmly — that France is mad, humanity stupid, and we ourselves are no more than a breed of badly-designed animals.
>
> What I have just said is true as far as it goes, but there is more. We must go on being in love with ourselves, the species to which we belong, and, most of all, our friends. We cannot permit ourselves to be deflected by the insanity that surrounds us on every side, and that, if we are not careful, insidiously influences our thinking until we, too, see the world upside down.
>
> Perhaps this chronic state of indignation is one of the necessary conditions of your continued existence, but I know it would be the death of *me*! Is it possible, you ask, to live in peace when the human race is so absurd? Speaking only for myself, which is all that my conscience permits, I am prepared to submit to the conditions of absurdity, reflecting the while that I, perhaps, am no less absurd than anyone else. What matters is that I begin to think how to improve myself, since I am unable to aid in the improvement of others.

Why, then, you will ask, do we write, if it is impossible to influence the thinking of others? My dear friend, I can reply only that we are unable to exert enough influence to reshape man's destiny overnight. If our advice is sound, if the mirror we hold up to society is accurate enough for man to recognize his reflection, and little by little persuade him to change his image, then we will not have lived in vain. Nor will we have written in vain; our self-love will have-served the compassionate purpose that, we like to tell ourselves, is our motive for spending our entire lives in the lonely, grinding work of creating a world on paper.

Work was still George's salvation, and although she promised Maurice and Lina she would slow her pace, they saw no sign that her labors were slackening. She continued to write three books each year for Buloz, and the public demand for her novels remained great, even though a new generation had joined the adult reading public. She also signed a contract to write essays for *Le Temps*, and her interest in the theater remained undiminished.

It disturbed her that most of her works were not reviewed by the critics any more, in part because she was considered old-fashioned in her approach, and partly because her output was so great that the reviewers convinced themselves her books were lacking in literary merit. Flaubert suggested that she read a few of the novels being written by Zola and some of the other young men who were currently making their mark, and she did, but was not impressed. In the spring of 1872 she wrote to her faithful correspondent:

Life is not made up *only* of criminals, rogues and scoundrels. There is more than a mere handful of decent people in the world, because, after all, some sort of ordered society *does* exist, and not all crimes go unpunished. It is true, I agree, that fools form the majority, but there is a public conscience which weighs upon them and forces them to observe decent standards of behavior. That rogues should be castigated and shown for what they are is right, even moral, but we should be shown the other side of the coin as well. Otherwise the simple-minded reader — who is in the majority — will react against such books, will become depressed and afraid, and ultimately will deny the truth of the portrait which their authors paint, because to do this is their only alternative to despair.

Work was not the only influence that kept George young and active; the other was her grandchildren. A desire to be near them kept her at Nohant for most of each month, and she appointed herself the tutor of the little girls. Each day they sat down with their grandmother in her study, and there she told them stories that emphasized the benefits of living ethical, moral lives. The Golden Rule, she taught them, was the foundation on which civilization was built, and she urged them, in simple ways, to live according to it.

She also spoiled the children outrageously, making them more clothes than they could wear, buying them ponies, and filling their nursery with toys. Lina and Maurice protested, but George, after the fashion of grandparents everywhere through the generations, blithely ignored the demands of her son and daughter-in-law. She admitted she was indulging herself as well as the children, but refused to alter her treatment of them. She could help them, she said, and they were her principal reason for being. Maurice and Lina found it impossible to argue with her.

In the spring of 1873, Flaubert and Turgeniev paid another visit to Nohant. The former, who tended to dominate conversations, wanted to spend his evenings discussing literature, and being a lifelong bachelor, was inclined to be somewhat intolerant of small children. But George insisted that her granddaughters attend the after-dinner sessions, and with the aid of the imaginative Turgeniev, invented silly game after silly game that sent the children laughing, singing, and skipping through the house. George was afraid that Flaubert's nose was out of joint, but if he resented the intrusion of the little girls, he successfully concealed his umbrage, and his conduct, as always, was impeccable.

In the summer of 1873 a potential cause of disturbance cast a long shadow over Nohant. Solange reappeared on the scene, and in spite of her mother's opposition, bought the nearby Château de Montgivray from her cousin, Hippolyte's daughter. George tried to block the purchase, saying she did not want the 'screech-owl', as she called Solange, keeping watch on Nohant. But shrewdness as well as dissolute living had earned Solange her fortune, and she outsmarted her mother by making her offer for the château through a third party.

Literally nothing at Nohant pleased Solange, who criticized the food, the work done by the servants, and the manners of her small nieces, who made no secret of their intense dislike for her. Maurice and Lina tried to be polite and exercise patience, but their efforts were futile, and they were forced to make it plain to Solange that she was no longer welcome at Nohant. She paid no attention, however, and continued to visit her mother.

George, who was reluctant to close her door completely to her only daughter, finally worked out a system whereby she could avoid a session of listening to Solange's complaints and criticisms. It occurred to her that her daughter usually stepped in, unexpectedly, an hour or two before lunch, and stayed for the meal without having been invited. So the old lady enlisted the aid of her granddaughters, and together they invented a game called 'Keeping watch for Aunt Solange'. Whenever she arrived at the house, one or the other of the little girls raced to find George, who immediately vanished into her study. Solange, who thought she was writing, could not force herself to break the habit of a lifetime by interrupting creative work, and more often than not left at once, neither seeing her mother nor staying for lunch.

In 1875, the politicians finally established the Republic on a firm, seemingly permanent basis. Caution tempered George's enthusiasm when she wrote to Flaubert: 'At last we have the Republic! But I rejoice only because Hugo is a Senator. As for the rest, who is to say they will not change their minds tomorrow and plunge us into chaos again?'

Now seventy-one years old, George finally gave in to the insistent demands of Lina and Maurice and cut her work output from three books each year to two. But she soon discovered she could not break the habits of more than forty years. She was not sleepy when the rest of the household went to bed, and thought it a foolish waste of time to spend hours lying wide-eyed under the covers. So, in order to make good use of the night, she began to write fairy tales for her granddaughters.

George's health remained remarkably good until the late winter of 1876, when she began to feel occasional stomach pains. But she had always been afflicted with what she herself called a 'writer's stomach', and was far more concerned about the health of Maurice, who was suffering from neuralgia, than she was about her own condition.

She resisted strenuously whenever her son and daughter-in-law suggested she see a doctor, so they finally resorted to a ruse, calling in a physician from La Châtre for the supposed purpose of treating Maurice's neuralgia. The doctor came on May 20th and prescribed some medicine for George's pains, but after taking a few doses she decided it was doing her no good, and threw away the bottle.

By May 29th her condition had worsened considerably, and she was forced to go to bed. She suffered greatly from stomach pains, but the local physician could do nothing for her, and at her request another, in whom she had great faith, was summoned from Paris. He tried various medications for twenty-four hours, and then brought in a surgeon, but all three medical men were afraid that an operation might prove fatal, as she had been weakened by an inability to eat solid food for more than a week.

On the evening of June 7th she seemed to sense that she was going to die, and asked to see her granddaughters. The children were brought to her, and she kissed them, told them to be good girls, and delivered a short homily on the blessings of hard work. Her pain was intense, but she made no outcry in the presence of the children, and refused to let them see she was suffering. Under no circumstances, she told Lina, did she want to upset or frighten them.

Maurice had unbent sufficiently to notify his sister that George was gravely ill, and suggested she come to Nohant if she wished. Solange arrived that same night, and took up the vigil with her brother and sister-in-law. The physicians were in attendance, but could do little to alleviate Georges pains, and several times during the night she cried, 'Oh, God, let me die!'

The end came about two and a half hours after daybreak, just as she was bidding Maurice and Lina a tender farewell. The date was June 8, 1876, and the greatest woman of her age, the pioneer in the crusade for sexual freedom and an author of the first magnitude, died three weeks prior to her seventy-second birthday.

That noon Solange shouldered Lina aside, took her mother's place at the lunch table, and issued an unending series of orders to the servants.

George Sand was buried in the private graveyard behind the chapel at Nohant, near the graves of her grandmother, her parents, and her adored granddaughter, Nini. At Solange's insistence a Roman Catholic burial service was held, the Archbishop of Bourges granting his permission. A large crowd was on hand, in spite of a rain that fell steadily all morning. Scores had come from Châteauroux and La Châtre, and virtually the entire population of the village of Nohant appeared.

A group of approximately twenty-five or thirty of George's friends came to Nohant for the funeral. Flaubert was there, and Alexandre Dumas the Younger, came from Paris, as did Victor Borie, Eugène Lambert, and a number of others.

Victor Hugo was ill, and therefore could not make the journey from Paris, but he wrote the funeral oration, and it was read on his behalf by his friend, Paul Meurice. Hugo said, in part: 'Can it be said that we have lost her? No. Great figures such as she may disappear — but they do not vanish. Quite the contrary. One might say that they take on a new reality.'

Turgeniev was unable to attend, too, having been away from Paris at the time the news was received. He returned too late to make the journey to Nohant, was heartbroken, and wrote a long letter to Flaubert, blaming himself for his failure to be present.

Flaubert's reply was crisp:

Don't berate yourself for what couldn't be helped.

You should consider yourself fortunate that you were delayed. I can't imagine what Hugo was thinking when he wrote his oration, but it was dreadful, so filled with cliches that I shuddered. I know that, wherever George may be, she shuddered, too, when she heard it!

Thank God a nightingale began to sing as Meurice stopped speaking, and when I caught the eye of Dumas I knew we shared the same thought: that song was a far more fitting oration for our beloved George Sand.

PRINCIPAL BIBLIOGRAPHY

Adam, Juliette Lambert, *Mes Premieres Armes Littéraires et politiques*, Lemerre, Paris, 1904

——, *Mes Sentiments et Nos Idées avant* 1870, Lemerre, Paris, 1905

Amic, Henri, *George Sand*, Calmann-Lévy, Paris, 1893

Barine, Arvède, *Allred de Musset*, Hachette, Paris, 1893

Billy, André, *Balzac*, Flammarion, Paris, 1947

Caro, Edmé, *George Sand*, Hachette, Paris, 1887

Charpentier, John, *George Sand*, Tallandier, Paris, 1936

Coupy, Étienne, *Marie Dorval*, Albert Lacroix, Paris, 1868

Davray, Jean, *George Sand et ses Amants*, Albin-Michel, Paris, 1935

Delacroix, Eugène, *Journal*, 3 vols, Pion, Paris, 1932

Dorval, Marie, *Lettres à Alfred de Vigny*, Gallimard, Paris, 1942

Doumic, René, *George Sand*, Perrin, Paris, 1908

Galzy, Jeanne, *George Sand*, Julliard, Paris, 1930

Jasinski, Rene, *Les années romantiques de Théophile Gautier*, Vuibert, Paris, 1950

La Salle, Bertrand de, *Allred de Vigny*, Fayard, Paris, 1939

Liszt, Franz, *Correspondance*, Grasset, Paris, 1934

Maurois, André, *Lélia*, Jonathan Cape, London, 1953

Moser, Franchise, *Marie Dorval*, Pion, Paris, 1947

Pourtalès, Guy de, *Chopin ou le Poète*, Gallimard, Paris, 1936

Sainte-Beuve, Charles-Augustin, *Correspondance*, 7 vols, Stock, Paris, 1947

Sand, George, *Diaries*, 1852-76, in Dept of Mss, Bibliothèque Nationale, Paris

————, *George Sand-Gustave Flaubert Letters*, Duckworth, London, 1922

————, *History of My Life*, 7 vols, Regents Press, London, 1901

————, *Intimate Journal*, Loring and Mussey, New York, 1929

————, *Letters*, 9 vols, Regents Press, London, 1896

————, *Works*, condensed ed., 38 vols, Regents Press, London, 1887

Sellière, Ernest, *George Sand*, Félix-Alcan, Paris, 1920

————, *Nouveaux Portraits de Femmes*, Emile-Paul, Paris, 1923

Seyd, Felizia, *Romantic Rebel*, Viking, New York, 1940

Silver, Mabel, *Jules Sandeau*, Boivin & Cie, Paris, 1936

Stern, Daniel, *Mémoires*, Calmann-Lévy, Paris, 1927

————, *Souvenirs*, Calmann-Lévy, Paris, 1877

Toesca, Maurice, *Une Autre George Sand*, Pion, Paris, 1945

Vincent, Louise, *George Sand et le Berry*, Edouard Champion, Paris, 1919

Vuillermoz, Emile, *Vie amoureuse de Chopin*, Flammarion, Paris, 1927

Winwar, Frances, *The Life of the Heart*, Harper, New York, 1945

A NOTE TO THE READER

If you have enjoyed this book enough to leave a review on **Amazon** and **Goodreads**, then we would be truly grateful. The Estate of Noel B. Gerson

Sapere Books is an exciting new publisher of brilliant fiction and popular history.

To find out more about our latest releases and our monthly bargain books visit our website:
saperebooks.com

Printed in Great Britain
by Amazon